THE NOT SO BIG HOUSE BOOK

Sarah Susanka

THE NOT SO BIG HOUSE BOOK

The Taunton Press

The Taunton Press
Inspiration for hands-on living®

The Taunton Press, Inc., 63 South Main Street, PO Box 5506, Newtown, CT 06470-5506
e-mail: tp@taunton.com

Photographer: Grey Crawford, except where noted

Library of Congress Cataloging-in Publication Data:

Susanka, Sarah.
  The not so big house book / Sarah Susanka.
    p. cm.
  ISBN-13: 978-1-56158-929-6
  ISBN-10: 1-56158-929-2
  1. Architecture, Domestic--United States. 2. Architecture--United States--
21st century. 3. Architecture--Psychological aspects. 4. Space (Architecture)
I. Title.
  NA7208.2.S87 2006
  728'.37--dc22
                                        2006011598

Printed in China
10 9 8 7 6 5 4 3 2 1

The following manufacturers/names appearing in *The Not So Big House Book*
are trademarks: Nintendo®, Lego®, Medite®, Plexiglas®, Hardipanel®,
Hardiplank®

Contents

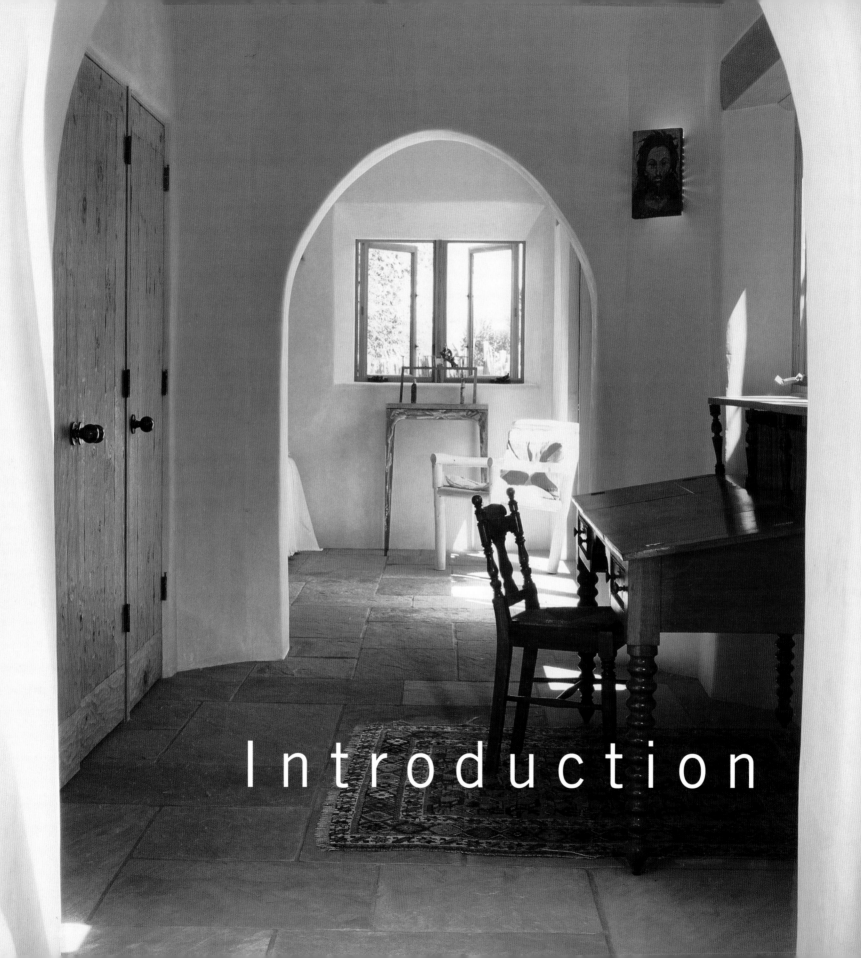

Introduction

The idea of a Not So Big House, a house that favors the quality of its space over the quantity, has evolved during the 15 years I've practiced architecture in the Twin Cities. Maybe it was the 1980s that created what I call the "starter castle" complex—the notion that houses should be designed to impress rather than nurture. More rooms, bigger spaces, and vaulted ceilings do not necessarily give us what we need in a home. And when the impulse for big spaces is combined with outdated patterns of home design and building, the result is more often than not a house that doesn't work.

When my husband and I, both of us architects, were planning our new house, we knew that we wanted a home that would inspire us and make the best use of the money we had to spend. Whatever we ended up with, we wanted our house to express the way we actually live. We started the planning process by considering an addition to our two-story 1904 four-square. We're not formal people, and the separation between kitchen and living space meant that we spent all our time in the kitchen—the tiniest room in the house. To change that, however, we would have had to add more space, which would have made our house bigger while leaving half of it still unused. That option didn't seem sensible. In fact, it seemed downright wasteful.

I quickly realized that our old house was designed for a pattern of life that was fundamentally different from the way we live today. So we decided to design our own house—which would be Not So Big—with each space in use every day. And it would be beautiful. I've designed big houses that are beautiful and small houses that had tight budgets; I wanted our house to combine the beauty of the big house with the efficiency of the small one. Rather than spend our budget on square footage we wouldn't use, we decided to put the money toward making the house an expression of our personalities.

We knew that by building such a house we would be going out on a limb, because the institutions that dictate the value and resale of houses demand all

about his own house, a suburban Colonial, and admitting that in 25 years his family had never sat in the living room. They lived in their family room. The banker, who at first appeared to be our biggest obstacle, became our strongest advocate.

So we built our house, and along the way many of the ideas that had been percolating in my subconscious came into being. I began to speak locally and nationally about the concept of the Not So Big House and found an extraordinary amount of confirmation from audiences. Even realtors, who perpetuate the conventional wisdom of resale requirements, were excited by the concept of building Not So Big. In fact, two realtors—a husband and wife team—approached me after one lecture and asked that I design a Not So Big House for them.

This book contains the work of more than 35 architects and related professionals who I have had the privilege of working with in our architectural firm in Minnesota. These colleagues have worked with more than 3,000 residential clients over the past 15 years. As a result of all this work, we get to see the aspirations, the struggles, the needs, and the realities of people who want new or remodeled homes. Architects build dreams, but we also have to help clients reconcile those dreams with real budgets. A house that favors quality of design over

the extra spaces that we knew we would never use. When we met with the banker and explained that our new house would have no formal dining room, he was dubious. But as I described to him my frustration with designing large houses with rarely used formal spaces, and my vision to put forward a different home model into the marketplace, his demeanor completely changed. Suddenly, he was telling us

quantity of space satisfies people with big dreams and not so big budgets far more so than a house with those characteristics in reverse.

It's time for a different kind of house. A house that is more than square footage; a house that is Not So Big, where each room is used every day. A house with a floorplan inspired by our informal lifestyle instead of the way our grandparents lived. A house for the future that embraces a few well-worn concepts from the past. A house that expresses our values and our personalities. It's time for the Not So Big House.

The Not So Big House isn't just a small house. Rather, it's a smaller house, filled with special details and designed to accommodate the lifestyles of its occupants. I've discovered living in my own Not So Big House that the quality of my life has improved. I'm surrounded in my home by beautiful forms, lots of daylight, natural materials, and the things that I love. Our house fits us perfectly and is unabashedly comfortable. My house feeds my spirit, and it is with this insight that I share with you how to make your house do the same. ■

"Not everything that can be counted counts, and not everything that counts can be counted."—Albert Einstein

S o many houses, so big with so little soul. Our suburbs are filled with houses that are bigger than ever. But are bigger houses really better? Are the dreams that build them bigger, or is it simply that there seems to be no alternative? Americans are searching for home in unprecedented numbers. Yet when we look, the only tools we seem to have are those we find in the real estate listings. But a house is more than square footage and the number of beds and baths. In one of the wealthiest societies ever, many people are deeply dissatisfied with their most expensive purchase. Which is where Paul and Laura come in.

I had just completed a lecture at our local Home and Garden Show. As I stepped from the podium, I was greeted by several members of the audience who wanted to thank me for saying something they hadn't heard before—that we need to value quality over quantity in house design. There was a couple in the crowd with a story about their own experience, a story that gave me the impetus

A Not So Big House exchanges space for soul, so that the quality of the space is more important than the sheer square footage.

Rather than spend their budget on spaces they never use, people who build Not So Big tailor their houses to fit their lives.

to write this book. As they approached me, I saw tears in the woman's eyes.

"We want you to come to our new house and tell us what you think," she said. "We just built it. We spent over $500,000 on it and we hate it. It's just not us at all. After listening to you, we think…" She paused and looked at her husband, who nodded. "We *know* that we have to start over. All we've got is square footage with no soul. We want the type of house that you describe. Can you help us?"

The next week, I drove out to the suburbs to see the house, past row after row of enormous structures covering the newly developed hillsides. These houses loomed in their treeless sites, staring blankly out toward vistas of more of the same. I felt as though I was driving through a collection of massive storage containers for people.

Paul and Laura's house was fairly typical of new, large subdivision homes. It had the required arched window topping off a soaring front entrance scaled more for an office building than a home. Inside the house, I was greeted by an enormous space, all white, with a cold marble floor. There was no separation between this vaulting foyer and the next room, which I assumed must be the family room, although there was no furniture in it (see the photo on p. 10). Laura ushered me into the kitchen, which was also oversized and made up of all hard surfaces that gave it the acoustics of a parking garage.

American suburbs are filled with big, expensive houses, but a bigger house isn't necessarily a better home.

She and Paul explained to me that until a year before, they had lived in the city, in a small, older home. Although they liked the house, their three boys were growing up quickly, and they were starting to feel cramped for space. The house had no family room, so the kids didn't have a place to be rambunctious. The couple found a piece of property they loved. The lot was owned by a builder, who made it clear as part of the terms of sale that he would be the one to build the home. They thought this would be fine—they didn't know any other builders and this one had a good reputation.

The builder showed them his portfolio of plans and explained that they could choose any one of them. Although they weren't particularly enamored with any of the plans, they picked the one that seemed to have the rooms they needed in the right relationships to one another: kitchen opening into family room, formal living room separated from family room to allow kids some space to play away from mom and dad.

It wasn't until the house was actually under construction that the feeling of uneasiness began to set in. As the framing proceeded, the heights of the spaces became clear, as did the proportions of each room. "All the rooms just seemed huge," said Laura. They asked to make some changes, such as lowering some ceiling heights and dividing a room in two to make each a more manageable scale. But such changes would be very expensive at this stage in the process, the builder explained, promising that, "When the house is done, you'll love it." However, the house didn't get better, and when it was finished, it was clear to both of them that they felt no affinity for it. It seemed ostentatious to them. The scale of each room was overwhelming.

Laura took me upstairs to show me the master bathroom. "Look at this," she exclaimed, "our previous bedroom wasn't even this size!" Although the couple now faulted themselves

This soaring living room was designed to impress, not to be a comfortable space for the activities of daily life.

almost anything would have seemed spacious compared to their previous home.

The outcome was that Paul and Laura had built a $500,000 house that was nowhere close to their dream of home. After spending almost three times the value of their previous house, they were deeply unhappy. They told me they felt no desire to make the house their own by furnishing it or personalizing it in any way. Their story was horrifying to me. And even more alarming is the fact that Paul and Laura are not alone. Over the last couple of years, more and more people who have lived in these impersonal, oversized houses have come to our office and asked, "Is there an alternative? Can you design us a house that is more beautiful and more reflective of our personalities—a house we will enjoy living in?"

The answer is, of course, yes. And the key lies in building Not So Big, in spending more money on the quality of the space and less on the sheer quantity of it. So this book is for Paul and Laura and for everyone like them, whether building from scratch or remodeling, who wants a special home that expresses something significant about their lives and values but who doesn't know how to get it.

The Case for Comfort

After designing homes for 15 years, I have come to an inevitable conclusion: We are all searching for home, but we are trying to find it by building more rooms and more space. Instead of thinking about the quality of the spaces we live in, we tend to focus on quantity. But a house is so much more than its size and volume, neither of which has anything to do with comfort.

for being naive, they were simply following the process that is standard to working with a builder and selecting from a stock set of plans. They were not offered an opportunity for input into the design. And they didn't know how to ask for or give the feedback necessary to make it an expression of their lifestyle and their values. Like many people building a new house, Paul and Laura didn't have the words to describe what they wanted, nor did they realize how important it was to have input into the "feel" of the house. If a builder hears that a home buyer wants a spacious family room, he reasonably assumes that they are asking for a BIG family room. To Paul and Laura,

Instead of quantity,
think quality.
Comfort is born of
smaller scale and
beautiful details.

11

Everything in this kitchen conspires to create a classic statement, from custom cabinetry to antique light fixtures.

When most people contemplate building a new house or remodeling an existing one, they tend to spend time focusing on floorplan options and square footage. But in a completed home, these are only a very small part of what makes an impression. What also defines the character of a house are the details, such as a beautiful stair railing, well-crafted moldings around windows and doors, and useful, finely tailored built-ins.

These details are what attract us to older homes. New homes should be no different. However, such details cost money. And unless people are working with an architect, it is unusual to spend much time thinking about these aspects of the design. Because most people start with a desire for more space than their budgets allow, anything more than basic space, minimally detailed, will exceed the budget.

It's the details that delight: An Arts and Crafts–inspired light fixture can make a bigger impression than a vaulted ceiling.

Natural light and a stained-glass window beautify a stair landing. In a **Not So Big House**, every space is considered to be an expression of the lives lived within.

People who are attracted to architecturally designed houses also tend to seek a higher level of detail. So a good architect will suggest reducing square footage to allow for more detail. It isn't unusual for an architect's estimate of square-foot cost to be half again as much as a builder's. The architect is simply aware that, given the client's desire for detail, a house without detail is not going to be satisfactory. We're already familiar with this design concept in automobiles. The quality and detail of a Mercedes, Lexus, or Jaguar are far more important than the size of the car. More space does not equal more comfort. In fact, size has nothing to do with the appeal of these cars. If you want nothing but space, you buy an equally expensive diesel truck.

I do not advocate that everyone live in small houses. What I do suggest is that when building a new home or remodeling an existing one, you evaluate what really makes you feel at home. In other words, concentrate on, and put more of your money toward, what you like rather than settling for sheer size and volume. This concept is just as applicable to someone building a very expensive home as it is to someone on a tight

The Not So Big House of the Past

Around the turn of the last century, two Englishmen warned that the machine age could very well destroy the quality of life. John Ruskin and William Morris believed that life needed to be rehumanized, and the first place to begin such an undertaking was in the home. Ruskin and Morris founded a movement that was called Arts and Crafts, and it encompassed everything from the design of textiles to the design of houses.

Our neighborhoods are filled with examples of Not So Big Houses from the past, like the Craftsman bungalow above.

An Arts and Crafts interior designed by Greene and Greene (right).

The Arts and Crafts home was custom-crafted and featured large fireplaces and built-in bookshelves and cabinets. In North America, the style was embraced by such architects and designers as Greene and Greene and Gustav Stickley. Other American architects, among them Frank Lloyd Wright, created styles that were also based on notions of craft and beauty. For those Americans who couldn't afford an architect-designed home, Sears sold a prebuilt bungalow—complete with built-in shelves, wood trim, and a front porch—which arrived in panels and was easily as-sembled. (In 1926, a two-bedroom bungalow was listed in the Sears catalogue for the affordable price of $626.)

Smaller houses still seem connected to a simpler time. Many of the older houses in our neighborhoods were built to offer solace in a changing world. Now, nearly 100 years later, we seem to have forgotten the ideas Ruskin and Morris were so passionate about. Houses are getting bigger and bigger, and, because square footage is all that is required, they are being built without the level of detail so important to humanizing life.

This room was designed to be a total expression of comfort, exemplified by the cozy scale, built-ins, and arched ceiling.

budget. While you might be able to afford a 6,000-sq.-ft. house, you may find that building a 3,000-sq.-ft. house that fits your lifestyle actually gives you more space to *live* in. In most very large homes, a substantial percentage of space is rarely used. And if you have a limited budget, this book will give you ideas on how to pare down the quantity of space you need so that you can put more of your money into giving the house some character.

Creating Comfort

The current pattern of building big to allow for quantities of furniture with still more room to spare is more akin to wearing a sack than a tailored suit. It may offer capacity, but at the cost of comfort and charm. Spaciousness, although it can look appealing in a photograph, just isn't conducive to comfort. Many of the huge rooms we see in magazines today are really only comfortable to be in when they are filled with people. For

No other space in a house says "comfort" quite like a window seat. Sitting here feels like an embrace from the house.

one or two, or for a family, they can be overwhelming. And when rooms feel overwhelming, they don't get used.

The Not So Big House, no matter its style, aims to be comfortable. Look up the word "comfortable" in any dictionary and you'll see a range of entries attempting to describe it. Webster's offers a wide variety of definitions, from "fitted to give tranquil enjoyment" to "free from pain and trouble." So how do we create comfort in the Not So Big House?

One of the tools that can help you determine what feels comfortable is to gain a better understanding of the proportions of space. Like most people, Paul and Laura were not able to understand from the blueprints what the space would feel like. Proportion literally refers to the relationship of the vertical to the horizontal dimension. It also includes the relationship to the third dimension, depth. Because we are human beings and come in sizes typically ranging from just under 5 ft.

to mid-6 ft., those three dimensions also need to relate to our human height. Some people can just tell when a space is pleasingly proportioned, while other people cannot. The ability to read a space this way is similar to an "ear" for music.

But not everyone agrees on what is well-proportioned space. Many people find Frank Lloyd Wright's much-acclaimed work to be oppressive, either because they consider it to be too ordered or because it's too constrictive for head height in some places. Wright used low ceilings to accentuate transitions between various significant places in the house, as well as at entryways, to give one the sense of needing to stoop, which is a gesture of reverence. On the other hand, the Prairie Style (the name his architectural style has come to be known by) liberated a new way of thinking about space and proportion in

Architect Frank Lloyd Wright was a master of proportion. He used variations in ceiling height to enhance character and comfort in his homes.

architectural design. For many people, the variations in ceiling height typical of his work greatly enhance the character and comfort of a home (see the bottom photo on the facing page).

Consider the foyer in Paul and Laura's suburban house. Why was it so unwelcoming? Well, with its tall ceilings and marble floors, it was designed to overwhelm and impress visitors, not to welcome. The proportions of their foyer were more suitable for a public building than for a house. When a space is overscaled, in relation to our own size, more often than not it doesn't feel comfortable.

The book *A Pattern Language* (Oxford University Press, 1977) has been a very useful tool in our office. Written by Christopher Alexander and a group of colleagues, the book consists of a collection of concepts, or patterns, that range from issues of city planning to those of individual room configuration. We use the book to help clients think about and describe how they want to tailor their house to their lifestyle and how to make it comfortable. One of my favorite patterns described in the book is entitled "Alcoves." It states that, "No homogeneous room, of homogeneous height, can serve a group of people well. To give a group a chance to be together, as a group, a room must also give them the chance to be alone, in ones and twos in the same space." It concludes, "Therefore…make small places at the edge of any common room usually no more than 6 feet wide and 3 to 6 feet deep and possibly much smaller. These alcoves should be large enough for two people to sit, chat or plan and sometimes large enough to contain a desk or a table."

What the pattern describes perfectly is how to make a space comfortable. By dividing a room into smaller spaces, it can be

A window seat is tucked into the second floor, allowing a cozy place for one within a house designed for entertaining.

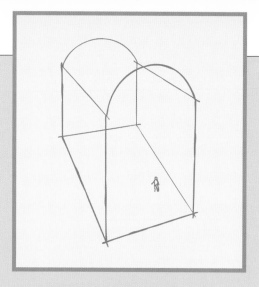

Finding Comfort

When I teach design, I ask first-year architecture students to collect data about places that make them feel particularly comfortable or uncomfortable. This is also a useful exercise for non-architects who want to understand better how the places that surround us affect us.

A big space, however inspiring, can be too tall for comfort.

Here's how it works. Equip yourself with a tape measure and a pad of paper. As you go about your daily routine, notice how you respond to different places—whether the place is as splendid as the rotunda in the State Capitol or as mundane as the copy room at the office. In each place you visit, notice how you respond. When I walk through the magnificent doorway at the State Capitol here in Minnesota, I feel awe and wonder. Physically, though, I feel very small, almost insignificant in this towering space, despite the beauty of the surroundings.

In smaller spaces, it's useful to measure the proportions of the room—and don't forget the ceiling height. As you measure, notice what constitutes the spaces that feel good to you. Try to determine if they appeal on an emotional level or in a physical way. And try to articulate why. Such spaces are the shapes that make you feel most comfortable and are worth incorporating in your own home.

used for a variety of functions while offering human-scaled spaces that are actually connected to things that go on in the house. I call this idea "shelter around activity," and one of the best examples of it is the window seat. The floor is raised, the ceiling is lowered and the walls are brought in to define a place for one or two people, from which they can observe the world. Sitting in a window seat feels like an embrace from the house. It is the epitome of comfort.

I designed a house for a single woman who loved to entertain. While many of the spaces in her house were suitable for large numbers of people, I wanted to make sure that the house had some places that would be comfortable when she was alone. Her window seat on the second floor is tucked into the geometry of the roofline (see the photo on p. 17), which offers shelter around activity and a bird's-eye view of the nearby lake.

One of my partners, Michaela Mahady, designed the living room shown in the photo on p. 15 to be a total expression of comfort. Not only does the fieldstone hearth bespeak comfort, but the small scale of the room also ensures coziness. The arch above the fireplace, the lowered soffits at the edge of the room, the soft lighting, the abundance of natural woodwork, even the overstuffed furniture—everything conspires to make this room one you want to spend time in.

Tailoring to Fit

Paul and Laura had embarked on a new house project because they needed a place for their boys to play indoors during the winter. But despite its size and cost, the house they had built still didn't offer this space. The would-be living room projected such a formality, because of its scale, that the whole family

In a house where every detail expresses the personality of its owners, a rope and a tree trunk become a stair railing and a load-bearing column.

The wooden railing features cut-out fish and trees, which express the family's favorite pastime and the house's North Woods location.

they were—to themselves or to the community. In fact, the house projected an image that they found fundamentally offensive. To them the house said "generic house of wealthy people," which wasn't at all how they saw themselves.

Clearly, what should happen before a house is planned or built is an analysis of the lives—the likes, dislikes, needs, and wishes—of the people who will live in it. Just as a tailor takes measurements before sewing a new suit, we should take measurements before building a new house. There are few things in life as personal as our homes. Personalizing a home, though, goes beyond decoration. Because it takes considerable thought and planning to make a house into a home, I advocate far greater participation in the design process by the people who will live in the house. Your house should be an expression of who you are, not something that's impersonal and generic.

A stair railing can be just a safety barrier, but if it's designed with the homeowner in mind, it can become a centerpiece for the house. In the examples shown here and on the previous page, the railings were custom-crafted to express something about the people who live there. The rope railing in the photo on p. 19, designed by an architect couple, came as a solution only after 10 other ideas had been abandoned. The husband, an avid sailor, loved the idea of the rope, which also works in a similar way to the organic form of the tree-trunk column. Both rope and tree serve a function, as well as imbue the house with personality. The photo at left shows a cabin on a North Woods island that was built as a weekend retreat for a family that loves to fish. The stair railing, inspired by the work of the Scandinavian artist Carl Larsson, illustrates both the woodsy location of the cabin and the family's favorite hobby.

shared one main living space—the kitchen/family room. If their needs had been given more careful analysis before construction, a very different solution would have evolved.

As my meeting with Paul and Laura continued they told me that their lack of desire to personalize their new home came from the fact that it communicated nothing at all about who

In this remodeled house, a favorite window was saved and reused in an addition, where it is now flanked with glass block and double-hung windows.

Windows can be custom-tailored to frame a special view or to make a striking interior statement. In the remodeled house shown in the photo above, the couple's favorite window was saved from the original house and moved out 8 ft. to the new face of the home. A glass-block transom and flanking double-hung windows were added to let in more of the south light. Circular windows are expensive, but they can also become a focal point for the entire house. In the house shown on p. 22, an 8-ft.-diameter circular window frames a spectacular view while also creating an equally splendid interior focal point that's visible from many parts of the house. A circular effect can be achieved less expensively, but with equal drama, by hanging a metal hoop inside a perfectly square picture window (see the photo on p. 23).

A circular window can frame spectacular views and become the focal point of an interior space.

How to Talk about Quality of Space

The language of quality is so much more hazy than the language for quantity. Without the language to describe what you want in terms of quality, there is no way to be sure that a house will be what you want, until it is completed. Unfortunately, at that point, it's too late to remedy mistakes. Here are some words that help identify the quality of space:

cozy, elegant, introverted, light-filled, spare, exciting, dramatic, sumptuous, homey, classic, masculine, welcoming, private, modest, impressive, delicate, friendly.

A circular effect can be achieved inexpensively by inserting a metal hoop into a square window.

Often a work of art or a special piece of furniture has particular meaning, and a house can be designed to accommodate such objects. The carved wooden owl shown in the top photo on p. 24 became a symbol of the owners' land, which was frequently visited by an owl, and of their first house, which had burned to the ground. When they designed their new home, the wooden owl, a survivor of the fire, was offered a special place by the front entrance, where it greets all who enter.

Another couple, who had collected art and furniture for most of their adult lives, wanted a retirement house that would be a backdrop for their collection (see the bottom photo on p. 24). So the wall in the dining area was recessed to create a niche just the right size for a special Japanese *tansu*, or storage chest. The painting over the buffet has its own display area, which was anticipated in the design process. White walls throughout the house provide a dramatic setting for the collection.

Houses are repositories of the things that have meaning to us. In this Prairie-influenced home, a carved wooden owl greets visitors from its built-in niche.

This contemporary interior was designed to showcase a collection of paintings and furniture, with a niche designed specifically for a Japanese *tansu*.

The garden shed shown in the photo on the facing page is modeled after a Wendy house, or an English child's playhouse inspired by the Peter Pan stories. In the process of remodeling a couple's Cape Cod home, Dale Mulfinger, one of my partners, discovered that the woman, an avid gardener, wanted a place to house her tools that would fit in stylistically with the house. Because gardening was her passion, Dale determined in the planning process to design for her a special place, rather than simply expanding the garage.

Tailoring is a basic ingredient of the Not So Big House. If you just make a house smaller, but still generic, it won't have any more appeal than its larger cousins. What makes the Not So

A tool shed designed for an avid gardener becomes a charming little house that matches the Cape Cod styling of the owner's home.

Keeping a Place Journal

In a three-ring binder, start to assemble data about the places in your life that make you feel comfortable and those that make you feel uncomfortable. Document their size, take photos, or make diagrams illustrating what it is within the space that evokes the response. Images of other spaces can supplement your notes—magazines are a great resource for this. Some current favorites for gathering images are: *Architectural Digest, Better Homes and Gardens Building Ideas, Better Homes and Gardens Home Plan Ideas, Better Homes and Gardens Remodeling Ideas, Elle Decor, Fine Homebuilding, Fine Homebuilding's* annual *Houses* issue, *Home Magazine, House and Garden, House Beautiful Home Building, Metropolitan Home,* and *Traditional Home.*

Big concept work is that superfluous square footage is traded for less tangible but more meaningful aspects of design that are about beauty, self-expression, and the enhancement of life.

Working with Paul and Laura, we started to identify what features they wanted in a home. These included window seats, a place for the adults to retreat to after dinner while the kids play in the family room, lots of built-ins and bookshelves, and a large amount of natural woodwork. In contrast to the 4,000-sq.-ft. house they are currently living in, their new house will be around 2,300 sq. ft. Despite its smaller size, it will cost only slightly less to build. This is because for this couple, quality and personality are important. And now they understand that that is where their money needs to go. No matter how big or how small you make it, a house will not be a home unless you, your architect, and your builder really craft it into a place that is tailored to the way you live, filled with the spaces and things that have meaning to you.

Cotswold cottages in England built from stone have lasted hundreds of years.

Built to Last

When I first started designing houses in the early 1980s, many of our clients were asking for help in making their homes energy efficient. When the tax credit for such strategies disappeared, most of the interest in energy efficiency left with it. At that point, my partners and I realized that if the homes we designed were to be energy efficient, it would be because we wanted them to be, not because our clients were requesting it. Like many other architects and builders, we continued to design houses that would minimize a reliance on fossil fuels. We also insist upon good construction practices, even though it is a rare client who asks for a house that will last for generations.

America is a country of pioneers. And, as Americans, we assume that the way to embody our dreams in a house is to build it new for ourselves. It's the exception rather than the rule for people to stay where they are planted. People don't assume that they will pass their home on to the next generation, so building for permanence has never held much appeal or value. But, gradually, this attitude is changing. Why do we love Europe so much? Because of a sense of history, which is told best by buildings built centuries ago and made to last.

Along with this dawning appreciation for building for the long term comes the recognition that we will take care of things that are beautiful. Beauty, more often than not, comes from careful crafting. And when a well-crafted object ages, no matter what it is, society almost always helps it to age well. Just look at the buildings our culture has chosen to preserve—all of them were well designed. Owner after owner of such homes has recognized the treasure inherited and cared for them lovingly.

Fallingwater, Frank Lloyd Wright's masterpiece, is an important part of America's cultural heritage. Its beauty inspires us to take care of the building, ensuring that it will stand for future generations.

The Not So Big House is built for the future by taking care of the present. Anyone who has driven past a construction site and seen the dumpsters filled with perfectly good building materials understands that there must be a better way. By building the Not So Big House with materials that are renewable and by limiting the expenditure to what will really make a difference to the quality of life, we can have an enormous impact on our lives today as well as on the future.

What I am proposing in this book is that our houses can express our personalities, that they can be designed to accommodate our changing lifestyles, and that they can be built for future generations.

"When shown into one of those polar parlors...the heart cries, 'Take me where the people stay; I didn't come to see the chairs.'"
—William C. Gannett

F or a residential architect, going to a party in a new house is like test-driving a new car—it's a chance to see how the house works under real-world conditions. When my husband and I recently attended the wedding reception of an old college friend, we were among 40 guests at the hosts' first big party in their new suburban home. The house was outfitted with all the trappings of a dream home—an impressive front foyer, an elegant living room, and a formal dining room. It seemed the perfect place for a wedding reception. If ever there were an occasion when the formal rooms of a house would be well used, this was it.

The reality was quite different, however—yet strangely predictable. During the entire party, the living room remained vacant except for the occasional guest who walked through to admire the art as if viewing pictures in a museum. Even the dining room, which was filled with a splendid display of food, was empty. Where was everybody? Crowded into the kitchen, where they were leaning on

every possible surface; or in the well-used family room, which had an assortment of comfortable furniture.

Every half hour or so the hostess would try to coax people out of the kitchen by calling out, "The food is in the dining room!" Whenever someone actually ventured into the dining room and returned with a plate of food, invariably there was a chorus of, "Where did you get that?"

Even though the family room and the kitchen are the most popular places in a home, many houses still feature beautifully appointed formal living and dining rooms that sit empty most of the time, awaiting the arrival of guests. Although life at the end of the 20th century is quite informal, Emily Post still rules over the floorplans of our houses, making sure that they mind their manners.

In most houses, the formal rooms for dining and living are dinosaurs—leftovers from the turn of the century when Victorian house design followed the social code of the day. Visitors were ushered into a formal parlor. Dinner was served in a formal dining room, typically located a circuitous distance from the kitchen. Children were seen and not heard. One hundred years later, these formal areas still define

Partygoers often assemble in the kitchen and family room, even when you don't want them to.

Living rooms are built for parties, yet during this gathering the room remained completely empty.

the house. It's as if visitors are presented with a stage set, while the people who live there spend their time backstage. We've put all the resources necessary into creation of the living room for our guests while we do without new carpeting in the family room. The front door is used twice a year, usually for parties, and the people who live in the house enter through the back door, past piles of dirty laundry and bags of bottles ready for recycling. The irony is that, even when guests do come over, they avoid the formal spaces created for them because they're *too* formal.

Yet we continue to live informally in houses designed for more formality. Since World War II, there's been an attempt to incorporate more informal places into our houses. Remember the den? The basement rec room? How about the wet bar, the party room, the pool room? Many 1970s suburban homes offered one or more of the assortment, but the formal living and dining rooms are still at the core of the footprint of a house. And beginning in the 1980s, a vast variety of rooms joined the roster of must-have spaces, including great rooms, entertainment rooms, lavish master suites, and spaces for the newfound fitness craze.

Rethink your house and you'll discover the places that are used everyday—this is the essence of the Not So Big House.

Essentially, however, today's houses still wear the architectural equivalent of a hoopskirt, even if the accessories seem more contemporary. While we've been busy evolving over the past century, most of our houses have not. Their evolution has been constricted by outdated notions of what we think we need and what the real estate industry says we need for resale. At the turn of the new century, most houses are designed for the turn of the last.

It's time to rethink our houses and to let them become expressions of the way we really live. A Not So Big House can be Not So Big because the "dinosaur" rooms are replaced with spaces that reflect the way we eat and the way we live. The floorplan of the Not So Big House is a map, not a fossil, that reveals the lives of the people who live in it today.

Formal living rooms are rarely used in most houses; they stand almost as a memorial to the way we used to live.

Rethinking the Room

When I was 10 years old, my elementary school teacher assigned the class a puzzle, which she wanted us to solve by thinking creatively. The solution offers the essence of how to think about design. Here's the problem: Without taking pen off paper, and using only four straight lines, connect the nine dots shown at the top of the facing page. At home I spent hours on the problem and grew increasingly frustrated. I knew my teacher wouldn't lie to us, that there must be an answer. Yet it appeared to be an impossible assignment. During the middle of the night, however, I awoke with the answer clear in my mind.

I reached for the problem and magically connected the dots with four straight lines. What I discovered was that, if I stayed within the box created by the dots, I couldn't solve the problem. Once I broke the confines of the outline, the problem solved itself. (If you have trouble solving the problem, you'll find the answer on the very last page of the book—but don't give up yet.)

Is there a way to think beyond ordinary boundaries to create a house that works better for us? This is the secret to designing a Not So Big House—the ability to think creatively, responding to needs and wishes, not to preconceived notions of what a house should be.

Instead of thinking of a house as a series of rooms, think of it as a sequence of places. One favorite place is a cozy spot by the hearth.

Without taking pen off paper, connect the nine dots with four straight lines.

Most people speak in terms of square footage and number of rooms when asked to describe a house: four bedrooms, three baths, 3,000 sq. ft. The idea that a house is composed of rooms for separate activities is fundamental to how it's been defined. But a room is an artificial construct, an attempt to put boundaries around space. The idea of the room can be replaced with the notion of places for various activities. What is your favorite place in your home? Is it a comfortable chair near the fireplace where you can enjoy a glass of wine and unwind after a day of work? Mine is a little book nook, a place just big enough for one that's carved into a corner of the living area. This place offers a cozy spot to read and a place to watch what's going on in the rest of the house.

In a Not So Big House, each space is defined by the activities that take place there. Think about what happens in the family room: There's a place to watch TV, a place to enjoy the

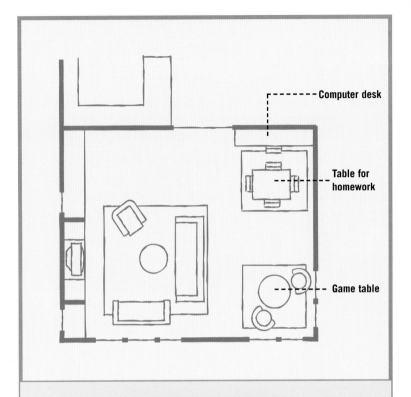

Computer desk

Table for homework

Game table

Saving Space with Alcoves
One space can accommodate three different activity places (above), each gravitating toward a corner. House the same activities in alcoves (below) and you reduce the square footage and use the space more efficiently.

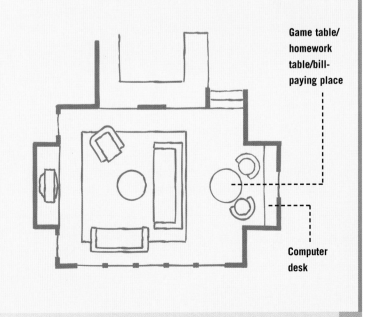

Game table/ homework table/bill- paying place

Computer desk

Understanding Where You Live Now

Take a look at your existing home. Now make a list of the rooms you have, along with the approximate square footage of each one. Under each room name, list what happens there. Under each activity, list the frequency of the activity and who does it. Finally, reorganize the list of rooms in order of most used to least used.

For most people, this exercise offers some surprises. A room that has significant square footage may not be used very often. This is a clear indication that you should rethink the space to see if there's another way to accommodate the activities it houses. In many cases, rooms such as the formal living room and formal dining room serve limited purposes.

Some people will discover that the formal living room is in use every day. In that case, the living room works. The point is to identify how you live and then tailor the house to accommodate those needs rather than just assume that every house has to have the same set of rooms.

fireplace, a place to do homework, a place to pay bills, a place to play Scrabble. When we think of the family room in this way, it's no longer merely a space bounded by four walls and a ceiling. It can be defined another way altogether: as a series of alcoves, each offering shelter around an activity and surrounding a central sitting area (see the drawing on p. 33 and the photo on the facing page). When this kind of thinking is extended to the entire house, a new definition emerges. A house is a sequence of places for all the different activities that happen there.

One reason houses have become too big is that they are planned with the idea that there needs to be a separate room for each activity. But look carefully at how you really live in your house and you'll discover how much space goes unused (see the sidebar at left). A house is Not So Big when it's composed of adaptable spaces, each designed to share various functions, each in use everyday.

Exercise: Understanding Where You Live Now

Kitchen   8 × 12 = 96 SF
Cooking
Making coffee
Eating breakfast & snacks
Reading paper

Dining Room   10 × 12 = 120 SF
Eating dinner
Entertaining (4-5 times per year)

Living Room   14 × 16 = 224 SF
Entertaining (4-5 times per year)
Reading
Listening to music

Foyer   5 × 10 = 50 SF
Coming & going in the non-winter months
Hanging coats
Greeting guests

Laundry   7 × 10 = 70 SF
Washing clothes
Hanging dry & drying clothes
Filing newspaper clippings

Bathroom   7 × 8 = 56 SF
The obvious - only one bathroom
so it all happens here

Bedroom #1   10 × 10 = 100 SF
Kid's sleeping place
Storage of off-season clothing

Bedroom #2   12 × 13 = 156 SF
Our bedroom
Reading in evening

Bedroom #3   9 × 13 = 117 SF
Storage of books - so it's really
a library
More storage of off-season clothes
Other crafts

Attic   10 × 24 = 240 SF
In home office space
Paying bills
Drawing
Designing
Internet access from computer here
Watching TV
Listening to music
Meditating
Reading
Also serves as extra bedroom
when we have guests

MOST TO LEAST USED
1. Kitchen   96
2. Attic   240
3. Bathroom   56
4. Foyer   50
5. Bedroom #2   156
6. Laundry   70
7. Dining Room   120
8. Bedroom #3   117
9. Living Room   224
10. Bedroom #1

The Not So Big House features adaptable spaces open to one another, designed for everyday use.

If you rethink the formal living room, formal dining room, kitchen, and family room, you'll discover a different model altogether, not unlike the way the nine dots are connected in the exercise mentioned previously. The core of the Not So Big House is an interconnected area that encompasses kitchen, living, and dining functions. All of these areas, which are physically and visibly open to each other, are shared by family and friends.

A balance between public and private space is essential to making any floorplan work. In this house, private spaces for adults are balanced by open areas for family activities. (Photo taken at A on floorplan p. 38.)

Public and Private Spaces

A realtor who had recently purchased a striking contemporary remodel of an older home called me with an odd complaint. Ever since she and her husband had moved into the house they had been fighting. An architect is typically not a marriage counselor, but I agreed to take a look. The house, with its white walls, high ceilings, and contemporary feel (see the photo at right), was ready for the pages of *Architectural Digest*. But as my tour progressed, the couple's problem became clear. There wasn't a single door inside the house, not even on the bathroom, which very stylishly featured a soaring arch to mark its entrance. The master bedroom had a half-wall that looked over into the living room. There was no privacy in this house for anybody, which clearly was creating tension between husband and wife.

The remodeling was fairly straightforward. Rather than build walls, we extended the half-walls with glass to provide acoustic privacy and to preserve the striking lines of the design. As for the bathroom, we added a door and filled the archway with a window that still allowed light to stream in.

Another client, living alone in a brand-new 5,000-sq.-ft. house, called me because she wanted to plan an addition.

When there are no doors to separate one space from another, a house offers no privacy.

When we met she confided that the house, believe it or not, felt too small to her—and she was right! In spite of its high square footage, the house was incredibly claustrophobic. There were countless rooms, each designated for a specific activity, and equally countless doorways that, when open, offered dead-end views of walls. There was nothing to look at beyond each room, no view of any other interior spaces—and deliberately so. In planning the house, the woman, who considered herself to be a terrible housekeeper, had wanted to make sure that her guests could not see into any of her messy rooms. She hadn't recognized that her need to add on was a direct result of this strategy.

Rather than add on, we reconfigured part of the existing space by opening up the maze of rooms into an open, public space. We kept the balance of rooms intact. As for the housekeeping issue, I gently suggested that she consider hiring some cleaning help.

To make any floorplan work, there has to be a balance between open spaces and closed, between public and private. Sometimes we feel like being with others, and other times we need solitude. A house should offer a hierarchy of spaces, each appropriate to its function and to our mood. The Not So Big House has at its core a public space

Family
room

Away
room

← A

B

Deck

Dining

A sitting area down the hall provides a private place for adults—in the Not So Big floorplan it's called the "away room." (Photo taken at B on floorplan.)

The plan shows how an informal living area can become the central part of the house when it's visible from many places.

composed of living, dining, and kitchen functions. It also allows for private spaces, which are acoustically or visually separate from the open areas.

One of my partners designed a house for a professional couple who wanted spaces for the family to gather together, as well as places for adults only. The light-filled living area shown in the photo on p. 36 is the most public space in the house because it's visible from the kitchen, from a more secluded sitting area, from a second-floor loft, and from an exterior deck (see the floorplan on the facing page). When the adults need privacy, they retreat to the sitting area just down the hall (see the photo on the facing page).

How public or private a space is depends on both its scale and its visibility. If a place is to be used, people need to be able to see it. A space that's visible from as many places as possible automatically becomes a public area. If a space is to be private, remove it from sight and locate it away from the main traffic areas—or put a door at its entrance. "Out of sight, out of mind," is a truth in house design.

When there is a proper balance between public and private places, something quite natural happens. All the spaces in the house begin to be used every day. The patterns of life are no longer constrained by the floorplan; they are expressed by it.

The Public Kitchen

Back when cooking was a private act, the kitchen was concealed behind doors, anterooms, and walk-through butler's pantries. In the Victorian era, the kitchen was so private that most family members never even set foot inside it—it was entirely the territory of servants. Later in the century, however, the woman of the house took over the kitchen, emerging from its confines only after taking off her apron and wiping the sweat from her brow. But today, we love to be in the kitchen, and no matter how tiny the space, this is where friends and family congregate.

The kitchen is the heart of the house, and the Not So Big House should have a big heart. If we acknowledge that the kitchen is where we want to be, then we should make the kitchen accessible and open to all the living areas of the house. Extend the kitchen so that it's visible from the areas where you live; once it is connected—physically and visually—to these spaces, then suddenly the need for a separate family room, sun-

Traditional Kitchen Placement

A hearth in the kitchen can offer a comfortable place for one or two people to sit, out of the way of food preparation but close to the center of activity.

room, and living room is gone. All that's necessary is a place for living, where family and visitors can gather near the kitchen.

You can even go so far as to offer a place to sit in the kitchen, by adding a hearth and a small cozy area where a few people can gather out of the traffic pattern of food preparation (see the photo on the facing page). This kind of space appeals to even the most citified folks, who long for the look and feel of the farmhouse kitchen. The image of this place, where bread bakes in an open hearth and sunlight streams in the windows, has captured our imaginations. The scale of this area is important to its success. It should be big enough for only a couple of easy chairs—the addition of just a few unnecessary feet destroys its coziness.

Double-Duty Dining

When a house is defined as a series of places for various activities rather than as a string of separate rooms, it's easy to see how often functions are duplicated in a typical floorplan. Many newer houses, for example, offer two or three rooms in which to eat. The first and most prominent is the formal dining room, which is usually a room set apart from the kitchen and main living areas. There is also an informal eating area, adjacent to the kitchen or a part of it. And sometimes there's a still more informal eating place at the kitchen island, where stools are pulled up to the countertop surface (see the floorplan on p. 42).

The dining room is not as universally neglected as the formal living room, but in many homes it is used only once or twice a year. Rather than put your resources into a room used so infrequently, why not create a place for dining that can do double duty—for everyday use, as well as for those few formal

The kitchen is the heart of the Not So Big House; connected to the living and dining areas, it's a gathering place for family and friends.

The Integrated Kitchen

Kitchen design has reached new heights of sophistication. But while a kitchen may boast the latest equipment and appliances, most kitchens still look fairly generic. When the kitchen is open to the rest of the house, the opportunity exists to integrate it visually. If a house features natural woodwork in its public areas, then the kitchen should feature natural woodwork as well. If a house makes a stark contemporary statement, so should the kitchen.

In simple terms, the materials that are used in the rest of the house are brought into the kitchen. Rather than use generic kitchen cabinetry, tie the kitchen together with the rest of the living area by installing custom cabinets. If you have a tile floor in the front entryway, consider running tiles as a backsplash along the counters. Choose carefully which kitchen gadgets are left out and which are stored. A hanging rack of well-designed implements, carefully placed, can become part of the kitchen's composition.

Tiles used in the front entryway can be repeated as a backsplash along the counters.

If you are using a center island, consider it as you would a built-in piece of furniture. The flooring materials used can also connect the kitchen with the living and dining spaces. Countertops, too, can make a striking statement. There are many resources to help you make your kitchen work exactly the way you want it to: As you plan for its usefulness, think also about its beauty.

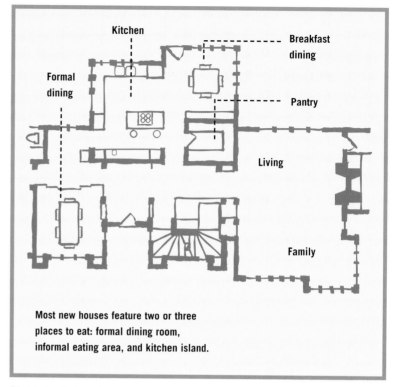

Most new houses feature two or three places to eat: formal dining room, informal eating area, and kitchen island.

Multiple Dining Areas

occasions? Just as a living area can work for both family and friends, so can one dining area function both for family snacks and for a dinner party. The top photo on p. 44 illustrates the key to making a place for eating work both formally and informally. The eating area was designed to accommodate a long table, which seats 6 informally and up to 12 or more on more special occasions with the addition of table leaves. Combining the informal and formal eating areas into one saves at least 200 sq. ft.

But what about the dirty dishes? Many cooks are concerned about guests seeing their messy kitchens. There are various solutions to hiding the detritus of meal preparation. A raised countertop between kitchen and dining area will obstruct the

Everyone loves to be in the kitchen, and the Not So Big House puts dining close to the place of food preparation.

43

view of the mess (as shown in the photo below). The sink and the dishwasher can be placed so they aren't in full view from the table. Or a series of sliding panels, illustrated on the facing page, can totally hide the kitchen.

If you enjoy the experience of creating a special atmosphere in a dining room that's separated from the kitchen—and don't want to give it up just to save a few hundred square feet—then this option isn't for you. However, remember that just because the dining area is informal in layout doesn't mean it will feel informal to your guests. An informal eating area can easily become a more formal space with some simple lighting strategies, which are addressed in chapter 3 (see pp. 66-67).

A dining area can do double duty, serving equally well for everyday use and for formal occasions, with simple strategies like special lighting.

A raised countertop between kitchen and living area helps hide dirty dishes from view.

A sliding partition between kitchen and dining room can be used to connect the areas or make them totally separate.

Before

After

This type of partition is a good solution when remodeling an existing older home to fit more informal lifestyles.

Remodeling for Double-Duty Dining

The most common addition to an older house is a kitchen remodel with adjacent family room. This addition almost always includes an informal eating area. Once this new space exists, what were the formal living and dining room are rarely ever used again.

The floorplans shown here illustrate a way to avoid the atrophy of the dining room. Two of the walls in the old dining room were removed to open it to the new family-room addition. Visible from the kitchen and family area, the dining area can now do double-duty: both as the informal eating area for the family and for special occasions, when closing the sliding doors creates a more formal atmosphere.

An away room is a place for acoustical privacy. This away room is adjacent to the family room but separated by French doors. It offers a quiet space away from the noise of televisions and stereos. (Photo taken at A on floorplan.)

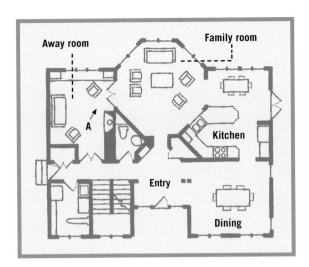

The Away Room

The "Away Room"

Imagine you drop by a neighbor's house for coffee. She ushers you inside her beautiful house, where one of the kids is watching an after-school special in the living area while another child is playing Nintendo. The teenager upstairs is listening to music—and it's not the harpsichord. Add the hum of a dishwasher to this cacophony, and you may wish you had never stopped by.

Because houses are filled with televisions, appliances, computers, and stereo equipment, they are filled with noise. In a more open floorplan, there needs to be a place that provides acoustical privacy. In our office we call this place the "away room," a term that refers to its function of providing escape (see the photo on the facing page). The away room can have several functions: It can be both the cozy and slightly more formal entertainment space where you can sit with other adults, and it can become a quiet place where adults can retreat to read or to work in the evenings.

In this house, the away room, smaller and less central than the classic formal living room, is the space for television viewing.

If the away room contains the television or the stereo, it becomes the place to watch or listen. Conversely, if the television or stereo is kept in the living area, the away room becomes the quiet area—a small, comfortable place away from the sound. Because the away room is separated from the more open living spaces by French doors or by distance, it can have a dif-

The everyday entrance to your house can be more than the back door—make it welcoming and beautiful. (Photos taken at A and B on floorplan.)

ferent style from the rest of the house. In a light and airy interior, the away room can be a cozy and book-lined alternative. If the house is filled with dark woodwork, then the away room can be filled with light.

The proportions of the room are important, as are its furnishings. A smaller scale—such as 11 ft. by 12 ft.—creates a cozier space. If the chairs are formal and uncomfortable, that's how you will feel. But if the away room is furnished with soft easy chairs, wicker rockers, and old family photos, it will offer a comfortable place for living.

The Entrance

The front door may be the most unused part of a house, especially in colder climates, opened only for visitors or for special deliveries. The everyday entrance to the house is usually through the back door. But why do we relegate ourselves to secondary status when it comes to the way we enter our houses?

Instead of thinking about the entry as just a front or back door, we can create a sequence of places and a more ceremonious greeting for ourselves than the passage from the garage, past the hot water heater, and through the laundry. Your everyday entrance should welcome you home. And that entrance

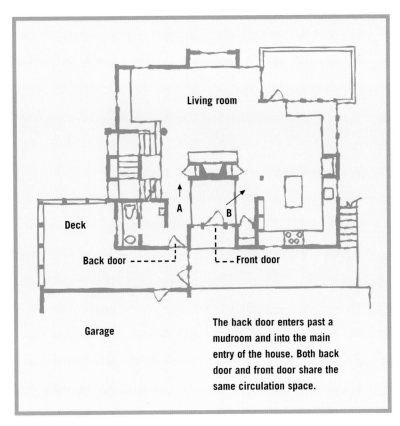

Combining Entries

Living room

Deck

Back door - - - - - - -

A   B

Garage

Front door

The back door enters past a mudroom and into the main entry of the house. Both back door and front door share the same circulation space.

from which you are welcomed home by the views of your house. The point is to save square footage and to give residents a pleasant entry to their own home.

If the garage can't be close to the front door, it's a good idea for the entrance to open onto a space that offers a view to a window or to some special feature of the house. The stuff of everyday life that gets crammed into back hallways—the cat food, laundry, and piles of newspapers—can be placed in planned-for storage areas. They don't need to be the first things that greet you when you get home.

It can be difficult to combine formal and informal entries if the siting of the house dictates that the front entry be located away from the garage and back entry. And the necessary clean-up before entering the house may require a different model. The example that comes to mind is a farmer client whose wife insists he shower before he enters the house. Their mudroom is quite large, replete with laundry and full bath.

Home Work

In medieval times, the grocer, the bookbinder, and the cobbler, along with their help and their families, lived above their respective shops. It's only been in the last couple of hundred years that living has been separated from work space. But very recently—within the last decade even—work has begun to come back home. Our firm has designed numerous home offices, many of which were intended for evening use but have since developed into full-time work spaces. The challenge when incorporating a new function into your house is to go beyond merely adding square footage. How and when do you work? Who will interrupt you? How private does the space

can be combined with what has traditionally been called the front foyer to create a space that is actually used (see the photos on the facing page). By having two different doors opening into the same foyer—one a traditional front door and the other from a garage or adjacent mudroom—you and your visitors can enter the house more ceremoniously. In this model, the garage is placed close to the front entrance (see the floorplan above).

In many areas of the country, there needs to be a place where kids and adults can remove snowy or muddy shoes and coats. One solution is to attach the mudroom to the entry, either as an anteroom to a front foyer or just around the corner. Take off your outdoor clothing first, and then step into the entrance,

French doors close off an office area from the master bedroom. This solution can offer the most private place to put a home office; in this instance, it allows a writer an escape from a young, active family.

need to be? What will your pattern of work be in the future? The examples illustrated here show five different approaches to integrating offices into the home.

Office attached to master bedroom A doctor who also writes books about health issues wanted to create a space within a 1926 Dutch Colonial where he could sit in a comfortable chair and read and also have a desk to work at his computer. He and his wife were facing the challenges of raising two active young children. It was determined that the most private place for the addition would be within the master bedroom suite. By adding no more than 80 sq. ft. to the master bedroom, we were able to create a distinctive reading nook and a workable office alcove (see the photo at right). The two sets of doors into the space—one into the master bedroom and then French doors that close off the office area—give him a kind of double-seal privacy.

Office in bedroom alcove A married couple contacted me about designing a weekend home. Because both of them were in professional positions, their weekend hideaway had to accommodate places to work. The woman, who is an attorney, didn't want her work space to be in the more public living area, so we carved a corner out of the master bedroom (see the top photo on p. 52). This nook, no wider than the desk itself, allows her

Through the French doors, the office area is actually an alcove tucked into the eaves of a low roofline. Many people would discard this area as unusable.

to study briefs while still enjoying the spectacular scenery. This option works well for people who are tidy—if your desk is usually cluttered you might consider an alcove that can be blocked from view with sliding doors.

Office in guest bedroom If you live in a house with a guest room, it can do double duty as an office. Putting an office in an infrequently used guest bedroom can be a good space-saving solution. The best way to double these two functions is to use a Murphy bed or a fold-out couch, so that the room doesn't stay filled with the bed platform. The size of this room should accommodate the bed both up and down. It's a good idea, however, to make sure there is at least 2 ft. 6 in. of clearance between the surrounding desk area and the bed. If the office computer is kept on a moveable cart, it can be rolled into another room during a guest's stay.

Office with separate entrance When my husband and I were designing our own home, we wanted a place with lots of counter space to lay out plans—and we knew that we needed a separate entrance in case clients came to the house. It also needed to be light-filled and pleasant to be in—if not, I knew we wouldn't use it. For us, the work space needed to be as interesting and as comfortable as the rest of the house.

An alcove in the master bedroom, created by a lowered soffit, can easily become a home office—a solution that works well for tidy people.

The site we chose to build on is sloped, and the office, along with its separate entrance, occupies the lower level (see the photo below). The main living spaces are on the main and upper levels. The separate level for the office removes it enough from the living spaces so that we aren't constantly distracted by the lure of the refrigerator and other family activity.

Office for evening work A computer consultant needed an office that would be close to the activity of his family but that had enough separation to allow work to get done. The office was placed in the loop of family activity, so that when the doors are open, it can be part of the rest of the house (see the floorplan on the facing page). If the doors are closed,

The author's own home office is filled with light and is as interesting and as comfortable as the rest of the house.

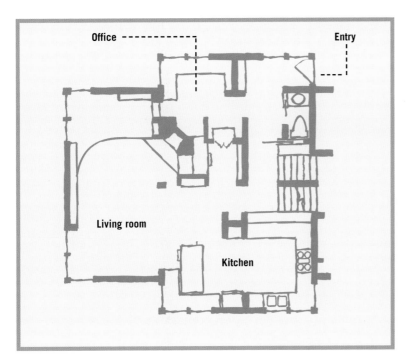

Home Office

though, he has acoustical privacy and his children know not to interrupt him. When a client comes to the house, he can close a door between the entry and living space, making the office entirely private.

If you're going to be doing a lot of work at home, it's better to create a space that is separate and private: Avoid making a home office double as the family control center. These are different functions and typically operate best out of different places.

Not So Many Bathrooms

The bathroom has undergone its own evolutionary process from water closet to luxury suite. American houses contain more bathrooms than any other culture's. Larger new homes feature one bathroom associated with each bedroom and sometimes even separate bathrooms for husband and wife. Add a

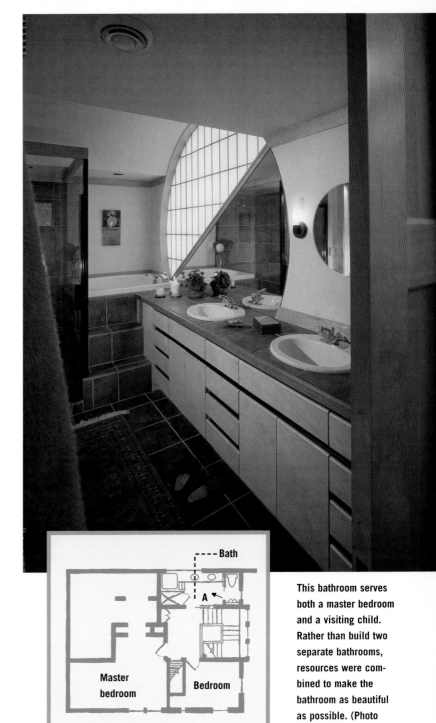

This bathroom serves both a master bedroom and a visiting child. Rather than build two separate bathrooms, resources were combined to make the bathroom as beautiful as possible. (Photo taken at A on floorplan.)

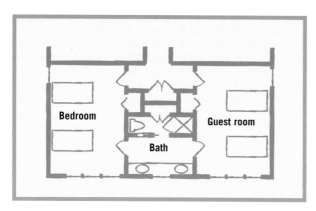

Bathroom with Two Entrances

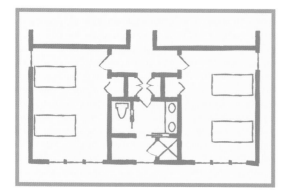

Two doors into one bathroom (above) can create an awkward situation for visitors. One entrance into the same bathroom (left) is a better solution.

powder room and a mudroom toilet, and you can have two or three bathrooms per resident. Why so many? The reasons are primarily for resale value. A private bathroom is considered to be a desirable luxury. Yet, bathrooms are one of the most expensive areas in the house per square foot (you could almost purchase a new car for every bathroom you build), so it's important to analyze whether such an investment is sensible.

The way bathrooms are planned to be used and the way they actually are used are entirely different. The model in most instances seems to be one bathroom for the adults and one for the children. In some families the master bathroom is used by the whole family, because the morning is the time when the family gathers socially. In other models, the parents' area is a private zone.

In designing a Not So Big House, there should be a concerted effort to cut back on the number of bathrooms. Here are a couple of strategies to accomplish that goal: Consider which bathrooms can be shared. The master bath is typically more an expression of fantasy than reality. With its whirlpool or soaking tub, the master bath implies a life of leisure and relaxation. The reality, in many families, is that the tub is used most often by children under the age of five. If you want to share your bathroom with your children, then plan accordingly. If you don't, then consider putting the soaking tub in a place where everyone can use it.

A common mistake is to connect a guest bedroom and another bedroom with one bathroom. This almost always creates an awkward situation for the guest, who may not be comfortable sharing a bathroom with whomever is on the other side of the door. In such cases, consider designing a bathroom with a single entrance, easily accessible from both bedrooms (see the floorplans at left). And by placing partitions between functions you can accommodate the needs of more than one person without any awkwardness.

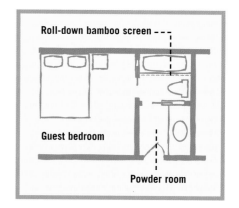

Powder Room/Guest Bathroom

Many people decide during the construction process to make the porch all-season. But a sunroom, which is an interior space, has a very different feel from a screen porch.

A powder room should be convenient to family social areas and also close to the mudroom entrance. The same powder room can serve both family and visitors, if you're willing to let go of expectations that the room will be pristine at all times, ready for the arrival of an unannounced guest. Frequently when I tell clients this, they still insist they need two powder rooms: one for family and one for guests. But if you stop and think about how often a guest stops by unannounced, you'll be able to reevaluate whether it's worth building a separate powder room for such a rare event. That's how bathrooms proliferate—we don't think about how frequently such events (a guest arriving unannounced) really happen.

If a guest bedroom is nearby, the powder room can even function as a guest bath. By hanging a bamboo shade or other screening device over the tub when the bath isn't needed, you can transform a bathroom into a powder room (see the bottom drawing on the facing page). Another strategy is to separate the shower or tub with a partition so that it's out of view.

If you eliminate unnecessary bathrooms, you'll save money and space. Use the space for a place just for yourself; and put the money toward making the bathrooms you do build more beautiful.

Sunroom or Porch?

What about those places in a house that serve no quantifiable function? The screen porch may seem to be just a place to enjoy a summer night. In a burst of practicality, many people decide during construction to make the porch all-season. It seems like

such a small change to add windows and doors, but the change will turn a place that would be used and cherished as a protected outdoor space into yet another sunny room in a house. A sunroom has a different function than a porch: A sunroom is an all-year-round indoor space, while a screen porch celebrates summer weather and the outdoors.

Newer houses in particular feature so many windows that several rooms in a typical house could be considered sunrooms already (see the photo below). In such a case, a sunroom often becomes yet another sitting room—beautifully appointed, but not much used. If your house has no similar space, a sunroom makes sense. One light-filled social space will get used, but two or more merely duplicate functions.

A screen porch isn't a luxury–it's an essential way to celebrate summer weather and the outdoors.

Living rooms in new houses often feature many windows. When you add a sunroom to such a house, it merely duplicates functions.

Older houses often have front porches that connect them to the street and the community beyond. In summer, the porch becomes the most cherished room in the house.

the thunderstorms and sunsets there. We were outside all the while, separated from nature by only a thin layer of mesh through which the mosquitoes could not penetrate. It very quickly became our favorite room in the house (see the photo on p. 57).

This experience is very different from sitting in a sunroom, which never gives you the impression you are actually outside, despite all the windows. The windows are a definite membrane between inside and outside. Even if you don't live in an area besieged with airborne pests, the experience of sitting on a

A porch doesn't have to be big. This three-sided porch, with elegant and minimalist detailing, transforms the house for summer living.

In Minnesota, where I live, the summer season is short and the air is thick with mosquitoes. If we want to be outside during the summer, we must have a screened porch. When I first moved here, I didn't understand this and very nearly converted the porch on the front of the old house I had just purchased into an extension of the living room. Luckily, I didn't have enough money at the time to follow through with my plans. After just a few weeks of summer, I realized that the porch was the living area for the few months of good weather, between June and September. We ate there, socialized there, watched

This writing nook offers a place for a poet to curl up on pillows and contemplate the view beyond.

porch, outside but protected by a section of roof, is delightful. The more sides of the porch open to the great outdoors the better: one is hardly enough; two is better; three is ideal.

A Place of One's Own

Whenever you tinker in the garage or retreat to a sewing room, you're expressing the need for a place of your own. Children get their own rooms, but a couple tend to share all their space with each other. Joseph Campbell wrote this about the need for personal space: "You must have a room or a certain hour of the day or so where you do not know what is in the morning paper. A place where you can simply experience and bring forth what you are and what you might be. At first you may think nothing's happening. But if you have a sacred space and take advantage of it and use it everyday, something will happen" (quoted in *Simple Abundance*, Warner Books, 1995).

Perhaps the search for the essence of this place—a room of one's own—has contributed to the scale of houses today: More and more rooms are planned in an attempt to create distance and separation. But all that's necessary to create a place for yourself is a very small area—truly just big enough for one. Tucked into an attic or carved out of a bedroom, such a place should encourage you to be yourself. A writer and poet I know made her personal space in a corner of the master bedroom (see the bottom photo on the facing page). By extending the windows from floor level to 2 ft. 4 in. off the floor, she can sit on cushions on the floor and have a bird's-eye view of the outside world as she contemplates her next poem. My own private place is an attic hideaway, accessible by a ship's ladder.

The author's own private place is accessible with a ship's ladder. Carved into an attic, it's a place of quiet inspiration.

Both a place for meditation and for writing, it is filled with things that I love and that have special meaning to me. It is a true expression of my inner self: a place where I find inspiration, clarity, and focus.

"Do not keep anything in your home that you do not know to be useful or believe to be beautiful."—William Morris

Anyone who's ever spent time on a sailboat already appreciates how the Not So Big House works. Each space within the boat is carefully tailored to serve more than one function. Everything from recycling bins to clothes storage is well considered. Because of this careful, thoughtful use of space, it's no great exaggeration to suggest that six people can live more comfortably on a 40-ft. boat than they can in a big, badly designed house.

The same kind of thinking that makes a sailboat both habitable and sea-worthy can make a Not So Big House work. As you pare down the actual square footage of your house plan, think about how to make various areas do double duty. For example, in a boat, the seats to the dining table double as beds (see the top photo on p. 62). In a Not So Big House, the fireplace hearth can also become a seating area with the addition of cushions. While storage in a boat is carved out of every possible place, in the Not So Big House it's been carved into the

A wooden boat expresses the essence of Not So Big: a place for everything and everything in its place.

Like a boat, this living area provides places that can do double duty. The hearth, for example, can become extra seating with the addition of cushions.

design of the house. When attention is paid to the usefulness of a house, there's a place for everything and everything is in its place. In architectural lingo, such a house expresses a "useful beauty."

But how do you make the Not So Big House work as efficiently as a 40-ft. boat? In this chapter, you'll learn about ways to make spaces do double duty, about planning for creative storage, and about strategies that will make your Not So Big House feel bigger. Through the alchemy of architecture, efficient smaller areas can be transformed into spacious, gracious spaces for living.

This Japanese interior is a living room by day and a bedroom by night. The futons and bedding are kept hidden from view in cupboards.

Doing Double Duty

I once spent several weeks with a Japanese family as part of an academic exchange program. Their house was extremely compact—and the way the family made it work was to change the function of the rooms over the course of the day. By day, the room Westerners would call the living room was used for more formal sitting and adult conversation. At night, this room became the children's sleeping area. The bedding, which was stored behind sliding doors, came out at night, and was then rolled up again in the morning (see the photo above). My room, which was truly tiny by Western standards, served per-

fectly adequately as both my bedroom and my study, because I rolled up my bed as well.

Although I'm not advocating that our homes should be as compact as the average Japanese home, it does seem as if our rooms have grown bigger to accommodate various activities and all their related furnishings. Rather than make an area larger, think about ways spaces can be shared. A home office by day can serve as a bedroom by night. An informal dining area can easily be turned into a place for formal dining with the addition of dimmer-controlled lighting. Consider other ways of doubling up: Can the away room also be an office? Or is it a place to listen to music? Is the guest bedroom a good place to put the television? Can the laundry hallway double as a place for guests to put their suitcases?

Allowing areas in a house to "moonlight" is one way to make them do double duty. And in the Not So Big House, the spaces where most time is spent should be able to accommodate a range of activities. The way to do this is to create spaces within a larger area that can be transformed to serve different functions.

Shelter around Activity

Creating shelter around a specific activity is a concept children instinctively understand whenever they make cozy hideaways out of cardboard boxes. What they're doing is creating a smaller space within the larger confines of their rooms. Adults exhibit a similar need for shelter when they go to a restaurant. Imagine you've arrived for dinner and you're the only one in

Children like to make cozy spaces for themselves out of whatever material is handy—in this case, a cardboard box gives a sense of shelter.

the restaurant. The waitress seats you in the middle of the room, but, if you're anything like me, you'll most likely ask for a corner booth, which offers a sheltered place where you can enjoy the restaurant as it bustles into life.

The alcove is the adult's equivalent of the cardboard box. Walls wrap around three sides of the alcove just as a restaurant booth does. Alcoves are a fundamental strategy for making Not So Big work. And they can be placed in virtually any space, from living areas to bedrooms. A room that has an alcove automatically does double duty by providing an alternative space within a larger space. The living area shown in the photo at left has two alcoves. One contains a window seat and a rocking chair; the other is more adaptable, changing function to suit the occasion—in this instance, Lego play time.

The Third Dimension

A floorplan encourages us to think in only two dimensions—length and width. Placing walls and doors is the usual way spaces are defined within a house, so most people think that they've finished with the design process once the floorplan is set. But the height of these spaces is what makes places feel

An alcove will make any room do double duty by creating a space within a larger area. This room has two alcoves—one for reading and watching television, the other in use as play space.

comfortable or uncomfortable. Have you ever been in an office building with room after room of 8-ft. ceilings? Uniform ceiling heights make any space feel homogenous. By raising or lowering the ceiling, spaces are enlivened and places within the larger area are created that are individually defined yet clearly part of the whole. In the photo of the dining area at right the lowered ceiling functions as the brim around a hat does, marking space.

Many people feel more comfortable under a lowered ceiling. A friend who was remodeling a warehouse space contacted me for advice. The loft, which had great light, turned out to be virtually unusable. The space was long and narrow—almost like a bowling alley. The only places that my friend felt comfortable in were the corners, where the two walls offered some shelter. A simple, inexpensive solution was to lower the ceiling at both ends. What had been unusable space was transformed into three spaces that could house various activities. The height of a space is critical to how it is experienced: Make sure to include the third dimension of height in the planning process.

Ceiling Height

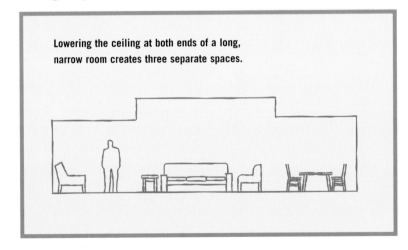

Lowering the ceiling at both ends of a long, narrow room creates three separate spaces.

The lowered soffit, put to use as a plate rail, gives a sense of shelter to the bench seating below.

Lighting for Formal Dining

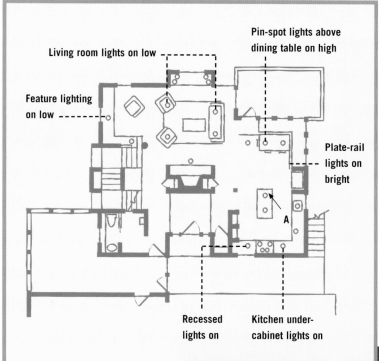

Pin-spot lights above dining table on high

Living room lights on low

Feature lighting on low

Plate-rail lights on bright

A

Recessed lights on

Kitchen under-cabinet lights on

Interior Lighting

Light is intrinsically connected to mood. A sunny day seems to express a cheerful mood, while a cloudy one might make us feel more introspective. Correspondingly, the use of light inside a house can transfigure a space. In the photos below, an everyday dining area is transformed by subdued lighting into an elegant place to entertain. By using brighter light, the same area can feed the family. Light is the primary tool for changing the mood of a space—and there are many sophisticated systems on the market that allow you to control each scene within the house with a series of dimmers (see the sidebar on p. 68).

Light can also be used to differentiate one place from another. If every area is lit to the same degree, a house can become very

Lighting is the most useful tool for creating interior ambience. Here, the lighting setting is for formal dining. The floorplan above shows how the various fixtures are set to create the appropriate mood. (Photo taken at A on floorplan.)

homogenous in mood and feeling. By lighting different areas with different intensities, various areas can be distinguished within a larger space.

Making More of the Practical

The year I turned 21, I spent part of the summer living with six other people on a 40-ft. sailboat. By day, we sailed the Puget Sound; each night, anchored by an island shore, we came to appreciate the level of detail in the boat's interior. Every square inch on the boat was lovely to look at—from the brass cleats on the bow to the vent stack in the latrine. As I design Not So Big Houses, I often think back to the level of detail on that boat and the ways it helped us live in relative harmony, despite

After-Dinner Lighting

Living-room lighting and feature lighting on medium

Pin-spot lights above table on low

Plate-rail lighting in kitchen and dining area on low bright

B

Kitchen under-cabinet and recessed can lights off

After dinner, the lighting system allows for a quick change of scene. Now the living area is illuminated and the dining area is more subdued. (Photo taken at B on floorplan.)

Lighting-Control Systems

Newer houses are filled with lots of different kinds of lighting, such as wall sconces, recessed lights, and pin-spot lighting. But more often than not, the proliferation of switches simply makes it easier to turn everything on rather than try to remember which switch controls what light. I first realized the need for more centralized control when designing lighting systems for new homes. When I visited my clients after they'd spent some time living in their new houses I discovered that they simply turned everything on when they walked into a room, completely negating the intended effect of having different lighting for different occasions.

There are a variety of lighting-control systems, which range in price, complexity, and flexibility. Some systems control the entire house, although these seem like overkill for the average homeowner. One house I recently designed for a couple included an expensive whole-house lighting system. In the bedroom, three scenes were offered—evening reading, morning dressing, and cleaning. The system controlled only two fixtures, however—recessed lights in the ceiling and bedside lamps. The homeowners were confronted with a variety of choices every time they walked into their bedroom, none of which exactly fit their intentions. They spent time trying to rename the functions, when all that was really required was two simple switches on the wall. In their case, the lighting-control system was complicating their lives, not simplifying it.

I prefer systems that control the main living area of a house, allowing the homeowner to control each "scene" by setting a series of dimmers that are then controlled by a single switch. Other systems allow even greater flexibility, but they require initial programming by a technician. These are significantly more expensive, and they offer more control than most people find useful.

The Lutron Grafik Eye System has six dimmer switches for different lighting loads.

Within the next decade or so, some sort of lighting-control system will probably be installed in all new houses—in the main living areas, at the very least. Lighting-control systems are just the beginning of what will become standard for all new houses as we develop ways to monitor and control from a single centralized location.

its cramped quarters. A boat's function depends on the crafting of its details. A Not So Big House's graciousness and livability comes from careful consideration of everything from the back hallway to the finishing touches in the kitchen. The practical places in a house, those unglamorous rooms where the work gets done, don't have to be unappealing. If you make the most of every space in a house—from the laundry room to the recycling center—you'll discover the joys of living Not So Big.

A laundry room doesn't have to look like a laundry room. Here, a sewing room also functions as a folding area for an adjacent washer/dryer. (Photo taken at A on floorplan.)

The Laundry Room

The laundry room is an itinerant space that travels upstairs and downstairs in floorplans, with no seemingly logical place to settle. In many older homes, it resides in the basement. In newer homes, it sometimes has its own spacious digs, complete with built-in folding and ironing equipment. The laundry room can also be found near the kitchen or adjacent to the master bedroom.

In designing a Not So Big House, I often ask clients a series of questions as we begin to think about the proper place for the laundry. Does it need to be an entire room, or could it be an alcove off a hallway? How much laundry does the household generate? Do you do large loads, or do you launder more frequently in smaller batches? Do you need an area to drip-dry

Laundry in the Sewing Room

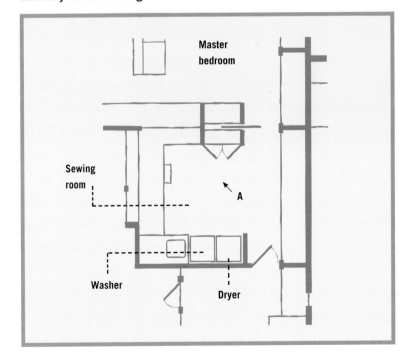

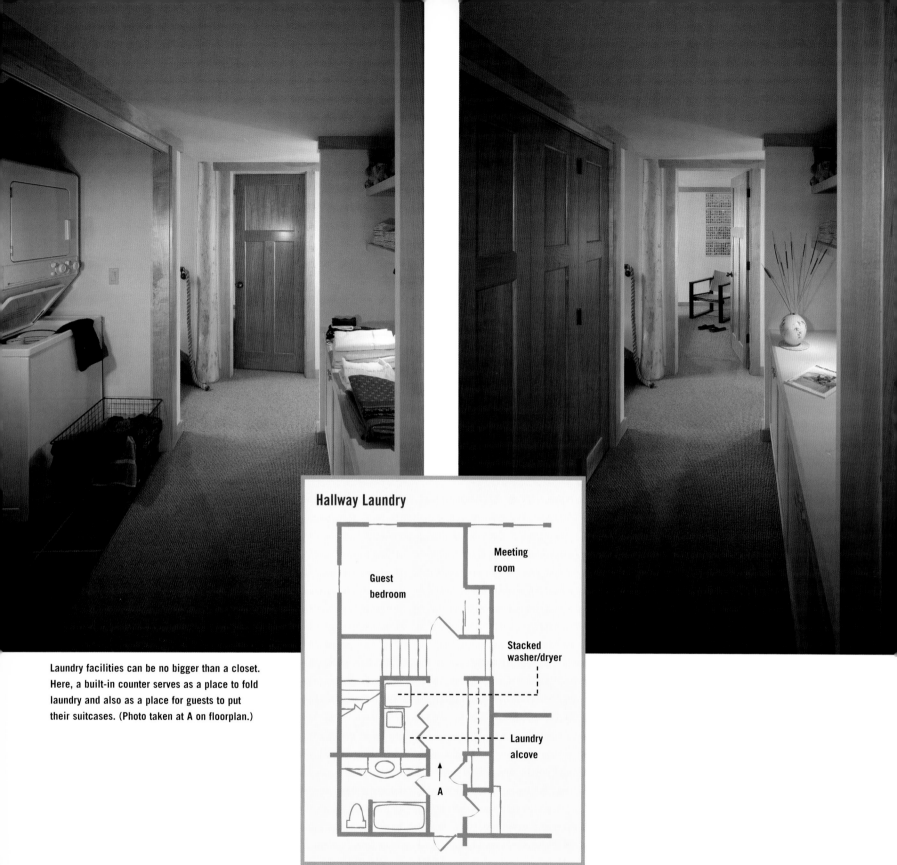

Laundry facilities can be no bigger than a closet. Here, a built-in counter serves as a place to fold laundry and also as a place for guests to put their suitcases. (Photo taken at A on floorplan.)

Hallway Laundry

Guest bedroom

Meeting room

Stacked washer/dryer

Laundry alcove

A

clothing? Would you prefer to fold clothes near the laundry area or elsewhere? Do you iron? If so, where do you like to iron?

Even though these questions prompt a variety of answers, one thing seems constant. While many people imagine they will do ironing and folding in the laundry area, they invariably take these activities elsewhere, either because they want to be near the rest of the family or because the laundry area is not a pleasant place to spend time in.

Depending on your lifestyle, there are various options for creating a place for the laundry. If you're an empty nester or a couple without children, a smaller area that's more similar to an alcove than a room (something adjacent to the master bedroom, perhaps) is adequate. Think about how the laundry area can be combined with another function: In the house shown on p. 69, it doubles as a sewing room. In my own house, the laundry alcove is covered with folding doors when it's not in use and simply blends into a hallway (see the photos on the facing page). A built-in counter along the hall can serve as a folding counter; and at other times it can offer a convenient place for guests to lay out their suitcases.

In some houses, the laundry doubles as the entrance from the garage. In this scenario, the main entrance takes everyone past piles of dirty clothes and detergent bottles. It's best to avoid placing the laundry here, but if it is the only spot you can find, it's a good idea to create a pleasant view to draw you beyond the clutter—either through a window or by hanging a favorite picture at the end of the way.

New Places for Not So New Things

What do junk mail, television, a bag of aluminum cans, a telephone, and a computer have in common? Each has no proper place in our homes. While the mail collects on the dining-room table and the cans accumulate in the kitchen, the computer resides in any number of places, from the office to the kitchen to the bedroom.

This mail center, located in a mudroom near the entrance, allows mail to be sorted and distributed to family members. The trash can is for recycling junk mail.

A Not So Big House includes space for each. A mail center near the entrance of the house (see the photo on p. 71) allows for separation of junk mail from bills and letters, which often end up in the kitchen. A kitchen mail center offers cubbyholes for each member of the family. And a kitchen island outfitted with trash cans can become a recycling center for cans and bottles.

A phone center can double as a kind of control panel for the house, hiding the thermostat and the air-quality and lighting-control system keypads (see the top left photo on the facing page). It can also house the calendar, family bulletin board, phone books, and address books. The use of a cordless phone keeps the area visually streamlined and allows for a minimum number of phone jacks in the house. The niche for the phone center shown in the photo was created from space in the fireplace chase. Its counterpart on the other end of the hearth is a broom closet. The wall on the backside of the fireplace defines the entry. The space between is filled with the main ductwork for the upper level of the house. In many houses, the bits and pieces of various controls are scattered throughout the building, for the convenience of the person who installs the system rather than for the long-term livability of the house. But this elegant solution brings all the controls together, mak-

A well-organized kitchen mail center has a cubbyhole for each family member. The work surface doubles as a place to pay bills.

Recycling for cans and bottles can take place where the waste is generated—here, it's in the kitchen island.

ing communication with the house and the rest of the world more efficient and more aesthetically pleasing.

As for the computer, it should find a place in the home that isn't makeshift. After all, the computer may be fairly new in our lives, but it is most definitely—in some form or fashion—here to stay. In designing a place for a computer, it's important to remember that printers, modems, external drives, manuals, disk files, and software boxes typically come with it—all of which need storage space in easy reach of the computer user. You can include space for the computer in a home office (see pp. 49-53), or you can put telephone jacks in public spaces where a laptop computer can hook into the Internet. As technology continues to introduce new tools into our lives, we must continue to update the way we think about the spaces we need in our houses.

In many houses, the real hearth of the home is the television. (Indeed, a recent best-selling video in Sweden was of a crackling fire!) The placement of the television often creates some acoustical and design challenges in the Not So Big House. The pattern of how the television is used is the best way to determine its placement. If watching television is an infrequent activity—or one that is more private—a good solution is to put it in a cabinet that can

This phone nook is the control center for the whole house, with phone, thermostats, and lighting and air-quality controls all consolidated.

The place for a computer doesn't need to be large, but you do need to plan for all the accompanying equipment.

In a room designed for television viewing as well as other activities, folding doors can conceal the set when it's not on.

In a room where television watching is the main event, the television and its surrounding cabinetry can be designed as a sculptural statement, as in this contemporary home.

be closed up, as shown in the photo at right on p. 73.

The family who owns the house shown in the photo on the facing page recognized that the television was the true hearth of their home. Rather than hide the television, they decided to make a sculptural statement with it. Its placement in the family area is actually adjacent to the fireplace, where family and friends can gather for either warmth or football, as the mood strikes. In my own house, I wanted to avoid having the blank face of the television staring at us at all times, tempting us to turn it on in our free moments. The wooden cabinet hides the television from the rest of the living area, while an alcove big enough for two allows us to keep the screen size small (see the top photo at right). Putting the television on a swivel base allows its position to be changed and lets it be seen from a variety of viewing points—a useful solution for media junkies (see the bottom photo at right).

When family members are trying to work or read, the noise of the television can be irritating. One solution is to create a space just for the television that can be closed off acoustically from the

Flanked by the side of a built-in cabinet, this television is designed to be visible only when sitting in an alcove. From the adjacent living area, you don't even know it's there.

A swivel base allows the television to be oriented toward different activity areas.

rest of the house (an away room). The key idea in creating a space for the television is to recognize your relationship to the TV—what it is and what you want it to be—and design accordingly.

Making Not So Big Feel Bigger

Square footage can be deceiving: Some big houses feel small, and some small houses feel big. The house shown in the top photo on p. 76 has a 900-sq.-ft. footprint, while the house shown in the photo below it has a 3,000-sq.-ft. footprint. The smaller space appears to be bigger because various strategies were employed to make it appear so. The image of the larger house feels smaller because views are kept short to create a sense of intimacy in the main living area. If you want to make Not So Big feel bigger, the following strategies will help you create a sense of spaciousness.

Diagonal Views

The diagonal line is used by both choreographers and theater directors to "activate the stage," in theater terminology. Similarly, architects use an imaginary diagonal line to create more dynamic

This small room feels big because there are long views sweeping from one corner of the house to the other.

This big room feels more cozy because the larger space is divided into smaller areas by the scale and placement of the fireplace.

A diagonal view, which stretches here from the kitchen to the piano alcove, not only makes a space seem bigger but also ensures that each area within is used on an everyday basis. The reason for this is simple: If you can see a space, you're more likely to use it.

spaces, which do in fact feel bigger. The reason for this is mathematical. Just as the hypotenuse of a triangle is the longest line, so in a square room, the diagonal view—from corner to opposite corner—is the longest dimension. If you create a number of diagonal views, you will focus on the longest view and so perceive the house to be larger than it is (see the photo above). Diagonal views can begin at the home's entrance. If you can

stand by the front door and see both opposite corners of the first floor, the house will automatically feel bigger. If you offer unobstructed sight lines to whatever space is diagonally opposite the kitchen, dining, and living areas, the house will seem bigger and more welcoming. When you see a space, you feel invited into it. And if you see a space, you use it more often.

Ceiling Height

A lowered soffit creates a pocket of coziness in a soaring space.

A ceiling trellis gives a sense of entry to the kitchen.

Why do we think that high ceilings make a space feel bigger than low ceilings? Our perception might come from hearing the basic measurement of the space: A room with an 18-ft.-high ceiling, for example, seems very big. And certainly, the volume of such a room will be bigger. But in some instances a high ceiling actually works against the perception of spaciousness.

In our architectural office, which is located in a renovated warehouse, the ceiling height in the conference room is 10 ft. 6 in. The footprint of the room is 10 ft. by 14 ft. When clients try to gauge the size of a space we've drawn for them, they often try to relate it to the dimensions of the conference room. But the ceiling height makes the room's floor area feel smaller than it would with an 8-ft. or 9-ft. ceiling. The reason for this is both mathematical and psychological. If the ceiling is the largest dimension, that is where our attention is drawn. We look up, marveling at ceiling height, instead of appreciating what the room has to offer at eye level. If the length and the width are longer than the height, then that is where our attention goes—the room feels longer and wider, hence bigger.

High ceilings are often considered more desirable than lower ceilings. This notion might come from a confusion between what is interesting and what is comfortable. Just because a chair is interesting to look at doesn't mean it's going to be comfortable to sit in. The same applies to a house. While we may reject a room with an 8-ft. ceiling because we perceive it to be run-of-the-mill, it can be more comfortable than a room with a high ceiling. Also, both high and low ceilings can be modulated with lowered areas. In the dramatic living room shown in the photo at left a lowered soffit creates a pocket of coziness within a soaring space. A ceiling trellis below a standard 8-ft.-high ceiling creates visual interest much less expensively than a 9-ft. or 10-ft. ceiling would.

Remember, though, that the proportion of the ceiling height to other dimensions of the room is important. A 10-ft. ceiling might feel right in a 25-ft.-wide room, but it can turn a powder room into an elevator shaft. Similarly, an 8-ft. ceiling in a large room will make the space feel like a generic office building.

And, obviously, if you're tall, an area with a 7-ft. ceiling may not feel comfortable. Frank Lloyd Wright, a man who stood 5 ft. 5 in. high, used lower ceilings throughout his houses and other buildings, believing if it worked for him it should work for everyone. In fact, his taller patrons find his architecture to be constricting.

Generous circulation spaces are critical to building **Not So Big**: A few extra feet at the top of the stairs can make all the difference. With a barrel-vaulted ceiling, this stair landing is a defined place, instead of just a passageway to somewhere else.

A few well-placed square feet can turn a stairwell into a stairway. The upstairs landing should beckon you with light; it should feel like a place in which there is generous room to move. Narrow hallways use up square footage that is better applied to living spaces. If you must have a hallway, find ways to introduce light into it, or put a lighted picture at the end so that you have something to walk toward.

Natural light in hallways makes them seem both wider and more inviting. Imagine this same space without the windows, and it would become almost tunnel-like.

Generous Circulation

In planning a Not So Big House, don't sacrifice square feet at the entry and in passageways. When you enter a house that doesn't give you enough room to comfortably take off your coat or move about, you automatically feel confined and unwelcome. While realistically there doesn't need to be a large amount of space at the front of the house, the proportion of the entrance can set the tone for the rest of the house. A large house with too-small circulation spaces makes you feel as if you're in a small house. Similarly, a smaller house with generous circulation areas feels bigger.

Windows frame the view outside and can also make a striking interior composition. Glass block used as a border creates a geometric pattern.

Let There Be Daylight

Light is integrally connected to our perception of space. Of all the qualities that people desire in a house, "light-filled" is among the most popular. Daylight, in obvious ways, makes a house feel welcoming. Windows connect us to the world, and by carefully planning their placement we can fill our houses with light and views. In Colonial times, fresh air was consid-

ered dangerous—and virtually windowless houses were shut tight at night to keep out the evil wind. Two hundred years ago, glass was expensive and difficult to find, and windows were used in construction quite sparingly. In the past 70 years, the number of windows used in construction has increased dramatically. But just like square footage, the number of windows does not necessarily make a house feel big. That's a function of how the windows are placed.

When placing a window, think of it not only as a frame for an exterior view but also as an interior composition, a kind of painting that is part of the wall. In the photo shown at left, a square window surrounded by glass block allows both views and a pattern of light to stream in. The window also functions as an important part of the living area's composition.

If you want good views of the outside, windows are best placed no more than 2 ft. 6 in. off the floor. If windows are higher than that, the view of the outside is limited—when seated you won't be able to see anything below the horizon line. This creates a sense of disconnection with the ground on which the house sits, a disconcerting effect similar to when you were a child sitting at the table, legs dangling, straining to reach the plate and see out of the window. In bedrooms, lower levels, and all seating areas, windowsills should be brought down so they don't obstruct views; by adjusting the sill, a connection to the outdoors is ensured.

Corner windows, two windows that come together in a corner, extend the diagonal views to the horizon. While a window in a flat surface defines only one direction, a corner window presents no boundaries to the view. A window that's placed right up to the edge of a ceiling without a frame makes a space

Windows placed up against the ceiling without frames make a space feel bigger because light bounces off the ceiling and walls.

feel bigger, because it becomes part of both the wall and the ceiling. In the photo on p. 81, the light reflected on the ceiling is a direct result of the window placement. Without the typical shadow cast by a window frame, the effect is striking: The ceiling seems to float. The window is simply a membrane between inside and outside, merely a surface that is a part of the wall. In fact, if you think about windows as see-through walls, then you can extend the connection between inside and outside (as shown in the photo below).

Sliding Doors

For many years pocket doors were flimsy contraptions outfitted with cheap hardware, which meant that the doors constantly fell off their tracks. The sliding door has come a long way: With heavy-duty hardware, any door can now be converted into a fail-safe sliding door.

The main reason to use a sliding door is to save space. There are areas of the house where the addition of the space needed for a swinging door would feel awkward. A 3-ft.-wide powder

The frameless windows in this house dissolve the separation between inside and out.

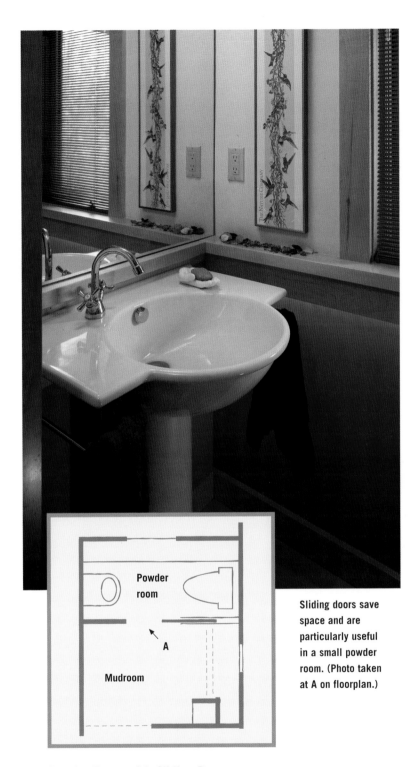

Sliding doors save space and are particularly useful in a small powder room. (Photo taken at A on floorplan.)

Powder Room with Sliding Door

Interior Views

Houses are usually designed to take advantage of outside views, with windows in just the right places to capture various scenes within the landscape. But we also spend a great deal of time looking within the house, and the composition of "interior views" is equally important. While a window frames an exterior view, ceilings and the edges of walls and floors frame interior views. If these views are thoughtfully composed, the house becomes beautiful to look at, from the armchair by the hearth or, as shown here, from the front entry through the living room.

The focal point of this interior view is a fireplace, framed by beams, columns, and the stair landing.

room, for example, won't accommodate the swing of a hanging door (see the photo and plan on p. 83). Sliding doors work particularly well in narrow spaces and in hallways (to hide laundry facilities, for example). In fact, the sliding door is an easy way to hide many different spaces you want kept out of view. A mudroom could have a sliding door, as could the kitchen, to conceal it when guests are over for dinner.

Connecting to the Outdoors

A Not So Big House will feel bigger if spaces for living are created outside as well as inside. As we saw in Chapter 2, porches and decks can increase living space considerably, especially in areas where weather isn't a great concern. When the roof offers shelter over the deck, the area becomes integrated with the rest of the house. And the extension of the roof line actually makes the house seem bigger from the inside. The courtyard house shown in the photos on these two pages was designed for a Minnesota woman who loves Italian architecture. Taking as inspiration the Italian cloister, the plan of the house allows for two circulation patterns—one inside, with views of the courtyard, and one outside, with views of the passageway. Two sides of the house are open and two sides are interior, allowing

The inspiration for this Minnesota house was an Italian cloister. With broad overhangs and precast concrete columns, a covered walkway connects the house with the outdoors.

the house to project its Italian image while making it useful in a northern climate. The seating area beneath the roof gives the sense of being inside, protected from the elements, but with views to the garden courtyard. From the inside, looking out, there is a layering of places that range from completely interior to partly exterior to completely exterior.

Creative Storage

While storage in many homes takes the form of a closet, in a Not So Big House storage is a strategic defense against clutter. In a Not So Big House, storage is designed for the way you live and the things you do. The hierarchy of how often the things in your life are used—from every day, to once in a while, to never—influences how storage is planned in a Not So Big House. William Morris, one of the founders of the Arts and Crafts movement, proclaimed 100 years ago: "Do not keep anything in your house that you do not know to be useful or believe to be beautiful." Such is the organizing principle behind storage in the Not So Big House: Every space is considered for what is useful; special places are planned to display what is beautiful.

The outside cloister is echoed inside by a long passageway filled with arched windows. It's the cold-weather alternative to the outside walkway.

Visually appealing kitchen storage is essential when the kitchen is open to the living areas. Built-in shelves, flanked by walk-in corner pantries, hold this cook's collection of cookbooks.

In each instance, storage corresponds to the place where the object is used: from a drawer in a window seat to a broom closet set into the fireplace area. Remember that the budget for your house will make an impact on the kind of storage you choose. Built-ins, in general, add significant cost to the overall price of the house. Very generally, you can assume that the cost will be analogous to a purchased piece of furniture of similar quality.

Creative Kitchens

In a Not So Big House, the kitchen is open to the living areas, so storage is essential to the way the kitchen functions and looks. The pantry is a very useful space: Make it as big or as small as necessary to fit the way the kitchen is used. If you are a gourmet cook, the pantry will be scaled to accommodate specialty items and equipment. If you'll use the pantry every day,

Pantries don't have to be walk-in size to be useful. A very efficient way to store kitchen supplies is to line a hallway with a pantry wall. In this instance, a 15-in.-wide dividing wall is a pantry on one side and bookshelves on the other. (Photo taken at A on floorplan.)

make it part of the kitchen. If you hoard items—buying jars of jam for next Christmas—it can be its own walk-in area.

The hallway that separates the kitchen area from the away room in the photo above is designed as a highly creative storage area (another example of "doing double duty"). The dividing wall, which is only 15 in. wide, becomes a very useful pantry area for the kitchen and creates bookshelf space for the

An L-shaped corner pantry was created from a former powder room in this kitchen remodeling. No bigger than a closet, it enhances the storage capacity of the kitchen.

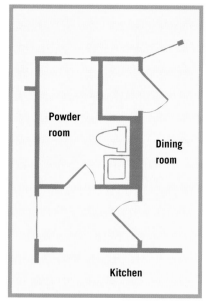

Creating Pantry Space: Before

away room. Walls at the edge of a circulation space can easily become fabulous pantries with the addition of 10 in. in depth (the width of a typical cereal box). In many ways, this is the most efficient kind of kitchen storage. Shallow storage makes everything visible and reachable.

The pantry shown in the photos and drawings on these two pages was literally carved out of a corner. It's no bigger than

3 ft. by 3 ft. and uses space that was formerly part of the powder room. Despite its odd shape, the pantry greatly enhances the storage capacity of the kitchen.

Another defense against kitchen clutter is the appliance garage (see the photo on p. 90). In recent years, the number of available kitchen implements has reached epic proportions. An appliance garage can hide appliances such as toasters,

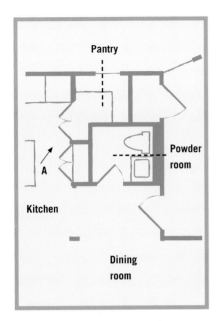

Creating Pantry Space: After

Although the pantry is oddly shaped, when the doors are closed it integrates perfectly with the rest of the kitchen. (Photo taken at A on floorplan.)

juicers, and breadmakers from view, yet keep them within easy reach.

The philosophy of the Not So Big House advocates that the things you use everyday are those things that have the most meaning. A client, planning for her retirement house, wanted a built-in cabinet in the dining room to store her heirloom china, which she planned on giving to her children. But while the fancy china had been cherished, it had never been used, so her adult children had no childhood memories of it. We decided to store most of the china in the basement, and made a special hutch in the kitchen to display a few choice pieces.

Most people would relegate the space under the stairs to a coat closet. But English designer John Ferro Sims transformed the space under the stairs in the London studio of the noted

Strategies for avoiding
kitchen clutter include
a hanging pot rack, a
center island, and an
appliance garage in
the corner. Stacking
the microwave and
wine storage above
the appliance garage
makes optimum use of
a corner space.

The space under the stairs in a London studio has been turned into a small jewel of a kitchen.

sculptor Henry Moore into a tiny but elegantly efficient kitchen (see the photo above and on p. 60). What most of us would consider wasted space becomes innovation at its finest in the hands of this designer. Here we see the very essence and personality of the Not So Big House.

Innovative Everyday Closets and Cupboards

Consider the convenience of having the extra roll of toilet paper where it's needed, instead of down the hallway. Storage in the living areas of the Not So Big House is always a convenient and sometimes obvious solution to an everyday problem

that can leave us stranded—pants around ankles—waddling to the laundry room.

The bedroom storage in the photo below shows the foresight of careful planning. In a bedroom that has limited space, the closet was designed to use every cubic inch to maximum effect. Built-ins, shelves, and mirrors, all behind folding doors, store clothes and personal items. This room does double duty: When the closet doors are closed and the futon is folded into a couch,

Consider putting storage where it's useful—adjacent to the toilet, for example.

This room is a symphony of storage. With built-in dressers, shelves, and mirrors, all enclosed in a wall cabinet, the room can do double duty as a bedroom or an away room. Notice the light fixture above the mirror—an ingenious way to give light where it's needed.

it functions as an away room. But with futon down and closet doors open, it becomes a combined bedroom and dressing area. The closet addresses a problem common with mirror placement. The recessed lights and the mirror are actually attached to the back of the door, ensuring that the light is in the proper location for using the mirror. In the bedroom shown below, built-in storage surrounds a fireplace hearth. Functional and beautiful, it becomes an integrated piece of the room's design.

Above: Windows, mirror, medicine cabinet, and sink are each typically given their own wall space. Here, they all happily coexist in an innovative design.

Left: Built-in storage around a fireplace makes a beautiful statement in a bedroom.

Any corner, nook, or cranny can function as storage. Here, the kneewall has become a triangular storage area; drawers under the window seat store blankets.

A common problem in bathroom design is the conflict between medicine cabinet, window, and mirror. Typically in new homes, the mirror takes up most of the wall surface above the sink, allowing little space for a medicine cabinet or window. People often assume that they can't put a window into the wall behind a sink because they need it for the mirror. But, in fact, the mirror doesn't need to be wall-sized. By breaking every rule in the book, the solution shown in the photo at right on p. 93 accommodates all three functions on one wall surface.

The guest coat closet is often scaled to accommodate 25 coats. The reality is that it is usually empty, or crammed with last year's Christmas wrapping paper and newspapers awaiting recycling. When guests do arrive, they typically traipse upstairs to pile coats on a bed. When you plan for coat closets in a Not So Big House, put them next to the front door. The closet doesn't need to be enormous, just big enough. When large groups of people visit, all the coats go into a bedroom.

Remember that the guest closet in the Not So Big House is only for guests: Your coats go into the mudroom.

You can't predict what you'll need to store in the next five years. But when you design your Not So Big House, keep in mind that storage needs increase the longer you live in a house. In the left photo above, the kneewall area could have simply been walled over. By putting doors to access the area, it becomes unusually shaped, but still useful storage.

Double-Duty Storage

Any space in a Not So Big House is fair game for storage, especially in living areas. The strategy is to find a spot that seems to take up no extra square footage. The bunk bed shown in the photo above doubles as a blanket or toy chest. Drawers in window seats and benches are a more practical solution than a lift-up lid, which is troublesome to raise when cushions are set on top of it. Stairways can offer wall space that is easily trans-

Above: The stairway doesn't have to be just an unadorned passageway. In this house, it's become a library. While the shelves offer storage, the books become a kind of decoration, visible from upstairs and down.

Left: This bed could easily be on a boat. Carved into a corner, it's surrounded by drawers and shelves, offering a maximum of storage in a minimum of space.

In the Not So Big House, even the space under the stairs can provide storage—in this instance, for shoes.

Storage can also serve as display. A plate rail that lines the kitchen shows off a collection of handcrafted plates. The rail continues into the dining area, artfully linking the two rooms.

formed into bookshelves with the addition of 10 in. to the width of the stairwell. The area under the stair steps is frequently unused, particularly in houses without basements. As shown in the photo on the facing page, one enterprising designer used the space effectively for pull-out shoe storage.

Storage as Display

A useful addition to a dining area or kitchen is a plate rail, which offers both storage and display. The plates that line the rail in the kitchen area shown in the photo above are both beautiful and useful. With dramatic lighting, they become a work of art, but on many occasions the plates are taken from the rail to adorn the table as functional items.

A client who had an amazing collection of beer cans asked for a built-in display in a recreation area (see the photo at right). A music-loving client wanted storage for his collection

Any collection is fair game for display. Here's a wainscot of beer cans.

When planning for storage, think beyond the confines of the cupboard. Beautiful things should be seen and displayed for everyday enjoyment.

Storage for a collection of CDs becomes a kind of wallpaper lining the room.

of CDs. By lining the walls, they become a kind of wallpaper for the room where he likes to sit and listen to music (see the photo at right above). If you have a collection of items, whatever they may be, that collection expresses something about who you are. It's an opportunity to integrate into the house the things that inspire you and give you pleasure. A Not So Big House gains its personality from the passions of its inhabitants.

In the built-in pantry by designer Fu Tung Cheng shown on the facing page, concrete, Douglas fir, and steel are combined to create a work of usable sculpture. That something as commonplace as a pantry can be transformed into such a beautiful object expresses the potential of how storage in our houses can enhance the experience of living in them.

In this built-in pantry, natural materials and elegant design create usable sculpture.

99

"Home is an invention on which no one has yet improved."

—Ann Douglas

Early in my career I worked with a young couple who were both successful professionals in the computer-software business. They saw in their future a big new house where they would live for the rest of their lives. They planned to have two children, at some indefinite point in their lives, so they would need two extra bedrooms—plus a guest bedroom—in addition to their own. The couple were convinced that their yet-to-be-born children would have no effect on their current lifestyle. In fact, to maintain their own privacy, they wanted to put the kids' bedrooms at the opposite end of the house from the master bedroom.

Anyone who has ever lived with small children will immediately understand that this approach to bedroom location is completely unrealistic. The direct result of placing a young child's bedroom far from the parents' is that the child will move into the parents' bedroom—for months, sometimes even for years. But my clients were undeterred; their vision of an existence unfettered by children

This house, at 800 sq. ft., is truly Not So Big. Designed for one person, it embraces the solitude of living in the woods. With its north face tucked into the hill, the house offers an enigmatic first glance as you approach.

remained. We began to design a house that had the bedrooms where they wanted them. Rather sneakily, I added a sitting room off the master bedroom, which was separated from the bedroom by French doors. I knew that this would, most likely, become the nursery. And I decided to let them discover this for themselves.

The one thing that's predictable about life is that it's unpredictable. You can have a little control, however. The process of making a house Not So Big allows you to tailor the house to your needs and to create spaces that can easily adapt and change with you throughout the stages of your life. In this

chapter, we'll look at a number of houses, each designed for people with distinctly different lifestyles: From a retreat for a single professional to a remodeling for empty nesters, these Not So Big Houses express the values and passions of their inhabitants. Although none of the homeowners are exceptionally wealthy, they've all built houses that work for them and that have enriched their lives.

A House for One

The little house that Kelly Davis designed for himself expresses his love of solitude and small scale. Davis, who is a partner in our architectural firm, is convinced that small spaces are more conducive to such everyday activities as reading, conversation, and quiet evenings in front of the fire, so he decided to design a house that was no bigger than 800 sq. ft. Fascinated with how space can be made to appear larger than it is, he was determined to create a warm, intimate house that would be as fluid and unconfining as possible.

The site Davis found to build on, just a few miles from his office, was a 35-acre mix of woods and fields on the Wisconsin side of the St. Croix River that overlooks the river valley and a distant limestone bluff. Capturing this view was essential, but he also wanted to make certain that the house would be protected on blustery winter nights. The house is, in effect, notched into the hillside: sheltered from the north winds by a windowless wall and a low shed roof, while the south side opens up with large windows and a clerestory to let in views, light, and warmth.

Davis has traveled widely and admires the traditional architecture of Japan. He used as inspiration for his house the

The house reveals its dramatic form slowly, first presenting a massive sculptural form (as shown in the photo on the facing page) and then opening up for views and light to the south.

Japanese concept of revealing vistas gradually, culminating in an element of surprise. The first indication of this is where cars park—at a garage/studio/guest room that's set about 300 ft. from the house. The only approach to the house is on foot, a kind of meditative walk through the woods that offers glimpses of the house and the view beyond (see the photo on the facing page). The house itself is a dramatic statement, with its powerful massing and sculptural form. Davis sustained this drama by setting the front door in a 7-ft.-wide alcove in the southeast corner of the house. (It's interesting to note that Kelly realized

that if he had placed the garage next to the house, it would have dwarfed the 800-sq.-ft. footprint.)

Inside, the house's open plan presents a feeling of spaciousness (see the photo and floorplan on p. 104). Long views extend from every direction, and a 50-ft.-long, 8-ft.-wide deck that's cantilevered over the hillside visible from the living area frames a view that's almost 75 ft. long from the living-room wall to the end of the deck. The living area of the house is anchored by a massive concrete fireplace, and spaces within it are defined by alcoves and built-in furniture, all of which is scaled appropriately to the house.

A soaring ceiling in the living area descends to create a sense of shelter for the built-in couch.

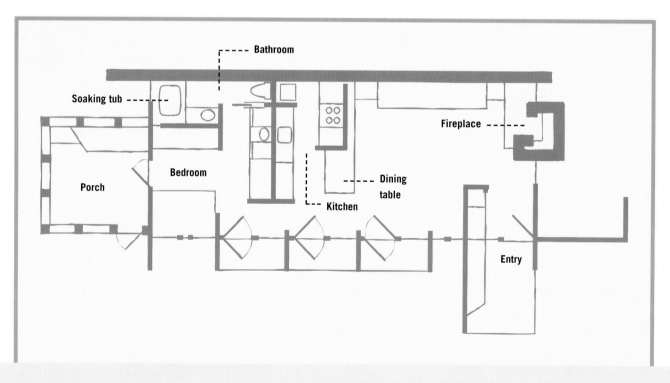

Bathroom

Soaking tub

Fireplace

Porch

Bedroom

Dining table

Kitchen

Entry

The small kitchen is screened from view by a partial wall but remains connected with the dining and living areas. The table can function as a countertop extension for the kitchen or as an eating area.

The bedroom, which is down a short, flat-ceilinged passageway, is hidden from the living area by a wing wall (see the photo on p. 106). A beautifully crafted bathroom connects to the bedroom. Davis wanted his house to be a retreat from the workaday world, so he purposefully did not include space for a drafting table and, hence, work he might otherwise have brought home. But a built-in desk and shelves in the bedroom allow the room to do double duty as an office where he manages his bills and correspondence. Should the need arise, the house is designed to accommodate the addition of a second bedroom and bath to the north of the existing bathroom. With an incredibly efficient use of space, and an impeccable eye for detail, this house is the epitome of Not So Big.

Because this is a house for one, there was no need to create acoustical privacy. The dining area is marked by a built-in table that's connected to the kitchen, which itself is partially shielded from the living area by a half-wall. Throughout the house, varied ceiling heights create shelter around specific activities and help activate the spaces: A soaring ceiling in the center of the living area is in contrast to a low ceiling along the north wall, which gives a more intimate feel to the sitting area. Wherever possible, Davis extended the inside to the outside. Windows are installed without frames, and a porch off the bedroom (shown in the photo at right) offers striking views in the summer months, as well as becoming a warm-weather bedroom. The roof, which cantilevers off the front and back of the house, also extends the impression of the house's size.

A screen porch located off the bedroom is for warm-weather sleeping; it's also a good place to enjoy striking views of a river valley.

The bedroom is really just an alcove, with a built-in bed sheltered by a lowered ceiling. The screen porch is beyond.

Designing for yourself can be both exhilarating and scary. While you can literally do anything that your budget allows, there's no one to discuss the ideas with; no one to counter your wishes. The challenge in this process is to realize that even if you now intend to live alone in the house for the rest of your life, the house can be a burden to sell if you make it too unique to your needs. Several years ago, I designed a house for a single man who wanted only one bedroom because he never had visitors. He had enough disposable income so that resale value wasn't a concern. He went ahead and planned for a single bedroom, complete with a whirlpool tub actually in the room. He saw no need for doors and, thus, the master bedroom (and its tub) was open to the living area below. A year after the house was finished, he fell in love. Unfortunately, his new partner did not have the same affection for his new house. The house went on the market, and stayed there for quite some time until an appropriate buyer came along, who was willing to remove the tub and add some doors, walls, and a guest bedroom.

When you're single, there's always the chance that the same thing could happen to you. When designing a home for one, how do you take into account the possibility for a change in relationship status? My suggestion (just as with designing for retirement years) is not to try to second-guess the future. Design sensibly, allowing the house to work for one or for two, but don't go overboard. My experience as an architect suggests that most new partners, when they move into a house that is so clearly an expression of the other's personality, will want a different space that expresses both personalities—even if the existing house is beautiful and comfortable.

This bathroom, complete with soaking tub, an abundance of natural woodwork, and a visible connection to the outdoors, reflects the owner's love for Japanese aesthetics.

Another thing to remember when designing for one is to make places that feel good to be alone in. To do this, select the two or three activities you enjoy doing most in the house and design places for those activities. Make sure there's a sense of shelter around each one. Even if you sit in a smaller space watching television or reading, you look out into the larger, more open spaces in the house. There's a big difference between being alone and feeling lonely—and nothing accentuates loneliness more than broad, open expanses of space. Smaller, more cozy places evoke a sense of security and introspection.

This contemporary Prairie-style house on a river bluff was originally designed as a second home for a professional couple. It's now a full-time residence.

A House for a Couple with No Kids

If a couple isn't planning to have children and is designing a house for themselves, the stereotypical plan of "three bedrooms up" really doesn't make sense. Obviously, a house for two does not need to be as big as a house for a family with children and, in fact, can be much more comfortable if spaces are scaled appropriately. While an away room is usually unnecessary, work spaces are usually important to the plan. Though some couples can easily share an office, often each will take a differ-

ent approach to organization. Recognizing these differences can help avoid a lot of potential arguments. Offices can also be useful for resale, especially when they can be easily converted into bedrooms. If you want an office to be able to function as a bedroom, make sure a closet is included or can easily be added later. When a couple are the sole inhabitants of a house, it is important to make sure that some spaces are comfortable for one or two people only.

The house shown at left was built by a professional couple in their mid-50s (Dianne and Bob) who approached me after months spent trying to design their second home themselves. They owned property on a river bluff, and they wanted a contemporary home that would be very different from the traditional house they owned in the city. However, both had strong opinions—strong and conflicting opinions. They needed an architect who could help give shape to their dreams and find common ground for both of them. The photos they had collected and brought to our planning sessions reflected their desire for everything to be open and visible. So the first design for their weekend house had a totally open floorplan with a wall of windows across the front of the house. While this seemed to be exactly what they wanted, I was concerned about

The relatively simple cubic form of this house allowed the owners to put more of their budget into windows. The living area features a wall of windows that captures a panoramic view. A window seat helps modulate the open expanse of space.

the lack of definition between the kitchen, eating, and living areas. An easy solution that maintains the sense of openness was to add a window-seat alcove in the middle of the wall of windows, directly across from the front door (see the photo on p. 109). The window seat beckons from the entry and also frames the spectacular outdoor views. Two built-in cabinets, designed especially for Dianne's collection of ceramic objects, flank the entrance to the living room, creating a kind of gateway into the main living spaces (see the photo on p. 100).

The form of the house is very simple, essentially a cube with two bays—one off the kitchen and the other in the window seat. Both bays extend the three stories of the house, providing alcoves in the kitchen, master bedroom, living room, and family room. The reason for the simple form of the house was economic: They wanted to devote as much of their budget as possible to windows in order to make the most of their spectacular view.

Specifically, the house was designed to take advantage of sunsets. Even the couple's bed is oriented toward the windows. But although there's a lot of glass, bands of trim and mullions help modulate the expanse of view, which creates smaller segments to frame the panorama. Without the trim and mullions,

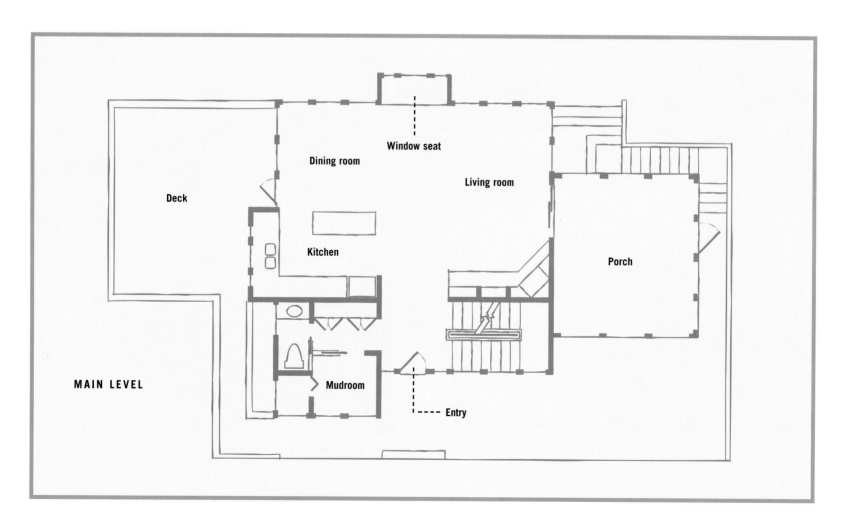

The kitchen's design is simple, with a minimum of detail. The main feature is a large window bay, which looks into the woods.

a large expanse of glass might make the homeowners feel as though they were living in a glass house.

The house—designed as it was to take advantage of the site—also had to function as a place where two professionals could take work home and actually get work done. Dianne wanted her office to be part of the rest of the house, and so we attached it to the master bedroom (see the photo on p. 112).

In many houses designed for couples without children, the main area of the house becomes what *A Pattern Language* refers to as "The Couple's Realm." The entire upstairs becomes the couple's suite, which is also a good place to put an office as well as a beautiful bathroom and generous walk-in closets. Dianne's work alcove offers her privacy and the best views in the house. Bob's office is a more defined room, located off the other side

An alcove in the master bedroom serves as an office area. The alcove is created by a lowered ceiling and a window bay that extends to two stories—on the first floor it accommodates a kitchen bay (see the photo on p. 111).

of the bedroom and attached to the bedroom with a sliding door. For Bob, the room becomes a kind of away room, offering acoustical privacy when he listens to music. Originally, the view wasn't as important to him as it was to Dianne. But, in fact, the view from Bob's study is quite lovely, and over time he's claimed the room as a place of his own.

The lower level is a basement on the bluff side of the house but completely exposed on the river elevation. Dianne and Bob often entertain out-of-town visitors, so both wanted to provide guests with their own spacious digs, allowing for privacy on both levels. With a family area, guest room, and bunk beds for kids, the lower level can easily accommodate an entire visiting family. Bunk beds, which take up only 18 sq. ft.,

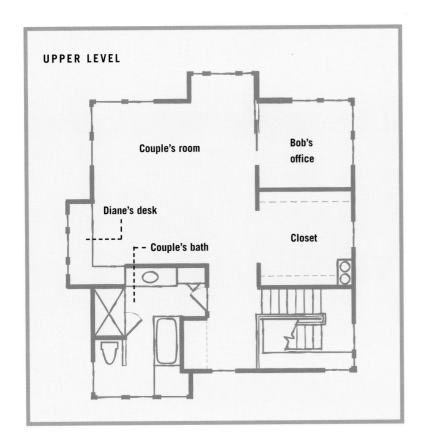

UPPER LEVEL

Couple's room

Bob's office

Diane's desk

Closet

Couple's bath

has views of the river valley—it feels like a weekend home, but it's convenient for more than weekend life. Although my husband and I were initially concerned about the extra cost of a city lot, when we factored in the expense of having both a city residence and a country residence, the city lot seemed like the more cost-effective solution.

When people begin planning a second home they often automatically think in more informal terms, allowing themselves to envision options that they might not even consider for their primary residence. The architects in our firm have designed many second homes. Again and again my colleagues and I discover that our clients are much more comfortable in their second homes than they are in their primary ones. For that reason, the second, or weekend, home is one of the biggest inspirations

take the place of an additional bedroom (see the floorplan at right).

The house has changed Bob and Dianne's lives. After a year spent in their Not So Big House, designed to express their personalities and accommodate their needs, they decided to make this second home their primary residence. They still commute to the city for work, but they've completely downscaled and now stay in a small apartment while they wait for the weekend. Their retreat has become their home; and this is where their hearts are.

While Bob and Dianne found their dream site outside of a city, many people who are interested in building a weekend home have discovered the appeal of building a retreat inside the city. My own Not So Big House is located on a city site that

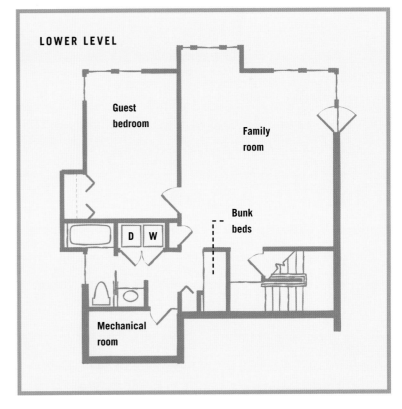

LOWER LEVEL

Guest bedroom

Family room

Bunk beds

D W

Mechanical room

This house is designed to express the charm of a European home. Everything about it nurtures the life of the family that lives there—down to the colorful awnings that cover an outdoor play space above the garage.

for the Not So Big House. The appeal of these weekend homes often is not just the location but the structure itself, which is designed to be comfortable, useful, and informal.

A House for a Family

Michaela Mahady, a partner in our firm, likes to encourage her clients and her students to capture the memory of houses from their past. Teaching a class on housing at the University of Minnesota, she encouraged her students to remember a place that had been important and to try and capture its essence. One of her students, Caroline, brought to class an intricate and beautiful collage of the house she had grown up in France. Ten

years later, Caroline and her husband, Peter, asked Mahady to help them design a house that would both express the charm of her childhood home and embrace the life of their young family.

Mahady, along with architect Wayne Branum, discovered that Caroline, a poet, and Peter, who is in the food commodities business, were able to articulate clearly the qualities they wanted in their new home. These included a home that felt like a tree house, a house where the family could dance together, and a house where daily life would happen in one spacious room. The site, quite wooded, also provided views of a small pond, and the architects knew that the family would want to be connected with the outdoors wherever possible.

The family who built this house not only wanted a beautiful place for daily life but also a room where they could dance together. The slate swath through the dining-area floor doubles as a dance floor, while the open living area is the core of the house.

115

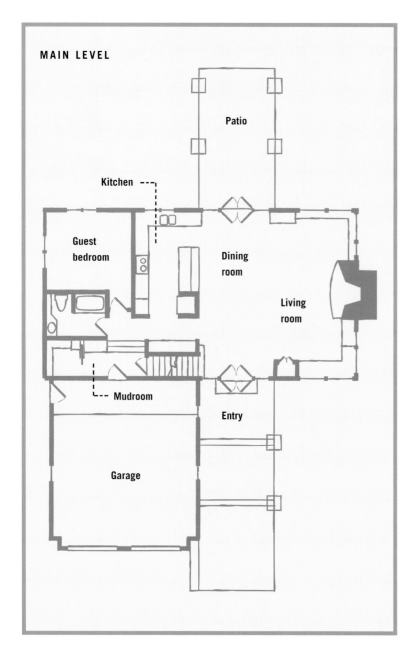

MAIN LEVEL

The kitchen completes the center for daily life. Open to the living area, its design enhances the first floor. The owners have personalized it with various collections, from dried flowers to cheese boxes.

The house's steeply pitched roof line lends the building a European flair, but inside the house materials such as Brazilian cherry and China green slate give a more contemporary flavor. The one room for daily living that Caroline and Peter requested offers a perfect example of designing Not So Big. The kitchen is open to the dining and living areas. Variations in flooring material and ceiling height, as well as alcoves, help define places within the large space. A green slate floor marks the dining area, which is also the "dance floor" the clients requested (see the photo on p. 115). The slate, which offers a stunning contrast to the Brazilian cherry on the living and kitchen floors, continues outside, as do the wooden beams, extending the space visually at both the front and back of the house and making an area where the family can dance outside. A cathedral ceiling over the fireplace creates a dramatic vault that is in contrast to lowered ceilings in the kitchen and dining area, as well as over the corner window seats. The architects integrated the kitchen visually by using the distinctive green slate of the floor as a backsplash and natural wood cabinets that echo the wooden beams (see the photo above).

With its steep pitched roof, the house has a European flair. One of the owners wanted to capture the essence of a childhood home in France. The slate floor continues outside, offering patio space in the warmer months.

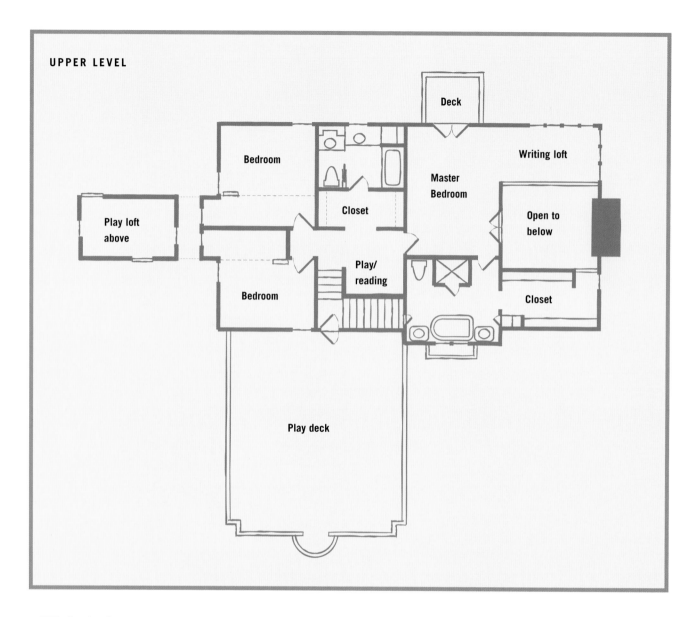

Deck

Bedroom

Writing loft

Master
Bedroom

Closet

Play loft
above

Open to
below

Play/
reading

Bedroom

Closet

Play deck

While the house encourages family togetherness on the first floor, upstairs it offers more private spaces, as well as places for both adults and children to play. Caroline and Peter's space contains a bedroom, a place of one's own for Caroline, who loves to sit on the floor and write, and a shared master closet and bathroom. Separated from the children's area by a door, the couple's realm is perched over the first-level living space, offering connection and privacy. A shared loft playroom con-

nects the two children's bedrooms (see the photo at left on the facing page) and is accessible by a ship's ladder. The stair landing has become another play space, at least in the winter, supplanted in warmer months by an outdoor area on the top of the garage: Shaded with colorful awnings in the summertime, it is a playground nestled into the treetops.

Since it was built in 1995, the house has become an even more personal expression of the family who lives there. With

Upstairs, there are places for children and adults to play. A shared loft playroom, accessible by a ship's ladder from the elder child's bedroom, connects the two children's bedrooms.

planned certain spaces for certain activities, they haven't been constrained in how they use the house.

As children and parents get older, the guest bedroom on the main floor, now occupied only when Caroline's parents come to visit, will become an adaptable space that can provide parents or teenagers with privacy. If Caroline and Peter grow old

The stair landing is big enough to serve as another play place. The little window offers views from the children's loft.

an inimitable sense of French style, Caroline has personalized the first floor with a painted mural that embraces the doorway (see the photo on p. 120) and displays of dried flowers and wooden Camembert boxes; perfume bottles catch the light in the windows. Her place of her own, with its windows on the floor, has recently become a temporary bedroom—with the mattress on the floor, she and Peter can look out the low windows and see the best views in the house. Even though they

This house offers plenty of evidence of how a family can make its mark. A hand-painted mural is a whimsical and personal addition to the stairway—even the skirt board sprouts grass!

together in this house, the placement of a guest suite on the first floor allows for the possible conversion into a master suite, if there were ever to be issues of mobility.

When you design a house for a family, if you plan to live there for any length of time, it's good to consider who you are today and who you will be as the years pass. Infants grow into teenagers, and teenagers into young adults who eventually move away to start their own lives. The house that at one time needed four bedrooms to accommodate children and the occasional guest can become virtually empty when kids leave for college.

The Not So Big House can be a house for a lifetime, if you think about how the house will age as your family does. The floorplans on p. 122 show a house for a couple—a computer programmer and a violinist—who have three children, ranging in age from seven to infant. The site they chose to build on in Colorado has panoramic views of city lights and mountain tops. Wanting to invest in their future, they determined that the location of the house was primary and so they spent more of their budget on the site than is typical. The house itself would have to be less expensive, with the idea that as time went by they could add to the original structure. We determined to design by level: giving them a finished lower level and first floor, with the opportunity to complete the second level and attic as time and finances allowed. On a flat site, the lower level would be a basement, but the significant sloping character of the site allowed us to put in three bedrooms with full-sized windows, with the result that the finished space feels like anything but a basement.

Why should a window just let in light? In this house, every windowsill is considered a place to display a collection. Here, a colorful row of perfume bottles catches the light and beautifies the view of a deck beyond.

The two youngest children, both girls, share a bedroom, while the older child, a boy, has his own, complete with a child-sized fort under the stairs. Both bedrooms are quite small, measuring only 9 ft. 3 in. wide by 14 ft. long. Built-in bunks, desks, and toy storage allow the rooms to function as much bigger spaces. An outdoor play area on the flat roof of the attached garage (see the lower right floorplan on p. 122) gives the children space to spread out during the good weather.

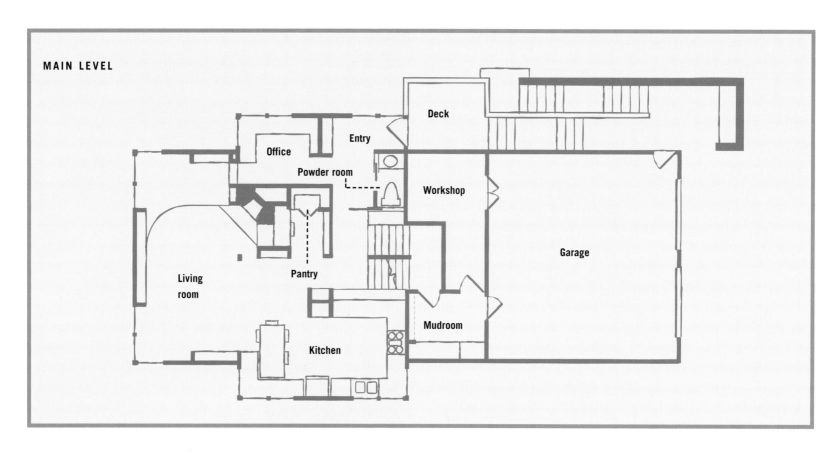

MAIN LEVEL

Deck

Entry

Office

Powder room

Workshop

Pantry

Living room

Garage

Mudroom

Kitchen

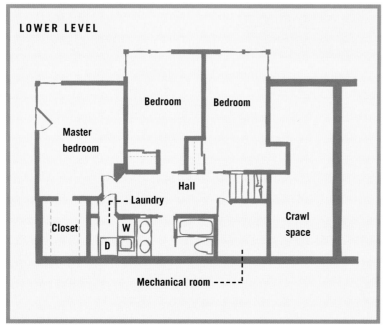

LOWER LEVEL

Bedroom

Bedroom

Master bedroom

Hall

Laundry

Closet

W

D

Crawl space

Mechanical room

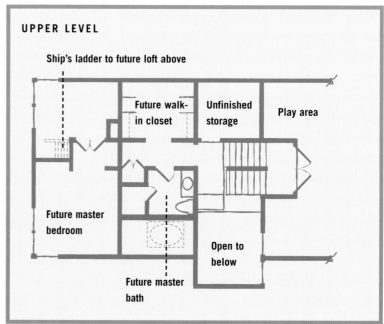

UPPER LEVEL

Ship's ladder to future loft above

Future walk-in closet

Unfinished storage

Play area

Future master bedroom

Open to below

Future master bath

A window in the kitchen allows the parents to keep an eye on the children—one of their biggest concerns was how to give the kids play space in such mountainous terrain. In the future, as their children get older, the couple has the option of enclosing the area above the garage and turning it into the away room, a place for the parents to escape. What is currently the parents' bedroom will eventually become one of the girls' rooms, when the parents complete the upstairs. The walk-in closet off the master bedroom is roughed in for a future bathroom, so that this room can, on occasion, do double duty as a guest bedroom when the daughter moves temporarily into her sister's room. This kind of flexible thinking for the future allows for one less bedroom.

The main level contains the family living areas, as well as an office for the husband, who likes the option of working at home. Upstairs, currently unfinished, there's room for a true couple's realm—with a walk-in closet, bath, and two places of one's own, one adjacent to the master bedroom, and the other in the attic above, accessed by a ship's ladder. This family has built the outlines of their dream. When the house is finished, it will be an expression of the lives they've made together.

It is, of course, impossible to plan for another significant way families can change—when a divorce or a remarriage happens and two families are "blended." Remember the *Brady Bunch*? ("And then one day this lady met this fellow, They knew that it was much more than a hunch, that this group would somehow form a family…that's the way they became the Brady Bunch.") The most important thing to do when designing for blended families is to give each kid a place of his or her own to

Children's bedrooms can be no bigger than a bunk; this one's tucked under the eaves, with a bookshelf forming the headboard. A drape offers privacy and creates a kid-sized hideaway.

retreat to. Such a space does not need to be large, and a good design solution might be to provide multiple bunk beds (as Mike Brady, an architect, did in the television series), each with a curtain or drape that gives them separation from the larger room. Although an adult might consider this space too small, most children love bunks precisely because of their "cocoon-like" quality, which makes kids feel safe and protected.

In all houses for families—blended or not—it's critical to provide a spectrum of spaces from public to private to allow for all the different kinds of situations that present themselves when you're raising children.

Designing for Kids

When I was designing a house for clients with a five-year-old daughter, the adults both embraced the idea of a place of their own for each of them. Toward the end of construction, Anna, their child, announced that she also wanted such a place. We found it under the stairs. I'll never forget standing there with her parents, seriously considering the design elements of this small place. The parents were seeking my counsel on how it should look. "Have you asked Anna?" I inquired. When we asked her what she wanted, she was very clear. "I see a tiny space with a green door with a round top and a diamond window in it," she announced, as if she were receiving some celestial vision—and that's exactly what she got.

Designing for children is one of the most gratifying aspects of my architectural practice. Kids are an architect's best audience. Not only do they embrace the idiosyncrasies of a design but they also figure out ways to use spaces that even the designer didn't realize could be possible. And they are almost always willing to tell you what they want, either by expressing it, as Anna did, or by their actions.

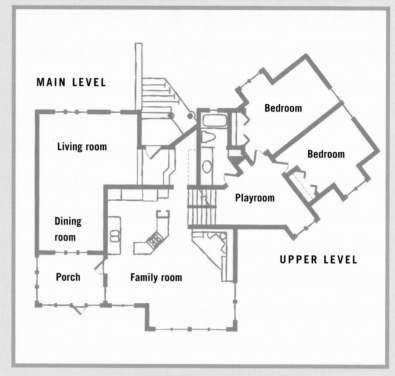

Children are bundles of energy who significantly affect the workability of any house design. Homes that work well for a couple without children may be totally impractical for a family with young kids. Anyone knows that children like to be where the action is. When they are little, they like to be close to their parents, so when I'm designing for a young family, I try to make sure there is a "loop" somewhere in the house—preferably close to the kitchen and family gathering areas, for children to race around without getting in the way of food preparation (see the floorplan at left). This loop adds a kind of planned-for race track that answers some of the challenges of creating a house for families with active kids.

As kids grow older, they still like to be close to the center of adult activity, which can create traffic jams in places of food preparation. By designing places where they can play and simultaneously see what the adults are up to, both the needs of parents and children can be met. In the floorplan above, the stair landing was expanded to become a playroom, a sort of anteroom to the

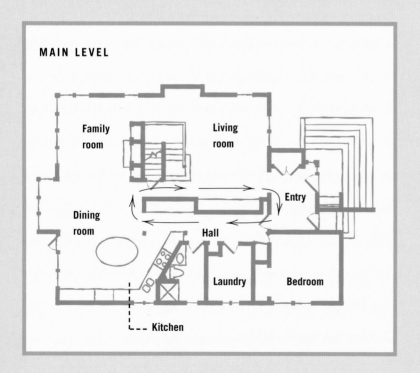

Kids love spaces that are scaled to fit their size. The desk area is tucked below a play loft, the envy of the neighborhood's younger set.

children's bedrooms. Perched on the landing, the children can keep an eye on mom at all times, without being underfoot.

Kids like places that are kid-scaled. A child's bedroom can really be quite tiny. I've seen successful rooms carved out of kneewall space, with just a bed and a curtain separating it from a play area. Kids also love bunk beds. One of the most successful space-saving solutions for kids' bedrooms is to design multiple

bunk beds. Not only are bunk beds like mini-jungle gyms but they also provide smaller spaces by creating a sort of stacked alcove where kids love to play and to sleep.

Remember when you design for children to plan for places that are kid-scaled, places that offer opportunity for play and invention. And watch the way your kids find ways to use spaces to meet their needs—we can all learn from their creativity and flexible thinking.

A remodeling for a retired couple added 500 sq. ft. to their weekend house. It also turned the home into a place where the owners plan to grow old together.

A House for Empty Nesters

When Fred and Marvel, an older couple whose children had left home, determined that their second home would become the house where they would retire, they contacted architect Kelly Davis to help them make it a place where they could grow old together. The original house had been designed in the 1980s by Mike McGuire, an architect with whom Davis had previously been in business. McGuire used the forms of Midwestern farm buildings to give the house a kind of rambling, organic shape. Davis, in planning a 500-sq.-ft. addition, was inspired by the original shape of the house and the farmhouse tradition of growing horizontally as the building responds to the needs of its owners.

The addition converted an existing screened porch into a master suite, and then extended the kitchen, on the opposite

Before

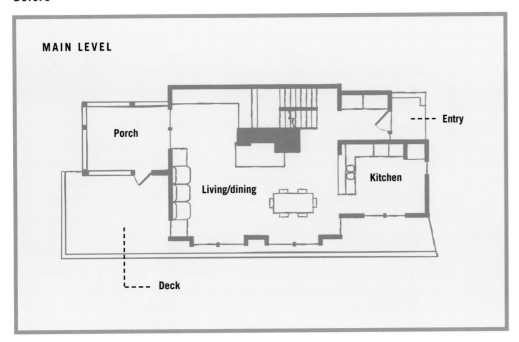

MAIN LEVEL

Porch

Entry

Living/dining

Kitchen

Deck

After

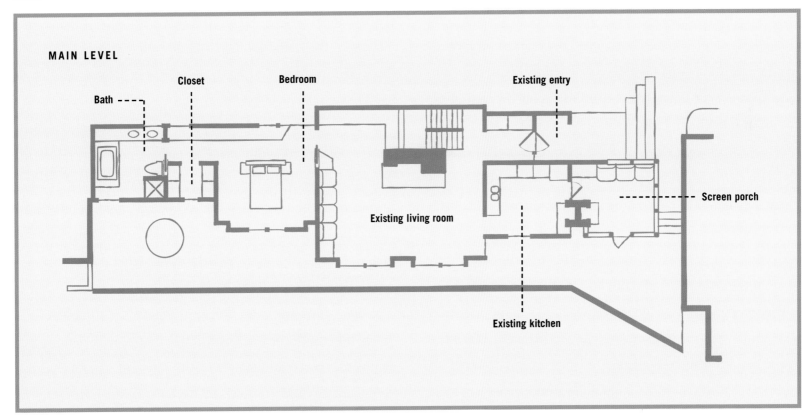

MAIN LEVEL

Bath

Closet

Bedroom

Existing entry

Screen porch

Existing living room

Existing kitchen

The addition extended the kitchen by adding a fireplace for cooking and a screened-in porch, located beyond.

end of the house, with a fireplace for cooking and a screened-in porch for warmer months. Essentially, the clients wanted to move downstairs, where their daily life could be centralized around the kitchen, a place where Marvel likes to plan and cook gourmet meals. Davis used the existing palette of materials to make the addition appear seamless: The pine ceiling and plank floor continue now through the bedroom area. A built-in storage system lines the corridor that connects the bedroom with the living area, a space-saving solution that gives Marvel lots more storage and an area for display (see the photo on p. 130).

The couple's concern about aging in the house has been addressed by putting all everyday living functions on one level. What had been the upstairs master suite is now reserved for guests or visiting family. And, thinking ahead, Davis made the

bedroom, bath, and kitchen addition all handicap-accessible by widening doors and being conscious of how a wheelchair could eventually navigate the space.

The house is a striking example of how architecture can provide a backdrop for the client to make a personal statement. From a basket hung from a ceiling rafter to the rugs on the plank floor, the couple's collection of Swedish-American antiques, handmade baskets, and ethnographic art adorn the house. Marvel, a potter, uses the yard as her gallery, placing various glazed forms throughout her gardens.

People can have quite different approaches to designing a house for retirement years. Some, like these empty nesters, recognize the potential for limited mobility and request that the living areas be on one level. I have had clients in this stage of

The owners of this home wanted to surround themselves with the treasures from a lifetime of traveling. A relatively simple living area, adorned architecturally with beams and large windows, becomes a stunning backdrop for their collections of baskets, weavings, and sculptural items.

life who purposefully build homes that require lots of going up and down stairs. Their attitude is that stairs are like built-in exercise machines. If they reach the point where they can't master the steps, then they will plan to move.

My very first clients in my professional career were a 65-year-old woman and her 98-year-old mother. The mother's eyesight was failing, and she used a walker to get around; nevertheless she was remarkably agile for someone of her age. She did have difficulty in the bathroom, because her right arm was weak. She requested a grab bar to the left of the toilet and asked to have the vanity countertop as close to the right side of the toilet as code would allow, so that she could use the edge to push

The addition of the bedroom to the main level integrates seamlessly with the existing house. A small hallway from the bedroom to the bathroom has a lowered ceiling and a built-in dresser, both of which help define the passageway as its own place.

off with her right elbow. Without such specific data about her particular infirmities, I could not have designed a bathroom that would have worked well for her. To have predicted the need for such elements when she was in her 60s would have been impossible.

But what *does* make sense is to employ some sensible strategies that don't cost a lot of money, or make the house "odd" in the eyes of the resale market if this is a concern. When I am designing a house for a couple approaching retirement, I suggest that we make the main level accessible from the outside by no more than one or two steps. Once inside, there should be no interior steps or changes of level other than the stairway to upstairs or downstairs. Designing this main level so that it can be a self-contained living unit allows the house to function in whatever way may be needed in that unpredictable future. Although the couple's realm may initially be upstairs on a second level, a main-level guest bedroom or den can be designed specifically to become the couple's area in the future, if necessary.

There are some other small considerations that can make a difference to the livability of the house as you get older. Making doors 2 ft. 8 in. wide throughout the house allows most wheelchairs sufficient clearance, without making the openings appear so wide that the house starts to take on an institutional look. Using lever door handles rather than knobs makes opening and closing doors easier for those with arthritic fingers and wrists. The addition of a plywood backer behind the drywall around the midsection of the main-level bathroom allows for easy installation of future grab bars, as it becomes clear where they are needed. Locating the laundry on the main

A bed doesn't have to be pushed against a wall. With built-in headboard and side tables, this bed takes center stage and creates a hallway that leads from the bedroom's entrance to the bath.

level, ideally adjacent to the couple's area, is a good idea. And the location of the oven and microwave should be considered so that the user doesn't have to bend down or reach up to take things in and out. Placing counter surfaces close to the refrigerator and ovens is also important so that items can be set down easily as they are unloaded.

A Not So Big House will age with you. You may have to make changes as time goes by, but these changes are easier and ultimately less expensive than trying to attempt to predict the future. Design for who you are today, recognize that there will changes—and make your house something that can grow and adapt as you do, rather than something complete and ready for a future that may never happen.

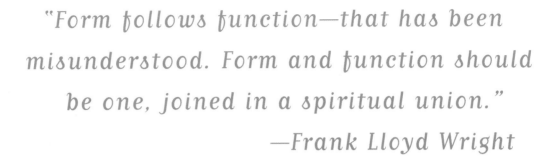

"Form follows function—that has been misunderstood. Form and function should be one, joined in a spiritual union."

—Frank Lloyd Wright

Every year, our firm has a booth at the local Home and Garden Show. This event is always a good opportunity to talk to people from all walks of life, many of whom dream of building a house. At a recent show, an older man came up to the booth to talk to us about building his dream house. He and his wife had spent at least a decade planning their retirement home. They had purchased the land some time before and had spent years compiling images of houses they liked. The man showed us a collection of articles, many of them about houses our firm had designed over the years. He seemed to be a fan of our work.

It was clear from the way he spoke that his dream house would be expensive: 3,000 sq. ft., with a high level of architectural detail. Unfortunately, and despite his dreams, his budget would afford him only a smaller (2,000 sq. ft. or so) standard builder home. Given the reality of his finances, I told him that the most sensible thing to do would be to find a set of architecturally designed plans (avail-

Dream houses like this one, with 3,600 sq. ft., a complex form, and lots of interior detailing, are budget-breakers for most of us. People often fall in love with a house that is several times more expensive than they can afford.

would have to start with a very simple, easy-to-build shape. As for details, using standard materials creatively would be the way to give the house the character he was seeking.

The basic problem with home-design books and magazines is that there's almost nothing in them that communicates to the public the hard facts about the costs of building a house. If the quality and character of a house are paramount, then there must be an understanding of the impact on cost.

Quality, Quantity, Cost

Building a house, more than any other undertaking, pits our dreams against our realities. When we think about dollars we tend to be very practical. Dreams, by their very nature, are often impractical. The reconciliation of the two is never an

able from a home-plans publication) and work from there. That way he could save on architectural fees, which can run 10% to 15% of construction costs. He called two weeks later, excited about a plan he and his wife had selected. They wanted to discuss the possibility of making a few alterations to it—expanding the kitchen and adding a bedroom. When we met and I saw the plan he had purchased, my heart sank. The plan was, in fact, substantially larger than the original house he'd hoped for, and in its detailing it was a high-style Prairie, with probably $80,000 worth of trim, which represented more than one third of his total budget. I knew the house itself would be at least four times the cost of his budget. (So much for saving architectural fees!)

I felt awful as I explained to him that the house was far beyond his range. If he wanted even a 2,000-sq.-ft. house, we

Building with simple forms and less expensive materials is one way to reconcile our dreams of home with the realities of our budgets.

Making Wish Lists and Reality Lists

To define what features you want in a house, it's helpful to use a couple of tools that architects often employ with their clients. Start by making a wish list. It should include all the dreams and visions you have for your home, even if you know that many of the items are beyond the scope of your budget. Think back through your life to all the houses, rooms, and places that have given you pleasure. Imagine including such places in your own home. Supplement the list with drawings and pictures—and anything else that helps describe your wishes.

Once you have completed this exercise, go through the wish list and identify which of the items are "musts," which are desirable but you could live without if necessary, and which are in the realm of dreams only. Then take the items that are in the must list and describe each more specifically. Now make a list of any items that were not a part of your wish list but are important to include in a list of needs. This is your reality list. The more specific you are, the more likely it is that your house will meet your needs.

Each of these lists is helpful to an architect, or to anyone working with you on the design. Although you must make clear what are dreams only, the two lists help describe not just the quantifiable aspects of your dream home but also the qualities that are important to you. In addition, they may tell you something about your life that you had not anticipated.

Several years ago I was working with a young female attorney, and one of the key elements on her reality list was a greenhouse—a BIG greenhouse. As I worked with her and got to know her better, I realized that the greenhouse she wanted represented a wish, not a reality. It was a wish for free time, and for something that could feed her soul. I made this observation, as tactfully as I could, in one of our meetings. The revelation proved to be correct. Her wish was an expression of her frustration with how busy she was, with no time for herself and no hope of finding any. The size of the greenhouse was simply an indication of the size of her frustration. She wanted something to bring her life back into balance and to reconnect her both literally and figuratively with the earth.

It's hard to see these contradictions ourselves, but they constitute one of the primary reasons that our houses get bigger than we really want or need. We accommodate our wishes, but often these wishes remain only wishes even after the place to realize them is built. If the wish is going to become reality, a change of lifestyle is needed more than a new place. If you can change your lifestyle, then the place for the wished-for activity is a sensible investment. But if you know that you aren't going to change, recognize this and move on. Developing a discrimination for what is a need and what is a wish can allow your house to become a place that has true meaning for you and relevance to the way you live.

Wish List
* I want a house that is small, beautifully designed, & unusual
* I imagine the view to the backyard to be something that you discover as you move through the house, & not immediately apparent.
* The entry process is really important to me. I'd like the main entry we greet guests at, and the entry we come in through on a daily basis to be the same one, or at least both doors arriving into the same space.
* I really like changes of level, but know how much these cost, and so would probably forgo such changes to keep costs down. Ceiling height variety however is very important.

Reality List
Kitchen: Don't need double oven
Design for 2' deep refrig.
Gas range
Built-in pantry
An island, ideally with barstools if there's room
Place for cat food, & cat dishes
Bread making supplies are key
Appliance garage for:
– bread maker
– coffee grinder
Ideally maple or cherry cabs.
No handles visible
No microwave
Small microwave
Place for cook books

Dining: No need for formal dining
Table to serve both formal & informal situations
Needs to be very comfort
This is our main ha...

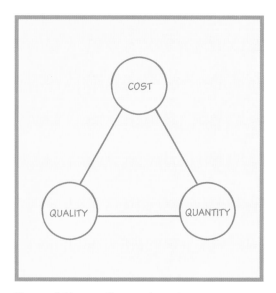

Three variables—quality, quantity, and cost—govern the decision-making process in house design and construction.

easy thing—and yet, in building a house, it's essential that the two come together. People's dreams are frequently two to three times more expensive than the realities of their pocketbook. The challenge is to find a way to bring dreams and realities in line with one another, without making people feel as though they've given up on their dreams.

Whenever I work with a client, I point out the three variables involved in reconciling dreams with realities: quality, quantity, and cost. Cost seems like the most obvious of the three: How much are you willing to spend to accomplish your dream? Often, what people think they can afford increases over the course of the project because they don't want to compromise on their dreams. The budget that at first seemed so absolute rises commensurately.

Quantity also seems like an obvious factor. Some people assume that they need a house of a certain size, because all the houses they've seen and liked are that size. But by going

through the process outlined in earlier chapters, you may find a way to reduce quantity and reallocate your money into higher-quality materials or detailing. For others, quantity is important, and the desire to live in a bigger space is what prompted them to consider building a new house in the first place. If size has nothing to do with your vision, then the quality of the space—the materials or character of the house—can be achieved with the reduction of square footage.

As you think about your own dreams and realities, it's useful to picture quality, quantity, and cost as the three points of a triangle. In designing and building a new house, two of these three variables can remain constant, but the third has to be adjustable. (Most houses are built with the quantity and cost fixed; the variable that has to give is quality.) Whenever I start to work with new clients I try to gauge where they fall on the quality-quantity-cost triangle. Are they the type who will want more space, even if they have to sacrifice quality of materials and execution to get it? Or are they astute observers of detail who will want fine finishes and craftsmanship even if the house has to be smaller so they can afford it? Or are they interested in both the quality and the size they have determined and willing and able to let the cost increase to accommodate both?

For clients who want to maintain both quality and quantity, I start the discussion by making sure they understand that this decision means higher costs. Allowing cost to be the variable offers the greatest flexibility in terms of design and fulfillment of dreams, but it's the rare client who has this option. If any party in the team—client, builder, or architect—is intransigent about the triangle and insists that no one variable can be flexible, then you simply cannot build the house. In this chapter,

In this addition, quality was the one variable the client refused to compromise on. No expense was spared—from elaborate trim-work to custom stained glass—and as a result the cost per square foot was very high.

Colonial-style houses are so prevalent because their form is very simple and therefore economical to build. They enclose a maximum of square footage with a minimum of surface area.

we'll look at a variety of projects, each of which illustrates the choices the clients have been willing to make in order to reconcile dreams with realities.

The Economical House

A realtor couple I know, who often work with wealthy clients, contacted me because they wanted to build their own home. Because they were so well versed in new homes, they knew that the houses they liked best were architecturally designed. While they were familiar with the high-end houses that our firm had designed, their own budgets dictated something that would be much more economical. As far as clients go, these two were pretty savvy—knowledgeable about how the detail and quality of a space can make it special but aware that their resources would preclude them from even considering many of the high-end homes they sold to other people.

There are certain decisions you can make at the beginning of the process to keep costs down. The first and most important is to keep the form or shape of the house square or rectangular. A complex shape costs a considerable amount more because there is more surface area per square foot of interior space. The outer "skin" of a building is typically the most expensive component of the house. Not only do exterior materials cost a significant amount, but making these materials keep the weather out is a significant undertaking, filled with complexity; and this of course costs money.

Have you ever wondered why there are so many Colonial-style houses built around the country? What is it about this form that is so appealing? The shape is very simple, and in terms of getting the most "bang for your buck," it encloses the most space for the least amount of money. In addition, the floors are typically 9 ft. from floor to floor, meaning that the house can be framed easily using standard 8-ft. studs and 10-in. to 12-in. floor joists (see the sidebar on pp. 140-141). Typically, there's a center bearing wall, which makes framing the floor simple, and there are no odd angles or vaulted ceilings. Every square foot of potential space is used for living area. When someone is looking for a way to make their dollars stretch the farthest, it's impossible to ignore the benefits of keeping the form simple. In general, the fewer corners you have in the exterior perimeter, the less expensive the house will be.

My clients were willing to start with a rectangular shape. But to avoid a boxlike feel, I planned for a "bump-out" in the stairwell, which would give the interior a dramatic, light-filled stairway as well as provide some visual relief to the exterior. This detail has since become a focal point of the house. The placement of the porch and the garage, flanking either side of the house, was intended to extend the house and to increase

The couple who built this house had a fixed budget. The primary money-saving decision they made was to minimize exterior construction costs so they could spend more on the interior detailing. The house has a very simple rectangular form, with a garage and a screened porch on either side.

A Construction Primer

The construction trades have developed a series of conventions that dictate which materials to use and the techniques for using them. These conventions are not absolute rules but rather indicate the methods builders have developed to achieve the best results with a minimum amount of decisions made in the field. Adhering to these conventions won't guarantee a minimum price, but it will help keep the cost down.

To understand this concept better, let's look at some of the component parts that go into building a house. The fewer changes made to the original size and shape of these components, the more money can be saved.

CEILING HEIGHT

The convention is 8-ft. or 9-ft. ceilings, although there's currently an increased use of the 10-ft. ceiling since materials are being made available that allow easier assembly of the

Manufactured and pre-engineered floor trusses, an alternative to standard-dimension lumber joists, allow for longer unsupported spans. Ductwork and wiring can be laced between and through the trusses.

10-ft. wall. The most common wall-finish material, drywall, is also readily available in sizes to fit these wall heights.

To build an 8-ft. ceiling, the most typical construction method is to use a "pre-cut" wall stud of $92\frac{5}{8}$ in. This dimension, used with one floor plate below and two horizontal plates above, results in a wall height of 8 ft., after allowing for floor and ceiling finishes. Pre-cut studs are also available for 9-ft. ceilings. A common mistake made by the inexperienced is to order 8-ft. studs, which result in an 8-ft. 4-in. ceiling when you add in the other necessary framing members. Although the added ceiling height can be a benefit, gypsum board is made for the pre-cut 8-ft. length, making the drywall process both more labor-intensive and expensive.

FLOOR JOISTS

The most common size floor joist used today is the 2x10. Large floor areas uninterrupted by columns or supporting walls require a floor structure that goes beyond the capabilities of the conventional 2x10 floor joist. The 2x10 board, which is actually $1\frac{1}{2}$ in. by $9\frac{1}{4}$ in., has a maximum span of about 15 ft. 6 in. when installed at the conventional 16 in. on center. In the past 20 years, more options have become available to achieve longer spans, such as manufactured floor joists and pre-engineered floor trusses (see the photo at left). These members are manufactured in depths ranging from typical joist sizes up to 24 in. or more and are available in almost all market areas. But, in general, the longer the clear, unsupported span, the more you pay.

FOUNDATION WALLS

Foundation walls, which are built into the ground and support all the weight of the house, are typically made of concrete or concrete block. The forms into which the concrete is poured are made of plywood or steel panels. As might be expected, multiple corner offsets, changes in elevation, and curved forms require more work and consequently cost more. In regions where concrete block is used for basement walls, it is typical to use a 12-in. block. This unit actually measures 11⅝ in. thick, 15⅝ in. long, and 7⅝ in. high. Including the mortar joints, it lays up in the wall as 16 in. long and 8 in. high. In some foundations that are not part of a basement (such as beneath a garage), 8-in. (7⅝-in.) or 10-in. (9⅝-in.) thick block is used.

ROOF FRAMING

Up until the 1960s most roofs were framed up one board at a time, a process referred to in the trade as hand framing. Although some builders still prefer this method of building a roof, this process is being replaced more and more by the use of roof trusses, which are prefabricated at a factory and delivered to the job site ready for installation (see the photo at right). These trusses can easily accomplish spans of 30 ft. or more and can be made in a wide variety of configurations. Because roof trusses are typically fabricated using computerized equipment to figure out the most efficient method of construction, almost any roof form that doesn't have living space within it can be made to order at much lower cost and with much greater speed than if the roof were hand-framed.

It is because of the advent of these factory-made trusses that we see so many more varied roof forms today than we did even a decade ago. Unfortunately, they are not always designed to be aesthetically pleasing. They are simply configured to cover the floor space below, which can result in some pretty odd-looking forms.

There is one form of truss that's popular today, called the "scissor" truss, that allows a vaulted ceiling inside. Another is the "room-in-the-roof" truss, or storage truss, which allows the use of some of the space inside the roof area but is more expensive than one without this option.

Before roof trusses became the norm and hand framing was the only option for roof construction, having space in the

Factory-fabricated roof trusses have made framing a roof much easier and faster, but they have also eliminated attic space in the majority of new homes.

roof that could be used for living space was a cost-saving option. Many people still have a great love for the look of the Cape Cod cottage, with its dormers bringing light into this roof space. But today, because of the gravitation to roof trusses as the norm, the roof form of the Cape Cod cottage no longer provides the cheap space option that it used to. As a result, people who prefer a smaller-scale, more cottage-like look can end up spending more money for a house that looks smaller and is indeed more compact.

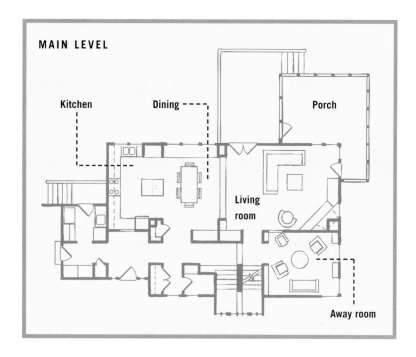

MAIN LEVEL

Kitchen · Dining · Porch · Living room · Away room

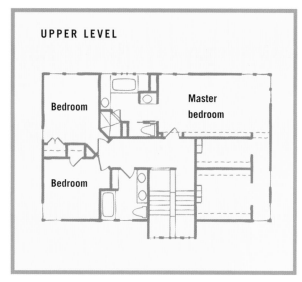

UPPER LEVEL

Bedroom · Master bedroom · Bedroom

The kitchen features standard builder materials like plastic laminate and flush-panel cabinets. With thoughtful design, these elements are brought together into an artful composition that transcends their humble nature.

the sense of its size. If necessary, the porch could have been built at a later time, if the bids had come in too high. When you're working with a tight budget, it's useful to identify sections of the house that can be eliminated or built later.

As for the quantity of the space, the couple were very willing to consider many of the Not So Big concepts, including a com-bined dining and living area and an away room (see the top floorplan at left). So, by reducing the quantity of the space by at least 500 sq. ft., more of their budget could go to the char-acter of the house. With its low-slung hipped roof and wide eaves, the house looks substantially bigger than its 2,100 sq. ft. To save additional dollars, a lower grade of cedar was used in an artful way on the exterior for trim and siding.

The one variable the clients were not willing to compromise on was character—or the quality of the interior space. The expense of a material doesn't always ensure that it's going to lend a house a sense of quality. If the material isn't used artfully, it's simply money down the drain. For this couple, quality was not connected with high-end materials but in how the materials were used. They were interested in using standard building materials, in standard sizes (like 8-ft. studs and off-the-shelf cabinets), which allowed them to save a substantial amount of money. By using economical materials in innovative ways, we were able to make the house more interesting architecturally.

In the kitchen, standard maple cabinets with a very simple design are integrated with a plastic-laminate countertop (see the photo on the facing page). Inexpensive tiles are used as a backsplash. Although all these materials could readily be found in any run-of-the-mill builder's house, the contemporary styling makes the house look infinitely more appealing. In the dining/living areas, alcoves, which are made by lowered soffits and interior wing walls, not by the exterior form, add visual interest and save money. The living area is distinguished from the dining area by two steps down, which enlivens the space and saves its long narrow configuration from feeling like a bowling alley (see the photo below). An away room adjacent to the living area doubles as an office and reading area.

Combining the kitchen, dining, and living area and leaving out the formal spaces reduced the square footage by 500 sq. ft., allowing the homeowners to spend more on interior detailing. A wood trim line marks the lowered soffit and continues around the perimeter of the interior walls.

But they quickly discovered that without this detail the bedrooms lost the unique character of the main level, so they determined to put the additional $500 for the trim back into the budget. It was money well spent: The consistency of the trim line lends the house an elegance and makes it look like a more expensive home.

The addition of corner windows in the bedrooms helps distinguish each space, as shown in the photo below. A striking

The bedrooms feature corner windows, which help make the rooms seem bigger, and the same trim line from downstairs. This detail unifies the two floors and transforms these simple bedrooms into spaces with greater personality and style.

The living room is two steps down from the adjacent dining area, which increases the ceiling height in this part of the house. Upper transom windows bounce light into the room from the bottom of the soffit.

The clients liked the use of an interior trim line, which is a feature of many of the older Arts and Crafts homes in the city where they live. This trim line became the primary interior detail, continuing through every space in the house along the upper soffit or above the windows. It is the principal feature that distinguishes this house from standard builder construction. During the construction process the clients thought they might save a little by omitting the trim on the upper level.

The mirror in the
master bathroom
extends right up to the
soffit and over to the
exterior wall, which
gives the illusion of a
room double the size,
with twice as many
windows. Glass block,
which comes down to
the tub, lets in light
but obscures the view.

A glass-block triptych on the stair landing brings light to both the upstairs and the downstairs. The clear blocks allow a sense of the view, while also providing some privacy for the residents.

glass-block triptych window on the stair landing enlivens both upstairs and downstairs. The two bathrooms are small, but the careful consideration of standard fixtures, cultured-marble countertops, glass block, and a well-placed mirror makes them seem bigger and more elegant (see the photo on p. 145).

This house, which is in the suburbs, is considerably smaller and less expensive than its neighbors. But by sacrificing only square footage and complexity of form, the owners have built a Not So Big House at a not so big price.

The Site and Your Budget

One of the first decisions to make when designing and building a new home is to determine how much of your budget will go to the site and how much to the design and construction.

The site you choose will significantly affect your budget. The lot that this house was built on slopes steeply from right to left and sold for less than most of its neighbors. The house was designed for the site and nestles perfectly into the slope.

While any realtor will stress the importance of "location, location, location," the fact remains that if you're building for the long term, you may choose to build in an area that has slightly less financial security, in terms of resale, but might have features that are desirable to you. For example, a good location for resale, such as an upscale suburb of new homes, will cost more money than a piece of land in an established neighborhood of small, postwar houses. A good rule of thumb is that a quarter to a third of an entire budget goes to lot cost and the rest to design and construction. If you want a highly detailed house on a limited budget, you might consider finding a piece of land that is less expensive so you can spend more per square foot on the house's construction. A banker can be a good source of advice on what the neighborhood you're considering can support in terms of construction cost.

Sometimes odd-shaped lots can be found that are less expensive, simply because people can't figure out or find a plan to fit them. In fact, nine times out of ten, this kind of lot will bring people into an architect's office as a last resort. From an architect's standpoint, a site that appears impossible can often lead to the most inspiring and ultimately exciting house design. The constraints of budget and of site peculiarities can create a very unique house. The house shown in the bottom photo on the facing page presented an interesting challenge: a site that slopes steeply from right to left. The doctor couple who approached our office came only because there was no plan on the market that could gracefully fit into this unusual piece of property. The solution was to make the house split-level, with the garage slightly more than half a level down from the main living area.

House Orientation

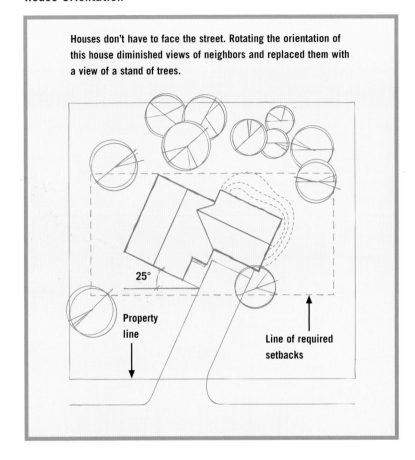

Houses don't have to face the street. Rotating the orientation of this house diminished views of neighbors and replaced them with a view of a stand of trees.

25°

Property line

Line of required setbacks

Taking advantage of the site features can make a home much more interesting, often without any additional expense. The site plan above shows a house our firm designed for a single father and his three children. The client's budget was extremely limited, and the site he found to build on was not particularly distinguished: The neighboring houses were very close and very plain. But the lot had a few nice trees and a location convenient to the client's office and the children's school. A simple solution we came up with was to rotate the orientation of the house by 25°, turning it so that it didn't look directly into its neighbor's windows. This solution cost no more money, and it improved the quality of life and views within the house.

A steeply sloped site can transform what would normally be the basement into desirable living space. This site slopes 9 ft. from the front entry to the back door. Windows in the lower level are low to the ground and offer views that are as appealing as those on the main and upper levels.

The slope of the lot allowed the lower level to accommodate some of the spaces the residents needed, reducing the square footage required on the main level.

30 ft.

10 ft.

40 ft.

10 ft.

In colder climates, a sloping piece of land can provide a distinct financial advantage when you're building Not So Big. Houses in cold climates require frost footings, which on a flat piece of land would create a basement level. If you have to have frost footings, it doesn't cost too much more to make this basement level another story of living space. A piece of land with a drop of 6 ft. to 10 ft. from front to back will lend itself to a "walk-out" plan, which allows a door from the lower level to open directly to the backyard. If you don't want this lower level to feel like a basement, you'll need plenty of windows, with their sills no more than 2 ft. 6 in. off the floor to keep you connected to a view of the ground beyond. This kind of plan allows you to reduce the square footage of the main and upper levels by redistributing living space to the lower floor. In the overall cost per square foot, this strategy can save you as much as a third of the cost of the house. The area is already there, so the cost of finishing it is significantly less than the cost of building an upper level from scratch.

The same strategy on a flat site will also save money. A "split entry" is the least expensive house you can build in a cold climate, where in some really cold areas frost footings are required to extend 4 ft. below ground. A split entry means that you enter the house halfway between the main level and the lower level, as shown in the drawing at right. Typically in such a house, the main living areas are upstairs and the bedrooms are downstairs. Without adding any more foundation than is required for frost-footing depth, you have a comfortable living level. Although windows cannot be as low to the floor, for someone with a limited budget this model buys the most space for the least money.

The site, perhaps more than any other factor, affects the quantity, quality, and cost of your house. The quality of a Not So Big House depends on making maximum use of every single opportunity offered by the site. Designing Not So Big means trading quantity of space for quality—and this idea should inform the lot you choose to build on.

The way the Not So Big House interacts with its site is symbiotic, but sometimes the features offered by a site aren't immediately evident. A client of mine was considering two lots on a city lake. The more expensive lot had unobstructed views to

Split-Entry House

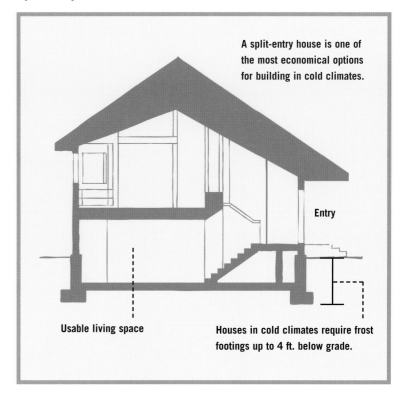

A split-entry house is one of the most economical options for building in cold climates.

Entry

Usable living space

Houses in cold climates require frost footings up to 4 ft. below grade.

the lake and to the houses beyond. The less expensive lot had no views because of the dense foliage. By trimming some of the lower branches, the view to the lake was opened but the nearby houses were still obscured. The client bought the less expensive lot, which turned out to be the most desirable.

Often the beauty of a piece of land is what inspires people to build a house worthy of that land. So when you're looking for a lot it's important to consider special features like long views, the presence of water, and distinctive trees and rock formations, which will ultimately affect the livability of the house. Most important is daylight. The pattern of the sun's movement will not only affect the orientation of the house but also offer perhaps the cheapest form of interior decoration: sunlight. The smaller the house the more profound the effect of the sun upon

This house was built for an owner who was willing to sacrifice square footage for interesting interior details.

it. Good resources for this topic include the books *Sun, Wind, and Light: Architectural Design Strategies* by G. Z. Brown and V. Cartwright (John Wiley and Sons, 1985) and *Passive Solar Energy* by Bruce Anderson and Malcolm Wells (Brick House Publishing, 1994).

The Middle Ground

Between the most economical of houses and the most expensive exists a broad range of possibilities, each again connected to one aspect of the quality-quantity-cost triangle. By increasing size, you increase cost; by increasing the level of detail, you also increase cost. The house featured in this section employs many of the principles of keeping cost down by using a simple form and structure, but it expands on the idea of quality of space and the craft of the details to become, as the client requested, "a little jewel."

The client, a church organist and choir director who teaches music, wanted a home where he could display various treasures from his travels as well as have space for a home pipe organ. He requested a bedroom that felt like a tree house, a screen porch, and a small deck off the master bedroom. From the kitchen, he wanted to be able to see the outside, the fireplace, and any guests he might be entertaining. Because he had traveled extensively in Asia, he knew he wanted the house to have a Japanese aesthetic. As for the size of the house, he needed at least 1,800 sq. ft., and he was willing to sacrifice any extra square footage to make the house interesting inside.

The site presented a few challenges: It is located on a busy street and slopes down to a marsh. So what would traditional-

The form of the house is a cube, a very simple and economical shape to build. A screened porch located above the garage extends the cube to the left. There are few windows on the front of the house because it faces a busy street.

architect determined that stucco would be easier and more cost-effective to maintain.

The architect's goal in designing the house was to take the very simple cube and give it as much visual interest as possible. This was achieved primarily through interior detailing. With simplicity as the guiding principle, Davis used a limited amount of wood trim to achieve a striking effect. Horizontal lines, valances, and window trim enliven the living areas. Lowered soffits carry ductwork to the upper floor and also provide varied ceiling heights, which are emphasized by lighting along the edge of the soffit. Niches for various treasures create

The back of the house opens up, taking full advantage of the sloped site to create a beautiful lower level that is filled with light and views.

ly be the front of the house needed to present a more private face, while the back of the house could open up for views. Remember, when you build deep frost footings, you get the chance to add a lower level that would just be a basement on a flat site. For architect Kelly Davis, the relatively tight budget, along with the site considerations, inspired a simple cube for the house form. While the client had originally specified wood siding, Davis was able to convince him that stucco would, ultimately, be a better choice for the exterior even though it would add $5,000 to the cost of the house. The maintenance of the wood exterior, especially on a three-level house, would also cost money. Wood requires frequent staining or painting, while stucco will last for decades without attention. The client and

Simplicity is this house's guiding design principle. The living area integrates carefully considered details, such as a trim line and a lowered ceiling along the wall between this room and the foyer, which marks the path to the porch.

interest on every level of the house. The grandfather clock, which has been in the client's family for 100 years, needed a special place. Davis carved an area out of the dropped soffit, rather than just make the ceiling height of the entire area taller. This creates a special alcove just for the clock—and the contrast of the two ceiling heights is striking.

In keeping with Not So Big precepts, Davis employed a number of visual tricks to make certain areas in the house appear bigger than they really are. The entry, which is between the main and lower level, measures only 6 ft. by 8 ft. (see the photo on p. 154). Open stair risers expand the sense of space; the entry's coat closet doesn't go all the way to the ceiling but

To accommodate a tall grandfather clock, the architect carved a niche up into the joist space rather than raising the ceiling height of the entire main level.

Open stair risers offer filtered views both up and down.
A small house like this one benefits from views connecting one
level to another, which makes it seem significantly bigger.

transforms into a display shelf, which is another way to make the entry seem larger. The alcove in the entry is a Japanese idea, a version of the *tokonoma*, which typically displays some sort off seasonal flower arrangement.

Because the house was designed for one person, issues of privacy were not important. So the house is quite open on each of its three levels. The main level uses Not So Big strategies, including a shared living and dining area, which is open to the kitchen. The dining area is distinguished by a two-story ceiling, which is opened up by two levels of windows (see the photo on p. 156). A two-story space is equivalent in cost to almost double the square footage of the area—in other words if the opening had been filled with floor and made into an upper-level room the cost would have been only slightly more. Thus, the cost per square foot of the entire house would have been lower. This client chose to spend money on drama rather than more living space. Although the main living space is relatively small (800 sq. ft.), in the summer months it's almost doubled with the addition of both a porch and a deck, which cover the garage below.

Upstairs, the master bedroom looks out over the dining area. A small study alcove, flooded with light from a large window that looks out to the street, is at the halfway point between the main and upper levels, almost like a big stair landing. The deck the client requested is just off the bedroom. Details enliven every area in the upper level, including the bathroom. A towel bar seems to be an extension of the trim line (see the bottom photo on p. 157); the mirror extends only halfway up the wall, allowing for windows to let in natural light while obscuring views to the busy street. The angle of the mirror allows the

MAIN LEVEL

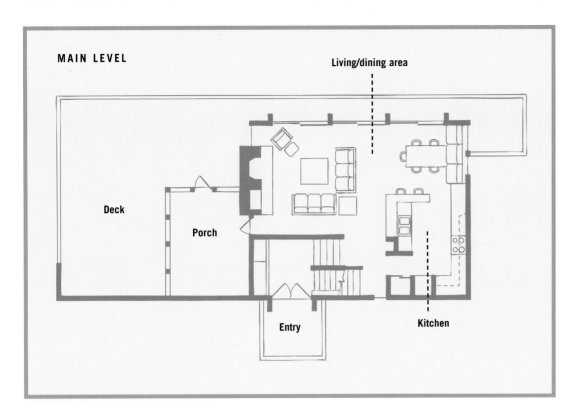

Living/dining area

Deck

Porch

Entry

Kitchen

UPPER LEVEL

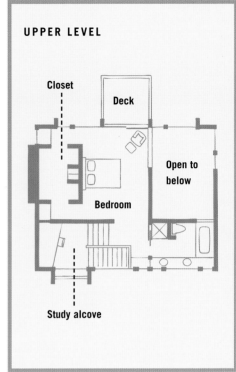

Closet

Deck

Open to below

Bedroom

Study alcove

BUILDING SECTION

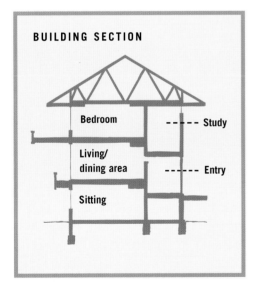

Bedroom — Study

Living/dining area — Entry

Sitting

LOWER LEVEL

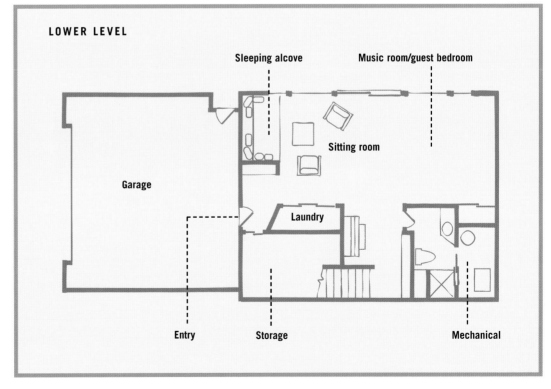

Sleeping alcove

Music room/guest bedroom

Sitting room

Garage

Laundry

Entry

Storage

Mechanical

A two-story ceiling in the dining area creates real dramatic interest on the main level.

The bedroom features a continuous band of maple trim, which aligns with the ceiling of the adjacent bathroom. Niches displaying treasures from the owner's travels are included upstairs and down.

same amount of reflection as would a mirror that goes to the ceiling (see the top left photo on p. 158).

The lower level of the house has become the music room, complete with home pipe organ. A built-in couch doubles as another bed, which the client uses whenever guests come to stay, allowing them the use of the master bedroom. The innovative details continue on this lower level, turning what might have been basement-like space into an extended living area. The client wanted an interesting floor but did not want to spend extra money on it. Exposed-aggregate floors are an economical finish for the lower-level floor. Because this level needed a concrete slab anyway, it cost only an extra dollar per square foot to use exposed aggregate for the finished floor.

Less expensive than most bathroom accessories, these custom-designed towel bars integrate perfectly with the aesthetics of the house.

High windows fill the bathroom with light. The mirror is designed to accommodate the windows and is set at an angle to reflect a greater area.

A lowered ceiling creates a special alcove for a built-in couch on the lower level. The couch doubles as a bed when visitors stay overnight.

The owner of the house is an organist, and the guest bedroom on the lower level doubles as a music room.

Wood dividers inset into the floor give it a more finished look and help limit any cracking that may occur with time (see the photo above).

The budget for this house was about 15% higher per square foot than for the house featured on pp. 138-146. The accumulation of so many special details gives this house a unique personality. Details were considered from the very beginning of

The finishing details are the most common items that can increase the cost per square foot in a new home. The faux finish on the walls of this room cost considerably more than a can of paint.

the design process, and they became the top priority. The client chose to purchase detail over complexity of form, and quality over quantity.

The most common items that can increase the cost per square foot of a new home are materials, fixtures, and finishes. For example, granite countertops, a hand-blown-glass light fixture, a whirlpool-tub faucet, a faux finish on a wall, imported wallpaper, and marble floors can each single-handedly break a budget. But, as shown in the house just profiled, good design can transform simple materials like concrete floors and laminate countertops. In architecturally designed homes, you don't need to rely on expensive materials, fixtures, and finishes to give the house its personality. What affects the cost is the quantity of whatever material is being used, as well as the

craftsmanship with which it is executed. Wood trim, used lavishly (as shown in the photo above), can add a substantial amount to the cost of the house, as can the fee for the high-quality finish carpenter who installs it. If the house for the music teacher had a similar amount of wood trim, the cost of the house might have risen by another 10%.

All wood—from pine to Brazilian cherry—is expensive. Some woods are also nonrenewable, such as hardwoods from tropical forests. Wood used on a broad surface, such as a ceiling, can also significantly affect the cost. And if you add an intricate coffered ceiling, the price is two to three times more than its flat-wood-surface counterpart. Similarly, a soaring ceiling can create real architectural interest, but you pay a premium for it.

Using the form of the roof as a vaulted ceiling costs more than the standard flat ceiling with a truss above it. The reason

A wood ceiling adds warmth to a room, but it also adds expense. The cost of putting wood on a ceiling is roughly equivalent to putting wood on the floor.

161

A two-story room is a wonderful space for entertaining, but its height makes it almost twice the price of its single-story equivalent.

A coffered ceiling is more expensive than a plain wood ceiling. There's more wood, and it requires significantly more craftsmanship to install.

for this is that any angle or curve simply costs more to finish and requires greater labor and skill than a flat surface. In short, when you deviate from a square box the price automatically goes up. This is why a simple builder house is usually less expensive. When you build a house that has special detailing you must assume that it will cost more, which is another reason to consider reducing square footage so that those special details are where the budget goes.

Exterior finishes can also affect the cost—and again the rule of thumb is that both quality of material and quality of craftsmanship cost money. In the Prairie-style house shown on p. 164, the exterior finishing looks expensive. But by using corner boards, or vertical pieces of trim at each corner of the house, a significant amount of money is saved. That's because the carpenter doesn't have to miter the edges of each piece of siding—a painstaking and expensive process. Although it has

Angles and curves can be beautiful to look at, but they are expensive to create. The curved ceiling that arches over the doorway to a deck looks effortless, but it belies the effort required to make it look so. The labor involved translates to increased cost.

Exterior finishing can figure prominently in a budget, but there are ways to reduce costs. The siding on this Prairie-style house butts up against corner boards at each corner of the house; without the corner boards, each piece of siding would have to be mitered and aligned perfectly with the siding on the adjacent surface.

This house, which, features siding with mitered corners, custom-colored windows, a cedar roof, and a brick base, is considerably more expensive than the one on the facing page, although both are at the high end of the residential market.

a similar aesthetic, the house shown above has a significantly more expensive exterior. The brick, while it is a durable building material, costs substantially more than wood siding; the custom color on the aluminum-clad windows adds to the price; and the wood shingles on the roof are typically five times the cost of a standard asphalt roof.

There are many less expensive alternatives to wood siding, such as steel, aluminum, and vinyl. And all of these products boast low maintenance. But the human eye is hard to fool, so a "fake" product has to be an extremely good replica of the natural product or it will leave the impression of being fake. That's

Four materials meet artfully on a house's exterior: tongue-in-groove redwood, lap siding, and Coronado stone (a fake stone product), topped with a concrete cap.

Increasing the ceiling height in this kitchen and dining area from 8 ft. to 9 ft. led to the inclusion of transom windows above the door and main windows. A change in stud length often has such ramifications throughout the house, which can add substantially to the cost.

a high price to pay. The only synthetic products I use are fake-stone products made of concrete, which can truly fool both the eye and the hand (see the bottom photo on p. 165).

Just as on the interior, angles and curves on the exterior cost money too. Every time you turn a corner or bend a wall, it requires a great deal more craftsmanship and precision by the builder or carpenter. The consequences of what may look like a simple angle in plan will ripple throughout the house. Floor-plans that look interesting on paper can in reality be extremely expensive to build.

Builders often encourage people to increase ceiling height from 8 ft. to 9 ft., telling them that the cost of the studs is only slightly more expensive. But the reality is that the increase in height mandates the addition of other products, such as transom windows, more cabinetry, and more trim to make the height look and feel right (see the photo above).

The High End

If cost is the adjustable parameter on your quality-quantity-cost triangle, then the potential to add character and detail to a house is limitless. The house shown below and on the following pages was designed by Michaela Mahady and built for the television series, *Hometime*. By most people's standards, it is not a small house. However, it does feature many of the Not So Big ideas on its main and upper levels, including a combined kitchen, dining, and living area and an away room (see the floorplans on p. 168).

The floorplans show the house's complexity immediately: If you count the number of corners, it's a pretty good indication of how expensive such a house would be to build. The curved roof form, multiple gables, unusually shaped windows, and stone terrace are all indicative of a very expensive structure. Although this house is significantly larger than any that's been shown so far, it is almost twice as expensive per square foot as the first house shown in this chapter. If the same level of detail were applied to a smaller amount of space, the cost per square foot would be even higher.

This home is much loved for its storybook charm, which comes from some expensive features, such as a curved roof, many dormers, custom-curved windows, and a stone base and chimney.

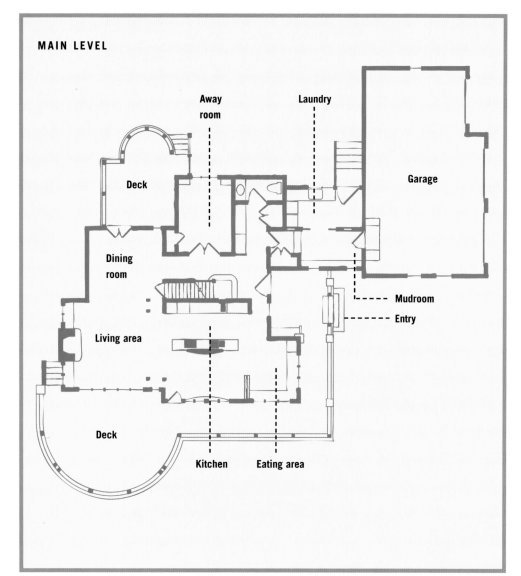

MAIN LEVEL

Away room · Laundry

Deck

Garage

Dining room

Mudroom

Entry

Living area

Deck

Kitchen · Eating area

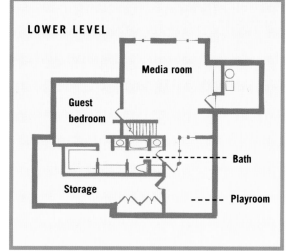

LOWER LEVEL

Media room

Guest bedroom

Bath

Storage

Playroom

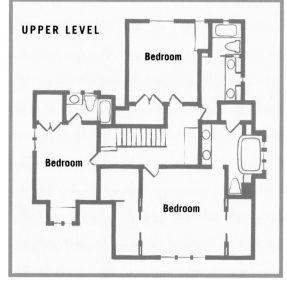

UPPER LEVEL

Bedroom

Bedroom

Bedroom

When you flare out a roof, a plywood web has to be added to the bottom of every roof truss to create the curved form before the roof sheathing is nailed on. And because the slope of the roof has changed, additional flashing and roof membrane have to be installed below the shingles to ensure that the roof won't leak. Every time you add a dormer to a house, you significantly complicate the roof framing, although dor-

mers clearly add a lot of personality to the house. Complexity costs money.

In a house where we're trying to keep costs down, my colleagues and I always use standard windows. The house shown here has windows that are curved and nonstandard in size, as well as upper transom windows used liberally on the main level. Again, these windows give the house a great deal of its personality—but simplifying this element alone could save several thousand dollars. The fieldstone terrace acts as a plinth on which the house is set; although stone is an inexpensive raw material, it takes a lot of labor to set it and, thus, becomes one of the most expensive building materials. If the stonework had covered the foundation alone rather than extending out to make a terrace, less stonework would have been required (and less additional cost). Although the terrace appeals to the eye and adds wonderful exterior space, it essentially adds another expensive foundation wall.

Every detail of this house is beautiful, such as this light fixture set into an arched frame between two symmetrical windows. Such details have to be thought out and planned long before the construction process begins.

From the maple woodwork in the kitchen to the fieldstone hearth beyond, the interior of this house is filled with high-end detailing.

Even the bathrooms feature woodwork throughout. Here, wood wainscoting lines the nook for the toilet and the tub surround. It lends an old-fashioned flair, but the details are luxuriously contemporary.

Special details like the surrounding panels for the exterior lamps, the brackets, the different colors of siding, trim, and shingles all take time and craftsmanship to apply. Inside, everything is custom-designed and detailed to the highest degree—from the kitchen cabinets to the granite and Corian countertops to the top-of-the-line appliances and the lavish use of trim. The detail continues even in more private and utility areas, like the bathroom. Even the stairs and the French doors into the away room have become works of art. In 1997 dollars, this house cost $775,500 to build, with 4,400 sq. ft. of finished space, which translates to $176 per square foot. (Over the last decade, prices have risen approximately 5% per year.)

The clients for the Prairie-inspired house shown at left on p. 172 requested a dramatic two-story living area where they could also feel cozy. Because budget was not a major constraint, I was able to come up with a dramatic solution that required some structural hijinks as well as a significant amount of glass and trim. Essentially, we created shelter around activity by "floating" the second story over the first, through structural beams that transfer the load to the mullion between the win-

dows on the main level. The beauty of the form that results is very appealing, but it is only an option when there are dollars available for such complexity.

Architect Joseph Metzler created the high-style Prairie kitchen and dining area addition shown at right on p. 172 for an Arts and Crafts aficionado. It is an example of a small addition that was very expensive to complete. While the original house features simpler Arts and Crafts detailing, the addition is

The stair railing goes beyond function to become sculpture; art-glass doors to the away room echo its lines. Together, these two elements create their own composition of light and line that is delightful to look at.

This room appears deceptively simple, yet it required enormous effort to make it look so. To make the beams that support the second-level window wall align perfectly with the mullions between the picture windows below, every detail had to be planned precisely in the early phases of the design process.

The addition to this home is Not So Big, but very expensive. While it added a combined kitchen/dining area, it also doubled the appraised value of the house.

highly decorated with trim, stained glass, and built-in cabinetry. Every material used is custom-crafted and top of the line, from the green-slate countertops to the custom light fixtures. Even the copper sinks were specially made. The walls are hand-glazed; stereo speakers are hidden in the corner behind a grill. The cost for this kind of detail begins with an architect's fees—

this kind of precision required more preplanning than a less detailed home, a computer model, and a very specific set of plans for construction. Everyone who works on such a project has to be top-notch, and you'll pay for their skills. In this addition, instead of using expensive furnishings and wallpaper, the architecture itself has been created to become the area's decoration. The cost, which came in close to $500 per square foot in 1997 dollars, almost doubled the appraised value of the house. In the right location, if you have the money available, such an expenditure on architecture can be a rewarding investment.

The greatest challenge in building or remodeling a house lies in making the best use of the dollars available. Building Not So

In this addition, architecture functions also as decoration. Notice the ceiling's trimwork, the lamps, the art-glass transom, the custom cabinets, and faux-finished walls. Details like these can double or triple the cost of the same square footage with a simpler design. Here, cost was of no great concern, so the issue of quality met no barriers.

Big requires a careful evaluation of needs and wishes, based not only on quantities but also, and more important, on qualities of space, light, and character. Our reliance today on the quantifiables of life often makes us settle for security over delight. Keep in mind that the reason you are building your house in the first place is to create a wonderful place to live on a daily basis. The quality-quantity-cost triangle can help you in your decision making, whether you have a tight budget and champagne tastes or an ample budget and a desire for an efficient, elegant environment. If you keep asking yourself what will enhance everyday living as you proceed with the design of your home, you'll ensure that the result makes the best use of the resources available and becomes a place that gives you pleasure every day.

A Timeless Classic

ABOVE **Situating the house and garage at right angles to one another and connecting them with a breezeway creates a view through to the backyard from the driveway and also makes the whole house seem less massive. The entry door, just to the right of the breezeway, serves guests and family alike.**

AS I SEARCHED FOR HOUSES ACROSS the country to illustrate the concepts behind building Not So Big, I discovered something I hadn't realized before: It's rare to find an architecturally designed house that doesn't have a vaulted or two-story ceiling somewhere in the design. Although higher ceilings can be dramatic, they add to the structural complexity of the house and thus increase the cost per square foot. And they don't necessarily make the house more livable or more beautiful. Extra money is invested on framing this expansive volume that could have been spent instead on the simple details and proportioning that really add to a home's comfort.

Stone lends this unassuming home a timeless quality that defies age.

This project from architect Peter Twombly is an example of a house without any tall spaces. It's a very simple structure and form, elegantly detailed with a minimum of fanfare. It's not ostentatious. It's not trying to be clever, unique, or outrageous. It's simply beautiful and comfortable. Let's see how he did it.

OPPOSITE **The kitchen in this house is a little like the helm of a ship, with a wide pass-through that looks into the dining and living rooms. The posts and beams that provide the structure for the second floor also serve to define the rooms below.**

Using a Belt Line

As was common in Shingle-style homes of the early 20th century, this house is banded by a belt line: a wide piece of trim below which all the indents of the main level occur and from which the windows appear to be suspended. A belt line is an excellent graphic device for composing a home's exterior. It organizes the upper and lower sections of the design and provides a graceful transition between materials. The only element that breaks the banding is the chimney, which serves to root the house firmly to its site.

On the front of the house (see the photo on p. 175), the lower section is mostly stone, while shingles are used on the sides, back, and upper section. With a higher budget, the architect might have selected to use stone for the entire lower section. It's not unusual to use a different color, as well as a different material, for the lower and upper areas—a characteristic you'll often see in older homes with a belt line.

If you're planning a belt line on your own home, you might try the following exercise to see what colors you like best: Take a drawing of the front face of the house, and make a number of copies. Then, use crayons or colored pencils to experiment with different colors above and below the belt line. Also, give some thought to the color of the belt line itself. It's typical to use the same color for the belt line as for the trim around windows.

This is a house with a very simple structure and form, elegantly detailed with a minimum of fanfare.

Peter's approach to the design resulted from a fairly limited budget, at least by architect's standards. As with many things of beauty, this economy of means led to a more elegant and satisfying result than an excess of showy details ever could. Think of a haiku. Its power to affect us comes in large part from the constraints imposed by its form, which is so restrictive that every word must transcend the structure. When it does, the effects are deeply moving. So it is with architecture. Peter knew that he would need to make the house very simple to build if it was to stay within budget. So spans were kept short, ceiling heights standard, and the entire structure was designed for conventional framing and lumber sizes.

The house is essentially a rectangular box, with small sections scooped out for the front entry and to either side of the piano alcove to give the front facade some visual interest. The only other

ABOVE Rather than standard spindles, this stair railing is made with 1x4s spaced an inch apart, with a keyhole cutout in every other board. Together with the elegantly proportioned newel post, the stairway looks quite different from the visual approach, yet it is simple and inexpensive to build. It's small touches like this that give a house a personality all its own.

LEFT The exposed rafters and graceful swoop of the roof edge add an artistic touch to the simplicity of the house. It doesn't take a lot to make a significant statement when the rest of the design is so restrained. The tiny hole drilled in the end of the rafter tail provides a subtle theme that's repeated in the stairway railing.

structural embellishment is the addition of a lean-to porch and kitchen eating area, which look out toward a pond to the east. What grows out of these constraints is a surprising amount of spatial complexity and variety.

One Entrance

The clients, Randy and Maggie, were moving from a standard builder's colonial, with an attached garage and a seldom-used formal entry. They assumed that their new house would have the same arrangement. But Peter pointed out that by separating the garage from the house with a breezeway, they could eliminate the garage entry to the house and combine the formal and informal entryways.

When a garage is attached to the house, it's almost inevitable that the family entry is through a laundry or mudroom—hardly an appealing welcome home. Meanwhile, the front foyer is lavished with dollars and pizzazz that are seldom appreciated. Creating a single functional and attractive entrance gives the family the pleasure of entering their home through a well-designed entry every day, and the strategy saves space in the process.

With this newly designed entry, guests and family now enter through the same front door. Just to the left are the mudroom, powder room, and study, making it easy for the kids to drop off their backpacks and for Randy and Maggie to set down their mail and briefcases. The view that greets them is of the window at the far end of the living room, which draws the eye in and acts as an invitation to the living area.

All the main living spaces are connected to one another visually,

but there's still a strong distinction between one place and the next.

Interior Windows

All the main living spaces are connected to one another visually, but there's still a strong distinction between one place and the next. The kitchen is defined by a wall that separates it from the dining and living areas, but there's a wide pass-through opening that connects the three spaces. Without this framed opening, the house would function very differently. When a space can't be seen, it is typically seldom used. Take away the pass-through, and the living room would be nearly invisible from either kitchen or breakfast nook. To socialize with someone working in the kitchen, you'd have to leave the living room. Most of the living in the house would thus gravitate to the breakfast nook and kitchen, and the living and dining rooms would go largely unused.

ABOVE **The breakfast nook is an excellent example of a large alcove. It's a small block of space with a lowered ceiling, filled with light and with views into a larger room beyond. We tend to gravitate to such comfortable corners. (Why else do we find ourselves asking for the corner booth when we go to a restaurant?)**

ABOVE Although this home has no vaulted ceilings or two-story spaces, the living room has been given a higher ceiling by dropping the floor two steps down. In this way, the living room is distinguished as the most important space on the main level. Unlike so many vaulted great rooms, however, this space remains eminently comfortable. It takes only a small increase in height to make a big impact.

Such a seemingly insignificant alteration can make a big difference in how one lives in a house. There are many houses, old and new, that could benefit from the implementation of this simple concept. But because we don't have a name for it, we don't know how to ask for it, and so it rarely gets designed. You can think of this visual access between spaces as a "connecting view" or an "interior window." By whatever name, the idea is to keep different activity areas in sight of each other so no room is isolated from the action.

Four Alcoves

Within the nearly symmetrical form of the main-level floor plan, there are four alcoves of varying shapes and sizes. An alcove is essentially a block of space attached to and opening onto a main living space. It houses a peripheral activity, so that more than one thing can be happening at the same time without the activities conflicting.

The largest of these alcoves is the breakfast nook. At 10 ft. 6 in. by 12 ft., it's the perfect size for a small table and chairs. With windows on three sides, it's also filled with light and views. From this cozy space, you can look out into the yard, so there's a sense of expansiveness. And you can also look into the house, through several rooms, so there's a sense of connectedness. This is the kind of space that people tend to be attracted to: a smaller space looking into a larger space. Make it larger and it would lose its appeal. Like a booth at a restaurant, scale is critical to comfort, and bigger is not necessarily better.

There's a second alcove made especially for the grand piano. Place such a piano in the main part of the room and it would dominate the space and add significantly to its formality. But put it in its own alcove, and it takes on a subordinate role. The beauty of its form can still be appreciated, but you don't feel that you're waiting for the concert to begin, as happens when the piano is center stage.

Architect:
Estes/Twombly Architects, Inc.
Builder:
Gardner Woodwrights
Size: 2,900 sq. ft.
Location:
southern R.I.

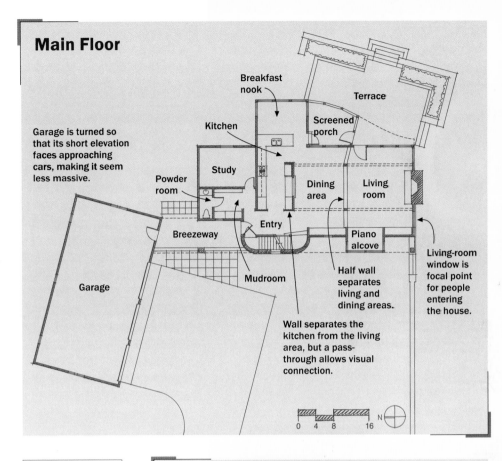

Main Floor

Breakfast nook

Terrace

Kitchen

Garage is turned so that its short elevation faces approaching cars, making it seem less massive.

Screened porch

Study

Powder room

Dining area

Living room

Breezeway

Entry

Piano alcove

Mudroom

Half wall separates living and dining areas.

Living-room window is focal point for people entering the house.

Garage

Wall separates the kitchen from the living area, but a pass-through allows visual connection.

0 4 8 16 N

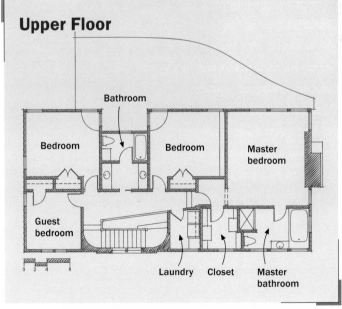

Upper Floor

Bathroom

Bedroom

Bedroom

Master bedroom

Guest bedroom

Laundry Closet Master bathroom

0 2 4 8

ABOVE Comfort is defined less by the furniture we choose than by the shape of the space, the quality of the light, and the crafting and composition of places for living. This spot by the living-room window, for example, invites you to settle in. It's the combination of chair, light, and alcoves that makes it so appealing. (PHOTO COURTESY WARREN JAGGER.)

The piano alcove is flanked by two smaller alcoves, which house built-ins and display places, creating a depth and variety of space that makes for a visual feast. This is an example of spatial layering. It gives the impression that the outside walls of the house are extra thick and that the alcoves have been scooped out of them to reveal a bit of the world beyond. It's this kind of depth and visual complexity that we've all but lost in new houses today. Instead there's the feeling that everything is paper-thin and could easily be blown away in a high wind.

Rooted to the Ground

The stone used for the front columns, the stairway enclosure, and the chimney adds to the sense of solidity and permanence that is so fundamental to this house. One of the reasons Randy and Maggie bought this particular piece of property was because they liked the old stone walls that ran across it. For them, the walls recalled a time when the area was farmland. In addition to rebuilding some of the existing farm walls, the owners wanted to use some of the stone in the house itself. Although stone is an expensive material to install, by selecting some key areas and locating the house to take advantage of one of the farm walls, a little has been made to go a long way.

Few things speak to us like stone—a simple, strong material created over millennia and solid as the earth. It lends this unassuming home a time-less quality that defies age, and chances are it will still have that quality 200 years from now.

The fireplace surround is made of Rhode Island blue granite with Belgian pavers used instead of regular firebricks, giving it a timeless look and feel. The mantle itself is made of maple, set upon stone brackets. And the sides of the stone-work are battered, or narrowed slightly, echoing the shape of the newel post at the entry. These are subtle moves, but the effect is striking.

LEFT The window in the stairway to the basement is set close to the ground, an intriguing puzzle, per-fectly aligned in the center of the wall and directly below the win-dows above. It's gone from just a window in a wall to an image in a frame, drawing you to take a closer look.

A House
for Today and
Tomorrow

W HEN BETH ASKED ARCHITECT
Murray Silverstein to design a cabin for her on a wooded site in Northern California, she wasn't sure whether she would make it her year-round residence or keep it only for weekend and vacation use. As a single woman, she didn't need a lot of space, but she wanted whatever she built to be beautiful and flexible—a place that felt like a retreat. What evolved is a house with the transformational abilities of a chameleon, despite a deceptively simple floor plan.

In order to appreciate this home's flexibility, we need to go back to Beth's original vision. She is a therapist by profession and was considering the possibility of living in the house year-round and also having her office there. She wanted a space that was professional and private, with a separate entrance so clients wouldn't have to walk through her living area in order to reach the office. In-home consulting practices come with their own special challenges. They need acousti-

A house designed to accommodate a variety of possible future living arrangements can actually benefit from the constraints imposed upon it.

185

cal privacy and a quality of quiet removal from the activities of the rest of the house, so that clients won't be uncomfortable talking openly. They also require ready access to a powder room, preferably one not in view of the living space.

These are, of course, the same qualities you find in a comfortable bedroom. To accommodate the restrictions of her budget and the small scale Beth was seeking, Murray realized that he could make that private realm do double duty. So he designed the second level to be divisible into two rooms—an office/study and a bedroom beyond. By nestling the house into the side of the hill to the northwest, he created an entry for clients halfway between the main and upper levels, allowing them to enter without ever encountering the main living space. The compact powder room on the landing could serve both the office and the bedroom. Meanwhile, family and friends enter directly through the solarium porch at the end of the beautiful flagstone path connecting house and driveway. Although Beth hasn't yet used the work-at-home option, her house is ideally set up for such an arrangement.

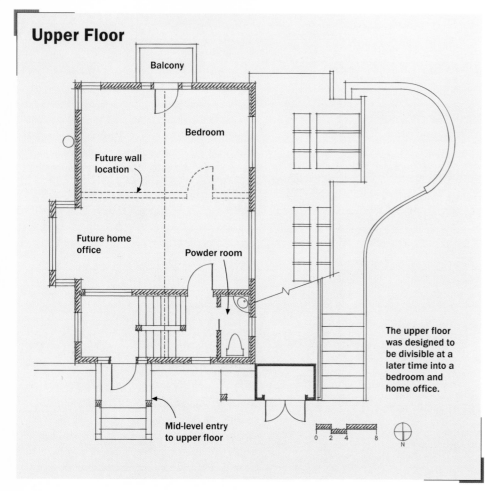

Upper Floor

Balcony

Bedroom

Future wall location

Future home office

Powder room

The upper floor was designed to be divisible at a later time into a bedroom and home office.

Mid-level entry to upper floor

0 2 4 8

N

ABOVE **With its steeply sloped roof and 5-ft.-high side wall, this bedroom feels both cozy and spacious. If the wall were raised to 8 ft., however, the room would take on the proportions of a cathedral—not a comfortable place for sleeping. Every dimension in our homes should relate to human scale. Taller doesn't automatically mean better.**

Architect: Jacobson Silverstein Winslow Achitects

Builder: Axel Nelson, General Contractor

Size: 1,150 sq. ft.

Location: Inverness, Calif.

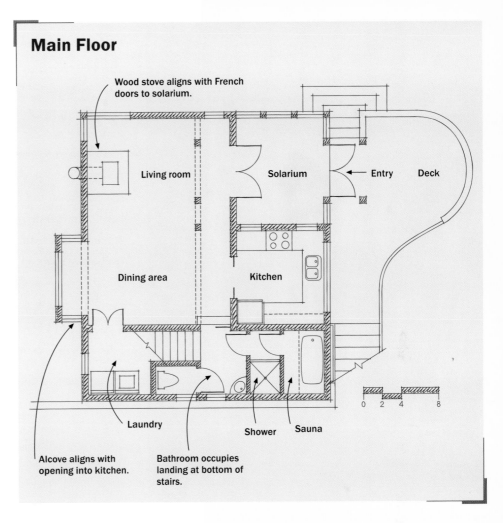

Main Floor

Wood stove aligns with French doors to solarium.

Living room

Solarium

Entry

Deck

Dining area

Kitchen

Laundry

Shower

Sauna

Alcove aligns with opening into kitchen.

Bathroom occupies landing at bottom of stairs.

0 2 4 8

Guest Suite with a Twist

Since Beth planned to have guests every once in a while but didn't want to have a room devoted to this purpose alone, she was willing to combine two functions that are an unusual pairing. The solarium porch is used primarily as an entryway, but when friends are visiting, it doubles as the guest sleeping area. Although in most houses an entry is one of the most public spaces in the house, in this home it can be turned into a very private space, thanks to the existence of the mid-level entry. The exterior doors are locked, the French doors into the living space covered with drapes, and the transformation is complete. Now it's a guest room or away room.

The One-Bath House

But what about a bathroom for the guests? When there's a bedroom on each level, it's a foregone conclusion these days that you must include a full bathroom on each level as well. Bathrooms are expensive, though, and guest bathrooms are typically seldom used. So Murray came up with a clever solution—one bathing area to serve both levels. The landing at the bottom of the stair-

Although in most houses an entry is one of the most public spaces in the house, in this home it can be turned into a very private space.

case is in fact also the main bathroom. A sliding door and two steps up separate it from the main-level living space. Directly across from the stair is the door into the shower. A door beyond that leads into the tub room. Lower the lid over the tub, and the room is transformed into a sauna. To the left of the stair is the toilet, in its own tiny room under the staircase to the upper level. And on the landing itself is the sink, tucked into a corner beside the window. Although this may seem a strange way to accommodate a bathroom, if every cubic inch must be used effectively, any space is fair game.

Defining Places

The rest of the main level is classic Not So Big in arrangement, with a single dining and living area and a kitchen that's open to both. When a formal dinner is in progress, Beth can close off the kitchen from view with sliding doors, but most of the time they remain open. The dining table has its own small alcove, just 7 ft. wide. The beams above it serve to mark off the space and give it a sense of enclosure, without lowering the ceiling or blocking the windows.

Often, in an effort to accommodate chair movement, dining spaces are made overly large and their intimacy is lost. Here, the space fits perfectly with the proportions of the house, and the table has become a favorite spot to sit. Without the alcove, though, the house would feel very different. There'd be no sheltered place to go to and no relief from the rectangular form of the room. Even when money is limited, including a small alcove like this one adds a spatial vitality that's well worth the expense.

ABOVE Placing a window at the end of a walkway draws you toward it. Remove the window and you'll be much less inclined to move in that direction. The two steps are part of the flight to the second floor and lead to the main-level bathroom. The landing houses the bathroom sink, tucked around the corner to the left.

RIGHT You pass through the shower area to reach the tub beyond, which is in its own cocoon-like room. When the lid is folded down to cover the tub, the room turns into a sauna. One space serves two functions, with a minimum of fuss, proving that a little creativity can save a lot of square footage.

When in Doubt, Line It Up

Another aspect of organizing space is used here that doesn't add any cost, yet is rarely implemented. Look at the floor plan on p. 187 and you can see that the dining alcove is perfectly aligned with the opening into the kitchen. The same is true of the wood stove, which is directly across from the French doors to the solarium. Aligning views and features in this way gives the whole house an integrity that's palpable. It's not something you will stop and take note of every day—in fact very few people will consciously observe such alignments. But the place will feel good, as though all is right with the world. Someone has taken the time to make a harmonious composition, and we appreciate it instinctively, even when we don't realize why.

Another ordering device used on the main level to add both character and comfort is the heavy timber walkway that leads from the entryway to the staircase. Although this area is still very much a part of the main living

TOP Why hide away the beautiful objects you own? Here, a collection of ceramics becomes the wallpaper for the living room. These mugs and plates are used every day and, when not in service, stored in this specially designed rack adjacent to the kitchen.

RIGHT An alcove creates a sense of shelter around the activity it houses. Although many alcoves have a lowered ceiling, here it is implied rather than actual, with the trim line between windows transforming into a beam that bridges the space. A ceiling doesn't have to be solid to create enclosure.

Shibui

In Japanese, the word *Shibui* is used to describe a quality of design that many Not So Big Houses possess. It can be an elusive concept to grasp, however, because we have no comparable word in our language. Words that combine to give a sense of its meaning include simplicity, elegance, beauty, functionality, restraint, reserve, refinement, and quietude. The term can apply to anything that has been designed, from an article of clothing to a piece of furniture to a building.

But none of these words describes how this quality comes into being. Though something *Shibui* looks effortlessly simple, even inevitable, it takes much labor and refinement to make it so. The quality of *Shibui* evolves out of a process of complexity, though none of this complexity shows in the result.

Shibui often seems to arise when an architect is striving to meet a particular design challenge. When you stop to think back on houses that have made an impact on you, they'll often be the ones where an awkward problem has been cleverly solved in a way that makes you think, "Well, of course! How else could it be?" When something has been designed really well, like the house shown here, it has an understated, effortless beauty, and it really works. It's simply *Shibui.*

It takes real skill to create an intimate small house that satisfies a complicated set of requirements—and does so without feeling confined.

space, it's also separated from it by the line of columns, lowered ceiling sections, and supporting beams. It's a little like the arcades you see in Europe, along centuries-old shopping streets. The kitchen and solarium are the shops, the main living area is the open-air plaza, and the walkway—the arcade—offers shelter as people come and go. There's a sense of order and layering about the arrangement that makes us comfortable because it helps us subconsciously understand what's going on: This is the path to get from one place to the next. And it's no accident that the windows at either end of the walkway are lined up along its central axis.

This little house has proportions that optimize comfort. Architects will be the first to admit that, although you can have fun designing a larger house with few constraints, it takes real skill to create an intimate small house that satisfies a complicated set of requirements—and does so without feeling confined. A house like this one, designed to accommodate a variety of possible future living arrangements, can actually benefit from the constraints imposed upon it.

The house has gone on to gracefully accommodate some unexpected new uses over the years. It's recently become a much-loved weekend home, not only for Beth but also for her new husband and baby. It illustrates well how a little forethought can extend the usefulness of a house as opportunities and lifestyle choices change without compromising its originally intended function—a quiet forest getaway for one. A house designed as beautifully and thoughtfully as this one can take on all manner of lifestyle changes—even the unpredictable ones.

BELOW As you enter the main living area from the solarium, visible here through the French doors, you emerge under the lowered timber walkway. The experience of entering is accentuated by the contrast between ceiling heights, which creates the experience of compression followed by release.

The Essence of Home

*I*N SELECTING NOT SO BIG HOUSES
for this book, I looked for dwellings that have an archetypal
quality—houses that resonate with the deep-rooted vision of
home that many people carry within their hearts and minds.
Features of this archetype include a
steep, single-gabled roof, usually with
one or more dormers; a centrally located entry with its own sheltering
roof; and a massive chimney, either at
the center of the house or at one or
both ends. These basic features, combined with pleasing proportions and
a well-chosen site, speak to us of
home. Not surprisingly, as we look
back through the history of the
house, we find dwellings from many
cultures that have this same general form. Architects refer to this
as "vernacular architecture"—literally, architecture that has grown
from the native building patterns of a culture.

> *The house embodies in its
> exterior form much of what
> we long for today—a house
> that says Home before you
> ever step through the door.*

ABOVE **A small sitting balcony is
aligned with the top of the stairs and
the middle dormer of the house—the
exact center of the floor plan. The combination of natural-wood newel posts
and handrails with white painted,
closely spaced spindles is a reference
to classic detailing and proportioning.**

OPPOSITE **Based on images from the
past but with a contemporary twist, this
house is almost symmetrical but not
quite. With its darker base, white
second-story dormers, bold green roof,
and central chimney, it is distinctive but
familiar. It resonates with the arche-
types that say Home.** (PHOTO COURTESY
JEREMIAH ECK.)

BELOW The windows throughout the main level are larger than normal, with a fixed upper transom set above out-swinging casements. The combination gives the look of an old-fashioned double-hung window, where the upper section was often shorter than the lower one. The raised platform of the window bay offers a comfortable place for overflow seating during parties and larger gatherings.

There is one house in particular that has spoken to many people in this way over the last few years. In my own architectural practice, clients would frequently bring in magazine photos of this house (first published in *Fine Homebuilding* magazine in 1990) and tell me how much they liked the look of the exterior. It was something they instinctively responded to without being able to say why. Designed by architect Jeremiah Eck for a couple who were building on land that their family had owned for generations, it embodies in its exterior form much of what we long for today—a house that says Home before you ever step through the door.

What Steve and Nancy were looking for was a modern version of an English cottage. Jeremiah drew from his knowledge of vernacular architecture and historical house forms to develop a design that would fit the needs of the couple and their two young children and reflect their love of the archetypal cottage. With its triple gables, steeply pitched roof, and massive brick chimney, it is an amalgam of imagery found throughout Europe, while also incorporating aspects of the American Gothic.

Building Character

The house is set at the edge of a wood that looks out toward the ancestral family home, across acres of meadowland. Like many other distinctive Not So Big Houses, it seems to have a face, with the two symmetrical gables like a pair of spectacles resting on the bridge of the nose—the third gable. As is typical of many American Gothic homes, the upper section (above the belt line) is made of wide wooden panels with vertical

The Effects of Color

*T*he color of a house can make a dramatic difference in how it looks and feels, but it's rare that we have the opportunity to see what a house looks like in two different color schemes. Thanks to the fact that Steve is a house painter and likes to experiment on his own house, we can see here the dramatic difference between the house as originally painted and how it looks today. When the house was new, Steve left the lower section a natural cedar color, stained with a semitransparent stain. Many people love this natural look, but it requires significant maintenance, with a reapplication of stain every two to three years.

Now Steve has applied a new coat of paint to both upper and lower sections, and the colors give the house a more playful appearance. Where in the original scheme the entire upper section was painted bright white, in the new version the trimwork remains white but the plywood and batten strips are a contrasting blue. In the lower section, the yellow of the siding contrasts only slightly with the trim, and since they are close in color to one another, the eye is drawn to the upper part of the house as the dominant form.

Color is a very personal issue, and one that can elicit some spirited debate among couples. Some people like the whole house to be the same color, while others prefer a darker base and lighter upper section, and still others like it the other way around. But the wonderful thing about color is that it's a relatively easy thing to change. And with the advent of computer-aided design and color modeling, we're able to see the effects of color choices *before* the paint is applied.

(PHOTO TOP RIGHT COURTESY JEREMIAH ECK.)

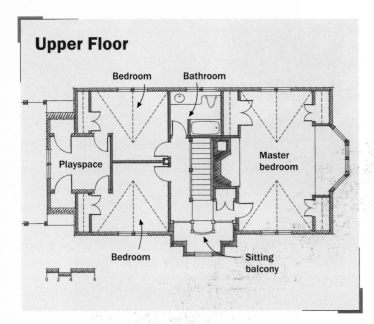

Upper Floor

Bedroom

Bathroom

Playspace

Master
bedroom

Bedroom

Sitting
balcony

0 2 4   8

Main Floor

Stairway and fireplace
separate the house into
two distinct sections.

Entry

Mudroom

Kitchen

Screened
porch

Laundry

Living room

Dining area

Formal entry doubles as
a place for bill paying.

N

0 2 4   8

batten strips, while the lower section has horizontal lap siding in a contrasting color.

This configuration serves to distinguish one section of the house from another. When we can identify an order to the parts of a design (in this case, main level, upper level, and roof), it gives us a sense of understanding—just as we use commas to break a sentence into phrases so we can take in the content more easily. Remove the commas and you might have to read the sentence a few times to understand what's being communicated. In the same way, if all the exterior surfaces of this house were of the same material and color, it would seem more monumental and, as a result, less inviting.

The trim width around doors and windows is important, too. In most houses today the only trim around windows is the brick mold, a narrow molding that comes with the window. The window looks almost frameless, as if it had been rather unceremoniously shoved into the wall. (Just visit any subdivision built in the last two decades and you'll see what I mean.) In this house, as in most Not So Big Houses, careful attention has been given to each window's framing. Most of the win-

Architect:
Jeremiah Eck Architects, Inc.
Builder:
Jarrett Vaughn Construction
Size: 1,750 sq. ft.
Location:
Holicong, Pa.

Small details combine to give the house a solidity and substance that would otherwise be lacking.

dows have a 3½-in.-wide piece of trim at either side and a deeper, 5½-in. board below the sill. In the case of the two triple-window sets on the main level, they are "hung" from the belt line, which serves as the head trim.

The double-hung windows in the twin gables are surrounded by more dramatic frames, again reminiscent of the American Gothic style. Here, the wide top casing is banded with an additional molding that extends about a quarter of the way down each side, further accentuating the windows' resemblance to eyes. All these small details may seem minor, but they combine to give the house a solidity and substance that would otherwise be lacking. They are characteristic of a house in which the available money has been spent on quality rather than quantity. It's the details that really make it sing.

Table at the Center

Inside, the house continues its interpretation of the past with a floor plan separated into two sections by the stairway and fireplace, a classic layout in many early American houses. Until the invention of extractor fans, the kitchen was often built either in an isolated lean-to structure or in a separate building, to keep the smells of cooking away from the living

ABOVE Without the half wall and columns, this spot by the wood stove would be an unsettling place to sit—at the bottom of the stairs and adjacent to the walkway through to the living room. But with them, this chair has a sense of shelter around it, making it more inviting and comfortable.

ABOVE The railing between the dining area and the staircase is transparent enough to allow an unobstructed view but solid enough to create a psychological separation. It's an implied wall—more like a lattice than a wall. It gives the stair a sense of enclosure while adding a wonderfully decorative backdrop to the room.

areas of the home. Since modern technology has eliminated this concern, Jeremiah has kept the lean-to form but opened up the kitchen to the dining area, creating one big room with the table as its focus.

When you consider the design of a home, it's important to look at family social patterns and recognize where people tend to gather. For many, the kitchen table is the place. It is only convention that encourages us to make it small and place it in a corner. If the room has an easy comfort like this one, the table can be large and centered in the room without it feeling formal. A table of this kind can still do double duty for both formal and informal occasions, but if it receives an extra nick or two from everyday wear and tear, it's not something you'll lose sleep over.

Just as in farmhouses of the past, the kitchen table is where the family congregates, and its central position puts it at the heart of activity. Adjacent to the wood stove, and with a clear view to the comings and goings of the stairway, it makes the dining area a place that feels vibrant and alive.

An Old-Fashioned Living Room

By contrast, the living room, which in this house is separate from the kitchen, is the quiet place of retreat for the adults. Although most Not So Big Houses have their kitchen, living, and dining areas open to one another, if you like to move into another room after a meal, then that's how you should plan your house. As always, build for the way *you* live.

LEFT **This house is full of personal touches that continue the theme of making new out of old. Here, an antique pediment perches above the window like a hat, and a charming old kitchen cabinet hangs above the stove, giving a little more storage and a lot more character to the simple kitchen.**

Up Close

In this home, the fireplace is an important social gathering spot that clearly sees frequent use. Together with the lattice frame above and bookshelves on either side, the whole ensemble suggests an old-world inglenook. But, as with so much else in this house, it's a contemporary version.

RIGHT Since the formal front entry in this house is rarely used (most guests and family arrive by the back door), it has been designed to do double duty as a place for paying bills. The antique desk looks like an appropriate piece for a foyer, but it can fold out into a desk when needed.

BELOW The comfortably furnished living room, centered around an old-fashioned hearth, is intended as the adults' realm for reading and after-dinner conversation. It is more separate from the kitchen and dining area than in many Not So Big Houses, doubling as a quiet away room. (PHOTO COURTESY JEREMIAH ECK.)

For Steve and Nancy, this adult realm of the house was an important and desirable feature that they knew they would use. They like to light a fire on winter evenings and to read and talk after dinner in a more elegant setting than the kitchen allows. By lowering the floor two steps and exposing the beams and flooring of the level above, Jeremiah has made the room almost 2 ft. taller than the rest of the main level, giving it greater visual and spatial weight. The warmth of the wood ceiling, the well-used fireplace, and the comfortable furnishings give it a very different feel than the typical formal living room. Like the exterior of the house, this room says Home.

The Personal Touch

Allowing your house to become a truly personal expression is one of the basic tenets of building Not So Big, and Steve and Nancy have missed no opportunity to give every nook and cranny of their home a colorful, lighthearted quality with the treasures they've collected over the years. There are small collections of special objects here and there, like the array of flower-patterned plates around the mirror at the bottom of the stairs and the coats of arms above the desk in the front-entry niche. There are also a number of "found" architectural objects dotted around, such as the wooden pediment above the kitchen window and the metal screen behind the bed in the master bedroom, which provides some psychological privacy without blocking the view. Often a house that's playfully composed encourages its inhabitants to continue in that same spirit, personalizing wherever they can, and giving the whole house an unselfconscious, friendly feel.

Finding someone to help you design a house that really expresses who you are can be enormously rewarding. It's as though the house both focuses and reflects the way you feel about life, to yourself and to others. So many people today live in houses that, they'll readily admit, don't really fit their spirits. A house like this one is made for the way its owners live and also expresses something more about their values and their delights. A house that's designed specifically for you and your family can enhance your life in a truly remarkable way. Until you've tried it, many houses will *seem* to satisfy, but after living in one that's really "you," you'll understand what coming home is all about.

BELOW A screen made of wrought-iron filigree separates the bed from the window bay. It shelters the head of the bed and still allows views through to the meadows and trees beyond.

A house that's designed specifically for you and your family can enhance your life in a truly remarkable way.

Doing More with Less

No ONE BUT AN ARCHITECT WOULD have dared to try to make the old summer rental cottage in Branford, Connecticut, into a year-round home for a family of four. But Matthew, who has his own architectural practice, and his wife, Beth, an interior designer, were undeterred by the diminutive size of the lot (less than a tenth of an acre) and the tiny footprint of the cottage. In fact, they used the 20-ft. by 24-ft. foundation of the original structure as their starting point and, with the addition of only two small bump-outs to the footprint, made a house that looks inviting on the outside and exudes charm and innovation within.

The house now has three stories and a basement instead of one story and a cellar, and every cubic inch of space is used every day. With only 500 sq. ft. on the main level, Matthew and Beth had to use all their combined inventiveness to make a place that is comfortable for a family to live in without feeling claustrophobic. The house is built vertically instead of horizontally, which is

The house utilizes the principles of building Not So Big to make a little space feel much bigger than it really is.

ABOVE **A pleasing graphic composition, the rear elevation is as thoughtfully designed as the front. The bright red door hints at the surprises inside.**

RIGHT **Unexpected materials are used throughout the house, like the oar instead of a standard handrail and the corrugated metal roofing as wall covering at the front entry. Overcome habitual thinking about how things are supposed to be used, and there's no limit to creativity.**

like thinking outside the box by prying the lid off. It takes this unusual configuration of space and the principles of building Not So Big to make a little space feel much bigger than it really is.

By using the basement level as a playspace for the children and by placing their own bedroom and the children's bedroom on two separate upper floors, Matthew and Beth have created 1,700 sq. ft. of living space. Each level is a treasure trove of clever ideas to make less do more. Most remarkable of all, this is done not through a minimalist approach but with a profusion of personal items, collections, and comfortable furniture.

What the Floor Plan Doesn't Reveal

In plan, the main level looks pretty stark—just an oddly formed square with a single U-shaped wall in the middle, which houses the refrigerator. If you were to see this floor plan in a house-plan magazine, you'd probably skip right over it. But this house illustrates the limitations of the floor plan as a device for gauging character. What you can't see in two dimensions is what makes this home such a delight.

The U-shaped refrigerator wall is a small item in the plan, but what it does three-dimensionally is very important. Essentially, the main level needs to accommodate five functions: entering, sitting, cooking, eating, and going up- or downstairs. If walls were added to partition the space according to function, every room would seem very small. But if the space is left completely open, there is little distinction between

Each level is a treasure trove of clever ideas to make less do more.

Architect:
Z:Architecture

Builders:
Matthew Schoenherr,
Michael Fuller

Size: 1,700 sq. ft.

Location:
Branford, Conn.

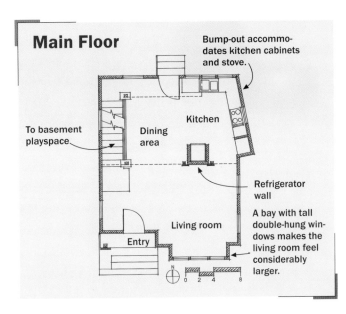

Main Floor

Bump-out accommodates kitchen cabinets and stove.

To basement playspace

Dining area

Kitchen

Refrigerator wall

A bay with tall double-hung windows makes the living room feel considerably larger.

Living room

Entry

N 0 2 4 8

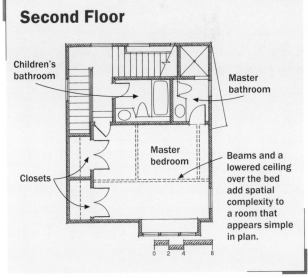

Second Floor

Children's bathroom

Master bathroom

Closets

Master bedroom

Beams and a lowered ceiling over the bed add spatial complexity to a room that appears simple in plan.

0 2 4 8

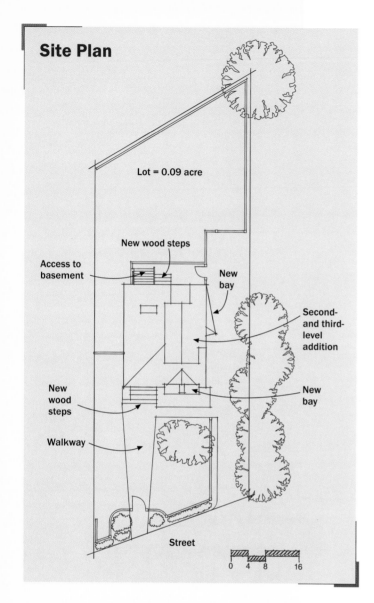

Site Plan

Lot = 0.09 acre

New wood steps

Access to basement

New bay

Second- and third- level addition

New wood steps

New bay

Walkway

Street

0 4 8 16

one area and another, and this also makes a space feel small. The refrigerator enclosure helps to break up the space by providing a separation between the kitchen and the living room, which partially obscures views from one to the other without the complete enclosure of a full wall. It's what I call a pod of space.

The refrigerator pod also serves as a large column. It aligns with the center of the front bay, giving the living room a feeling of symmetry. And finally, from the dining area, it identifies the right-hand edge of the kitchen. Combined with the lowered ceiling over the kitchen and dining area, the four main quadrants of the floor plan are all defined by this simple 36-in. square. Quite an accomplishment for one small box!

Ceiling Magic

On the second level, the master bedroom looks like a regular rectangular room on the plan, but in the photo on p. 209 you'll see that the space itself gives a very different impression. The ceiling is full of unexpected detail, which derives from the structure required to support the kids' room above. There are parallel beams and a lower paneled ceiling over the bed that aligns with the window bay. And the west end of the room is vaulted, following the lines of the roof above. Though not a large area, it provides a high wall surface for Beth's collection of dinner plates (antique and otherwise) and lends a spatial complexity that is quite invisible in the floor plan.

In the kids' upper garret there are more surprises, including a closet that in plan looks perfectly ordinary but which in elevation provides food for some serious head scratching (see the photo on p. 211). The two doors into the closet have transom windows above them, which trick the eye into believing that the doors lead outside.

This house illustrates the limitations of the floor plan as a device for gauging character. What you can't see in two dimensions is what makes this home such a delight.

LEFT The refrigerator is concealed behind this narrow wall, which is the only interior wall on the main level. The flanking columns, made of steel channel concealed behind 1x8 trim, help support the floors above. The opening between kitchen and living room is just wide enough to allow easy communication between the two spaces but narrow enough to screen the sink area from view.

ABOVE When a room is bright, it feels more spacious. The bay window in the tiny 10-ft. by 12-ft. living room makes the space seem significantly larger, thanks to the flood of south light and tall double-hung windows. The bay acts like a light box, bouncing sunlight off the side walls and deep into the room.

RIGHT When the original house was built, money was tight, and the couple had resigned themselves to living with plywood floors for a while. But then Beth had an idea. Why not use wallpaper? This image shows their first wallpaper floor covering, which lasted about three years. (Photo © Candace Tetmeyer.)

The bedroom is topped off with a vaulted ceiling painted with golden stars, which at night gives the distinct impression that the room is open to the sky. It is, in many ways, a magical space.

A Tower of Alcoves

The 2-ft.-deep bay added to the front of the house is another strategy that adds lots of character with minimal means. On the exterior, the two-story structure is painted and detailed to look almost like a tower (see the photo on p. 202). It is distinguished from the rest of the shingled exterior with white clapboard siding and houses all the street-facing windows. Its effect on the interior is even more pronounced, creating alcoves in both the living room and master bedroom, which combine with the windows to work like light boxes. Sunlight bounces off the side walls and into the room, and the light-filled space creates a wonderful illusion of expansiveness. Although the square footage added to each room is minimal—16 sq. ft.—the effect on the perceptible scale of each room is dramatic.

Wallpaper Where?

If you're wondering what the material is on the kitchen and dining-area floors, you're not alone. When I first received snapshots of the house from Matthew and Beth, I called with that very question. I'd never seen anything quite like it. The answer? Wallpaper. Architects don't usually like wallpaper even on walls (we're a purist bunch), but on the floor?

LEFT The master bedroom has a bay identical to the living room's, but here the effect is to define a separate space, delineated by the beams in the ceiling and the paneling over the bed. These are the kinds of details that don't show up in a floor plan but make an enormous difference in how a room functions and feels.

Up Close

The fish handrail and wallpaper floor are two of the innovative ways the owners personalized their home. There is even a wallpaper rug below the dining table, made by using a room border for the edge and a different paper for the center. The wallpaper is applied just as on a wall, with two coats of polyurethane added once it's down to give some protection to the surface.

When they first finished remodeling the house, having done most of the work themselves, they simply had no money left for floor coverings. Matthew had reconciled himself to the fact that they would have to live with the plywood underlayment for a while. But Beth had a better idea. Although it would last for only a year or two, she suggested laying down wallpaper, adding a urethane finish, and calling it good for the time being. As an interior designer, she loves to make frequent changes to her home anyway.

ABOVE Displaying family history and memories creates a connection back through time and helps children to build a sense of continuity and belonging. In this house, the walls along the stairway to the children's bedroom make a perfect gallery for family photos.

The wallpaper floor was like a license to redecorate. The first wallpaper floor lasted three years, and they liked it so much that they put in another, which gives the house a completely different look and feel.

For innovators like Matthew and Beth, the canvas that their house provides will in all likelihood be a constantly changing, very personal masterpiece for many decades to come. If, like them, you let your imagination roam, and don't let keeping up with the Joneses bother you too much, you can make a house that's packed with ideas, full of fun, and a pleasure to live in. And in most cases, the size has nothing to do with its success.

ABOVE Most kids prefer to sleep in the upper bunk, but in this house there's an even bigger attraction than simply being on top of the world. The large, round window offers views to Long Island Sound, turning this bunk into a window seat as well as a place to sleep.

LEFT The inventiveness in this house extends to optical illusion. Looking at the transom windows above the two doors, you assume that the doors themselves lead outside. But in fact they provide the access to the children's closets. The closet roof aligns with the door headers, so there's enclosed space below.

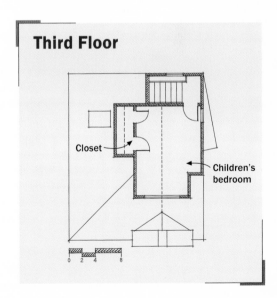

Third Floor

Closet

Children's bedroom

0 2 4 6

A Farmhouse for Our Time

WHILE MANY OF THE NOT SO BIG Houses being built around the country today are modern in style and spirit, there's nothing to say that you can't apply the same concepts to traditional house forms. This Minnesota farmhouse is a perfect example. When architect Jean Larson asked clients Susan and David to bring in pictures that illustrated the look and feel they wanted for their new house, what they came up with had a definite, traditional theme. They clearly liked simple, clean lines—almost spartan, some might say—and were attracted to the classic forms of Midwestern farmhouses. Since their land was in the midst of farm country, Jean felt that this was a good starting point for the design.

This house is reminiscent of the farmhouses of the past but designed for a more contemporary lifestyle.

Many classic farmhouses from the turn of the last century have an L-shaped plan, with four main rooms: kitchen, dining room, living room, and parlor, each occupying one quadrant, with a mudroom/rear entry added on to one side. A wraparound

OPPOSITE A section of the wraparound porch is screened in to serve as an outdoor room in summer. As in classic farmhouses, the roof slope of the porch and other lean-tos is very shallow (only 4-in-12), while the main gable roofs are much steeper (12-in-12).

213

Main Floor

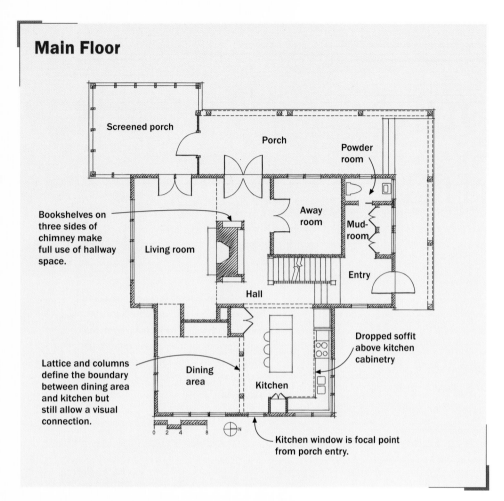

Screened porch

Porch

Powder room

Bookshelves on three sides of chimney make full use of hallway space.

Away room

Mud-room

Living room

Entry

Hall

Lattice and columns define the boundary between dining area and kitchen but still allow a visual connection.

Dining area

Kitchen

Dropped soffit above kitchen cabinetry

0 2 4 8   N

Kitchen window is focal point from porch entry.

porch completes the floor plan. Susan and David wanted a house that was more open than this classic plan, but they still liked the idea of identifiable rooms. The result is a house reminiscent of the farmhouses of the past but designed for a more contemporary lifestyle. Rooms are more open to one another, and views connecting one space to the next have been widened, but the classic farmhouse plan is still very much apparent.

Back-Door Living

In updating the plan for today's lifestyle, Jean reasoned that out in the country nearly everyone comes to the back door, while the formal front door remains largely unused. So, why not make the back door the acknowledged main entry and allow the location that would have been the front door to be the main access to the wraparound porch instead? The strategy works perfectly. Friends and family alike enter through the same doorway, with the garage set a short distance away, just off the knoll of the hill. Meanwhile, the double doors onto the porch extend the living space of the home's interior out into the surrounding landscape.

LEFT **When part of a room is bathed in sunlight, our eye tells us there's more around the corner, and we want to go and explore. Without the windows, though, it's not nearly as enticing.**

Rooms are more open to one another, and views connecting one space to the next have been widened, but the classic farmhouse plan is still very much apparent.

BELOW The lattice separating the living room from the entrance to the away room completes the rectangle of the room without enclosing it with a solid wall. This makes the room feel bigger but preserves the formal proportions of the room. In summer, the French doors can be thrown wide open to connect indoors and out.

RIGHT **A tightly spaced lattice separates the kitchen from the stairways. Allowing the spindles—in this case, painted 2x4s—to run from floor to ceiling gives this wall a composed look and creates a strong sense of the room's edge. With a more typical railing, the room would extend to the back wall of the stairway. It would appear bigger but less tailored.**

BELOW **Instead of using narrow hallways, this house connects the rooms with usable spaces, like this library wall at the bottom of the stairs. The window defines the end of the axis through the house, giving a perceptible order to the overall composition.**

Pathways and Implied Walls

The plan has two central pathways that channel both view and movement and separate the four rooms from one another. They're not really hallways but spaces composed of parts of other rooms. Looking through from the porch doors to the kitchen window, for example, you look directly along one pathway, past bookshelves across from the stairway, and then into the kitchen beyond. The window at the far end of this porch-kitchen axis performs a very important function. We are attracted to light and instinctively tend to move toward it. Without this focal window, the draw of the kitchen would be significantly reduced. The passageway between the away room and kitchen is also a usable space—a cross between a library and a stair vestibule.

Openings between rooms are wider than would have been typical in farmhouses of the past, allowing a better view into the adjacent space. The dining area is open to the kitchen, for example, but the room is still defined with a lattice that hints at where the old farmhouse wall would have been. The connection between the living room and the away-room hallway is defined in a similar way. You still have a definite sense of the edge of the room, but the space and view flow out beyond the implied boundary.

At the stairway there's a more substantial lattice—one that looks like a decorative wall from the kitchen side but allows a view through to the kitchen for someone descending the stairs. The lower level of the house is not yet finished, but by leaving

LEFT In a classic farmhouse, there would be only a small door connecting kitchen and dining room, but for today's lifestyle the two rooms need to be much more open to one another. The wide-spaced lattice and columns suggest where the old wall would have been, but the view is wide open.

BELOW To make the most of the farmland vistas, the kitchen work area is wrapped with double-hung windows. The inset cabinets, deep porcelain sink, and maple butcher-block countertops are all reminiscent of an old farmhouse kitchen, while the electrical outlets and period light fixtures have been gracefully integrated to make it work for today's cook.

the stairway open, with a door at the bottom instead of at the top, there's a suggestion of more living space below. And when the lower level is eventually finished, it will feel much more connected to the rest of the house.

A Light-Filled Kitchen

We spend much of our lives in the kitchen today, yet all too often this room is poorly lit and uninspiring. For Susan and David, a light-filled kitchen was high on their list of priorities. One of the pictures they brought to show Jean at their first meeting was a photo of a restored kitchen in a Victorian home, with many windows and wide sills for plants and other kitchen paraphernalia. Jean took this image as the inspiration for their

ABOVE With its almost symmetrical gable-end design, corner boards, and simple trim framing double-hung windows, the house looks like it's from an earlier time. The woodwork surrounding the upper vent at the top of the gable is the kind of detail that can make a big impression with only a small amount of effort.

RIGHT The wider trim around windows and doors and the shape and size of the baseboards are typical of an older home. It's these seemingly insignificant finish details that give a house much of its character.

kitchen. She wrapped the corner with double-hung windows and pulled the kitchen cabinets 4 in. in from the exterior wall to make room for a widened sill. This gives the illusion that the wall is thicker, a reference back to the brick and stone walls of old farmhouses.

What about the lost upper cabinets, which had to be sacrificed to make way for the windows? This kitchen has two substantial pantries: one at the end of the corner countertop and the other across from the island. As long as provisions are made for storage to replace what is lost to windows, a kitchen can function perfectly well. In fact, many people prefer a pantry because the storage space can be laid out more efficiently and made more accessible.

A lowered soffit runs the full length of the kitchen work surface, from the refrigerator at one end to the smaller of the pantries at the other. This soffit, which is the same depth as the countertop below, does a number of things. It creates an alcove, in which the kitchen work happens. It fills out the frame around the windows, giving a greater sense of depth to the wall. And it provides a surface from which to hang the light fixtures, which in this home are period pieces, not the typical recessed cans we've become accustomed to today.

Keeping It Simple

While many Not So Big Houses make a visual statement with bold color schemes, this house succeeds through subtlety. With walls painted a slightly darker color than the bright white trim, the whole house takes on a quiet elegance. The trim itself has a simple profile: The 1x6 baseboards have a piece of cap molding, and the 1x4 trim around the windows and doors has an added backband. These interior details lend the house the proportion and character of its early 20th-century ancestors without creating an overly careful replica. The same is true of the exterior, with its white clapboard siding, corner boards, and symmetrical windows at the gable ends. The steep 12-in-12 roof and wraparound porch complete the picture.

When we imagine what a farmhouse should be, for most of us it's pretty close to this new home. Our modern tract houses—with their vaulted, textured ceilings, white walls, casement windows, and predictable trimwork—aren't the houses most of us want to come home to. Here we have an example of a house that, through restraint and an appreciation for the past, puts forward a familiar but definitely upgraded vision for the future. It's a farmhouse all right— but a farmhouse for our time.

Architect:
SALA Architects
Builder:
Al Hirsch & Sons
Size: 2,400 sq. ft.
Location:
Chaska, Minn.

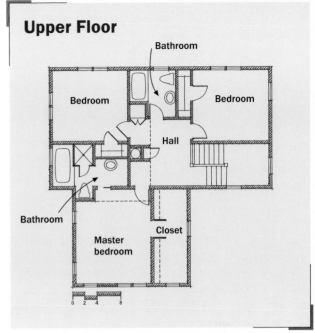
Upper Floor

Perfect Pitch

Builders and architects often refer to the pitch of a roof as a ratio of rise to run, or height to length. You'll hear professionals discussing a house with a "10-in-12 roof" (written as 10:12), which is fairly steep, or a "3-in-12 roof" (written 3:12), which is gently sloped. The first number in the ratio (the rise) is the number of inches the roof rises for every foot of length. The second number (the run) is always 12, for the number of inches in a foot.

Because roof pitch isn't well understood, it's not uncommon for a change to be made in roof slope during design or construction that ruins the look of the house. This farmhouse has a much steeper roof in the two-story sections than in the one-story lean-tos. If the lean-to roofs were built with the same slope as the main house, they would look completely out of proportion, and all resemblance to the farmhouses of the past would be lost.

As you drive around your own neighborhood, notice the difference that roof slope makes to the look and feel of a house. Notice, too, the houses that don't look quite right. Often this is the result of a roof with a slope that doesn't fit the style of the house it shelters.

A Jewel in the Suburbs

Sᴇᴛ ɪɴ ᴀ ꜱᴜʙᴜʀʙᴀɴ ɴᴇɪɢʜʙᴏʀʜᴏᴏᴅ of look-alike single-family homes from the 1940s and '50s, Jim and Julie's house is undistinguished from the outside. But step in through the front door, and you're in for a surprise. This house is a veritable jewel box of clever storage and detailing ideas—an extraordinary example of what's possible when you approach design with a playful, inventive spirit and a commitment to doing more with less.

Over the past decade, a miraculous transformation has taken place within the existing walls of this 1,500-sq.-ft. 1950s tri-level. Jim, an interior designer by profession, used his skill to rethink the house and make it a home filled with character, detail, and vitality. Julie used her graphic-design talent to make every surface a composition of color, texture, and light. Both love the unexpected, and both enjoyed the process of letting the house evolve. It took the change well, emerging with the flexible durability needed to accommodate an

This house is an extraordinary example of what's possible when you approach design with a commitment to doing more with less.

BELOW The chopping block and microwave work area illustrates how standard materials can be used in creative ways to make something both functional and delightful to look at. All it takes is a little ingenuity.

Up Close

The television is cleverly concealed in a well-crafted cabinet at the end of the lower kitchen cabinet run. The television faces into the hearth room: As in many homes today, the hearth *is* the television.

active family that includes seven-year-old daughter Racheal and two golden retrievers. Together Jim and Julie have created a home that is both fun to look at and a pleasure to live in.

Opening Up the Rooms

When the couple first moved in, the house had a standard floor plan, with distinct formal and informal spaces. A wall separated the dining room from the kitchen, which was designed, like many homes of the era, as a place solely for food preparation. And, as in most homes today, most of the living took place in the tiny kitchen and breakfast nook, while the formal rooms, which were visually and physically set apart, remained unused. By opening the kitchen and dining room to one another, the house automatically feels bigger because you can see farther, and the entire area becomes the social hub of the house.

Other special touches add to the feeling of spaciousness. In the kitchen, the cabinets are held away from the walls and ceiling to make the room feel bigger. (It would be more typical to make an L-shaped counter at the far corner of the room.) Eliminating cabinets above the peninsula also minimizes the visual separation between the kitchen and dining areas. Jim refers to the peninsula itself as the "runway" between the refrigerator and the chopping block. Thinking about the way food is

Designer:
Garramone Design
Builder:
Jim Garramone
Size: 1,500 sq. ft.
Location:
Evanston, Ill.

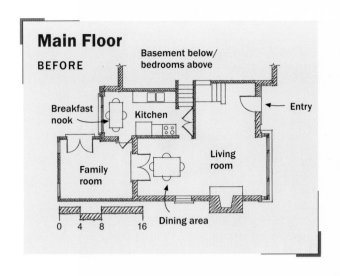

Main Floor

BEFORE

Basement below/ bedrooms above

Breakfast nook

Kitchen

Entry

Family room

Living room

0 4 8 16

Dining area

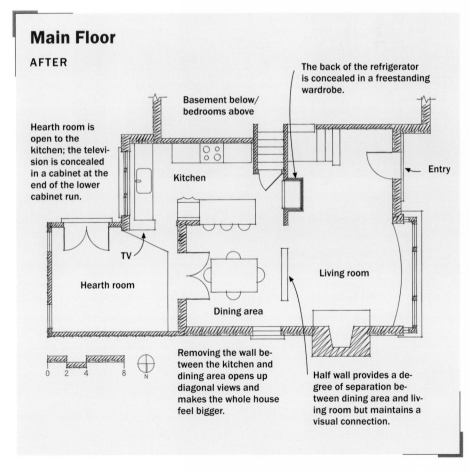

Main Floor

AFTER

The back of the refrigerator is concealed in a freestanding wardrobe.

Basement below/ bedrooms above

Hearth room is open to the kitchen; the television is concealed in a cabinet at the end of the lower cabinet run.

Kitchen

Entry

TV

Hearth room

Living room

Dining area

0 2 4 8   N

Removing the wall between the kitchen and dining area opens up diagonal views and makes the whole house feel bigger.

Half wall provides a degree of separation between dining area and living room but maintains a visual connection.

ABOVE AND RIGHT **The refrigerator installation is a wonderful example of creativity, turning a space-wasting liability into an asset. From the kitchen, it looks like a normal refrigerator. Move into the entryway, and you see a finely crafted freestanding wardrobe—in reality, a camouflage for the back of the refrigerator.**

moved through the space is especially important in a small work area.

Making the Most of the Ordinary

The chopping block is a standard end-grain model with added front and back edging detail (see the photo on p. 222). The sculpted front edge is rounded so chopped vegetables can be swept into a bowl held underneath—another example of adding inexpensive and creative detail. The back edging provides a place for knife storage just where you need it—a wonderful example of useful beauty.

Above the chopping block, a standard medicine cabinet—its mirror replaced with cork—serves as both a bulletin board and spice cabinet. Most upper cabinets are 12 in. deep, but that doesn't mean that they all have to be. The shallower cabinet allows for better visual access to the chopping block—always a plus for a work surface. What looks like a built-in microwave cabinet below the chopping block is, in fact, a clever use of a standard cabinet door. The microwave sits on a shelf, and the surrounding door panel has been cut to fit, with holes above and below to allow for ventilation.

The door to the basement also uses ordinary materials in

ABOVE This shallow cabinet stores Rachael's drawing and coloring paraphernalia and provides just enough separation between the dining and living areas. The top is soapstone, to match the kitchen countertops. Reusing a particular material around the house lends continuity and integrity.

RIGHT The gentle curve of the bookshelf window seat is an elegant touch that gives the whole room a softness. Introducing curves in nonstructural elements like this adds beauty without excessive cost.

unexpected ways. Jim and Julie replaced the glass in an old French door with a porcelainized steel blackboard, which serves as a message board for the family (see the photo on p. 224). As a bonus, while magnets won't stick to the new stainless-steel refrigerator, they will stick to the steel panels in the French door, allowing it to replace that essential family display area.

Attention to Detail

The careful attention to detail continues in the living room, where the window bay beautifully illustrates the effect a soffit, or lowered ceiling, can have on a room (see the photo on p. 225). If the ceiling height of the rest of the room continued out to the window wall and the bookshelf below were removed, the room would have more volume, but, contrary to what you might expect, it wouldn't feel bigger. If anything, the room would feel smaller. It is the contrast between the two ceiling heights, and the development of two distinct "places," that gives this room its beauty and uniqueness.

LEFT The house has functional works of art at every turn, and this English phone booth is certainly the most unexpected of them. The bedroom level is separated from the main floor by a short flight of stairs, with a landing between the two that used to have a standard railing. Now the phone booth sits there, and one moves through it almost like a gate between the two living areas. Its novelty gives the whole house a sense of whimsy that anticipates more surprises to come.

LEFT On a wall of the hearth room are these narrow shelves, used to display a constantly changing exhibit of photos and drawings.

BELOW There's a comfortable connection between the hearth room and the kitchen, allowing for conversation between the two.

A 36-in.-high storage wall has been located between the dining and living areas, giving some separation between the rooms while still maintaining a visual connection (see the photo on p. 225). The wall allows the living-room furniture to be pushed against it, which effectively increases the floor area available. Without its presence, the chairs would need to be farther away from the dining-room table in order to look right. So by defining the boundary between spaces while maintaining the connecting views, a small space can be made to comfortably accommodate more items.

The Hearth Room

Some further creative remodeling provides a quiet space while opening up yet another vista to the kitchen. The brick wall visible in the photograph used to be the exterior of the house.

A platform bed doubles as couch, table, and sitting area. The cushions at either end are built around a steel frame for back support. The swivel side tables offer room for a cup of tea and a paperback.

A porch had been added, which Jim and Julie turned into a hearth room that also functions as an away room of sorts. Because the hearth room is separated from the dining area with French doors, one person can watch TV here without disrupting anybody in the living or dining area. When the TV is not in use, it is hidden from view with bifold doors (see the photo on p. 222).

A Not So Big Bedroom

Although the existing bedrooms in the house are not large, Jim and Julie made the most of limited space by designing furniture that serves multiple functions and by keeping broad expanses open to maximize the sense of space. This feeling is further enhanced in the bedroom by the mirrored doors behind the bed, which both serve as a piece of art and double the apparent length of the room. On one wall is a wonderfully clever and beautiful storage area. Rather than building a standard closet, Jim made the available space into both hanging area and dresser, decorating the doors to look like a wall of drawers. The whole composition has become a work of art.

An Illusion of Space

The bathroom off the master bedroom presented a particular challenge, both in the use of space and in access to light. A typical arrangement in a small bathroom like this one is to have a tub with shower rod and curtain that extend across the end of the room, which decreases its apparent size. Here, with a retractable shower rod, the full dimension of the room is apparent.

The selection of fixtures also allows this bathroom to live larger than its diminutive size would suggest. The bath itself is a deep soaking tub. And the pedestal sink opens up more floor space, again increasing the apparent size of the room. As a final touch, the mirror over the sink extends all the way to the ceiling, reflecting the room and adding yet another illusion of space. No opportunity is missed in this house to make an everyday necessity into an inspired composition.

ABOVE/RIGHT Jim's love of Shaker cabinetry inspired this closet wall. Cleverly designed to look like a wall of drawers, the upper "drawers" are in reality doors that open to reveal a very efficient hanging closet. The lower drawers really are drawers.

Three Easy Pieces

This cabin is divided into three separate pieces: a living cottage on the left, a sleeping cottage on the right, and a silo that houses both bathrooms. Together, the three pieces are reminiscent of the random assemblages of farm structures in the neighboring countryside.

TAILORING A HOUSE FOR THE WAY ITS occupants really live is a fundamental Not So Big concept. When I first started thinking about how to accomplish this, I realized that the best model we have for comfortable, informal living is the weekend cabin. It's designed to be both welcoming and functional and usually includes a strong connection to the outdoors. Rooms are cozy—certainly smaller than we expect in a year-round house—and there are no superfluous spaces. Yet often these weekend retreats make our spirits soar. There's something about their scale and simplicity that gives them a warmth that's missing in a larger home. The idea of nesting, or cocooning, is becoming more and more appealing in our busy lives, but we seem to think we can do it in spacious mansions, when a true nest or cocoon is really a cozy and secure haven, just big enough to accommodate its residents.

It's a rare space that's too small for comfort, but it's not at all uncommon for one to be uncomfortably big.

OPPOSITE This cabin in the woods has an archetypal quality that speaks to us of home in simpler times. There's much about a cabin that can help us understand better what we are missing in our new homes today.

231

ABOVE **A covered link between the sleeping and living cottages frames the view of the lake beyond, creating a striking vista as you approach the house.** (PHOTO COURTESY FREDERICK PHILLIPS.)

Architect:
Frederick Phillips
& Associates

Builder:
Young Brothers
Construction

Size: 1,200 sq. ft.

Location:
Washington Island, Wis.

This cabin is a perfect illustration of how it works. Here we have an unembellished version of a house, reduced to its spatial essentials but with the qualities of comfort we're so eager to find. It came about when architect Rick Phillips was asked by his mother and stepfather, Kay and Ted, to design a year-round lake cabin for the family on their island property at the tip of Door County Peninsula in Wisconsin. The site was a five-hour drive and a half-hour boat ride from Rick's home in Chicago, and his frequent weekend visits to the site gave him plenty of time to think about the design.

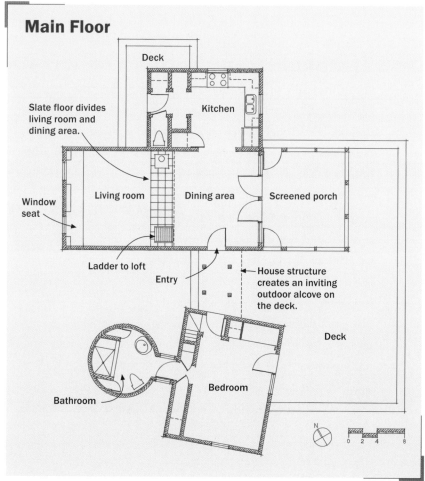

Main Floor

Deck

Kitchen

Slate floor divides living room and dining area.

Living room

Dining area

Screened porch

Window seat

Ladder to loft

Entry

House structure creates an inviting outdoor alcove on the deck.

Deck

Bathroom

Bedroom

Shelter around Activity

Rick knew that one of the most important spaces for his parents would be the deck, a place to sit and look out at the water. But a deck without a sense of shelter tends to be little used, because it makes you feel vulnerable and exposed. However, if you add some sort of structure to provide a shelter around the various activities, it's suddenly inviting. This can be difficult to do with a traditional rectangular house form. So Rick got creative. His long drive to the property took him past a multitude of farms, with their random collections of agrarian buildings—silos, barns, storage sheds, farmhouses. These images inspired him to consider a similar combination of forms for the cabin. By breaking the structure into three distinct pieces, he could create an outdoor alcove with a sense of containment on three sides.

When Kay and Ted saw the scale model Rick had made to illustrate his concept, they loved the idea. He suggested that each of the three forms contain one of the main functions—living in one, sleeping in another, and bathing in a third—and that they keep the size of each space to a reasonable minimum. Kay and Ted wanted a place that was relatively inexpensive to build and didn't want rooms

ABOVE **Sometimes a room is most comfortable when its dimensions are small and it has only a few strategically placed windows, focusing your attention inside rather than out. This living area—with its two symmetrically placed windows, flanking bookshelves, and long window seat—has a distinctly Scandinavian-cottage feel: plain in style but cozy and inviting.**

LEFT **The kitchen, which is an alcove off the main rectangle of living space, contains just the bare necessities, with open shelves instead of upper cabinets. The lower cabinets and flooring are made of natural cedar, which gives this simple room a deep richness.**

No matter how large or small a house, the need for different levels of privacy is a critical design element.

that seemed designed more for large gatherings than for family living. To them, the cabin was a place of retreat from the hubbub of city life, and they weren't interested in having a lot of space to maintain.

Fear of "Too Smallness"

In the final design, the living room is only 14 ft. wide, which most people would consider too narrow. But at this dimension, the couch and chairs can be nestled against opposite walls of the room and still be a comfortable distance apart for conversation. The window seat that runs the length of the far end of the room completes the sitting circle and provides space for an additional guest or two.

All too often, we increase the size of a room in the planning phase, for fear it will feel too small. But making this room even 2 ft. wider would dramatically reduce its intimacy. It's this fear of "too smallness" that is driving our houses to reach proportions more appropriate to giants than humans. And in the process, we're losing the very quality that makes us feel at home.

The Shape of the Ceiling

The main level is straightforward in plan: just a long rectangle with a kitchen alcove opening off to the north side. From the plan, you might imagine that the living and dining areas would look very similar, since they're almost identical in shape. But the ceiling heights and forms are quite different, giving the spaces a very different feel. In the living area, the ceiling is gently sloped,

Up Close

A low wainscot runs around all the living spaces in the house, creating the effect of a waterline around the main level. The darker coloring of everything below this line emphasizes the lower section of each space, adding a visual weight that subtly encourages you to sit down and stay a while.

The bathrooms on both levels are enclosed in the windowless silo, giving each a cocoon-like feel. The rooms aren't dark, though. They get ample light from the short, window-filled walkway (visible in the exterior photo) that connects them to the bedrooms.

following the lean-to form of the roof above, with a view to the upper-level loft. By contrast, the dining area is sheltered below the loft and has a flat 8-ft.-high ceiling that's paneled with wood, giving it added visual weight.

The difference between the two spaces is further accentuated by the wall of French doors at the far end of the dining area, which open onto the porch beyond. This is the source of most of the light and views and so tends to lead one outward, while the living area is inward looking and encourages nesting. What looks almost boring and undifferentiated in plan is far from it when seen in all three dimensions.

Public and Private

In any cabin, there's often a lot of shared time, but there's also a need for varying degrees of privacy. Despite its small size, this cabin offers a full spectrum of spaces. There are those that are clearly very public, such as the living and dining areas. Then there's the loft, a semiprivate space where the activities below can be heard but not seen—useful when you want a private space without feeling isolated from the rest of the family. And finally, there's the complete privacy offered by a separate structure for sleeping, where noise from the living cabin can't even be heard.

No matter how large or small a house, the need for different levels of privacy is a critical design element. A home can look very beautiful but actually be quite unlivable because there's no place to be alone. Or it can go to the opposite extreme, with every space so separate that there's no sense of focus, no central gathering place. This cabin gets the balance just right. If you want a house to work well, it's important to place the main living areas where they can be seen easily from several other places. The main spaces gain much of their vitality from their visibility.

The private spaces should be tucked away, off the beaten track, where someone seeking privacy can draw back from the social center and know that they'll be left alone. The places in the middle of the public/private spectrum, like the loft in this house, can be designed to participate in some of the energy of the focal gathering places but give the occupants the option to engage in the activities or not, as they choose.

Even when a house is very small, there's no reason it can't offer a spatial and social variety of places for living. When we design each space to enhance the activity it houses, rather than worrying about whether it is big enough for the rare occasions when we have extra guests, our houses benefit enormously.

We can learn a lot from a weekend cabin like this one. What we seek in our year-round homes is some of the ease and informality we see here. This comes from building only what you need, tailoring it to fit your *real* lifestyle, and crafting it to bring delight to the senses. It sounds easy, but there are a lot of countervailing forces at work to convince us otherwise. Just keep in mind that it's a rare space that's too small for comfort, but it's not at all uncommon for one to be uncomfortably big.

ABOVE The covered link provides protection and enclosure for the deck. If you imagine these two structures without the connecting roof, the space looks more like a hallway than a sheltered place.

LEFT There's something fascinating about a round window. When placed at the center of a gable, as in this loft, it symbolizes both focus and inspiration. The effect is dramatic and worth the added expense.

A Sense of Flow

ABOVE AND RIGHT **By** enclosing the existing carports and extending a colonnade beyond the face of the house, the architect completely altered the sense of entry. (PHOTO AT RIGHT COURTESY BERNIE BAKER.)

WHEN IT COMES TO HOUSING needs, empty nesters are faced with a real dilemma. The house that served so well while the children were growing up no longer works so well for two. Yet they want to stay put because they've developed close relationships in the community over the years. This is where their friends live. This is the place they love. Fortunately, there is an answer: Take your existing house, one designed for the way you lived half a lifetime ago, and transform it into the house of your dreams—a house that fits the way you live today.

This is what Sally and Gary did. Until they met architect Bernie Baker, they were starting to despair of ever getting the house they wanted. They'd been trying to find an architect who understood their desire to completely transform their home, and they knew that applying cosmetic solutions to problem areas wasn't going to be enough. Although a major remodel would be expensive, they loved their wooded canyon site and had no de-

This house uses the principles of building Not So Big to make an adequate house into a really comfortable home, tailored to the lives of the people who live there.

OPPOSITE **The colonnade continues on the inside of the house, serving as a spine that defines the circulation space and organizes both rooms and views. New windows extend all the way to the roof, minimizing the distinction between inside and out.**

239

ABOVE The brick courtyard between the two garages serves as a light-filled anteroom to the house. Standing here, you are welcomed by the house before ever stepping across the threshold.

sire to leave. Bernie was the first architect they'd met who understood. He told them that what their house needed was a sense of flow, both of movement and of views, something sorely missing prior to the remodel.

Redefining the Entry

In the original structure, an unassuming split entry, you were greeted at every turn by obstructing walls, dark hallways, and visual cues that misled. As you walked into the old house, for example, the view led your eye directly to the master bedroom. Visitors to the house felt drawn to a room that was part of the private realm—not a direction they were welcome to proceed in. Meanwhile, the lower level, where the main living areas were located, was shrouded in darkness.

Bernie recognized the need to redefine the process of entering the house, to give the appropriate cues as to which way to proceed and to make the descent into the main body of the house a pleasant and inviting experience. Just like a choreographer, he composed a remodeling with a new theme and variations, superimposed on the bones of the old house. The result is a home that, though not a lot bigger, has integrity and style. It uses the principles of building Not So Big to make an adequate house into a really comfortable home, tailored to the lives of the people who live there.

Entering is an extraordinarily important part of experiencing a house. If you're not welcomed by the house as you enter, it's difficult to remedy the negative impression once you're inside. So Bernie started back at the driveway with design strategies that would help to establish a sequence of places to draw you into the house. He enclosed the two carports on either side of the entry walk, added a skylight above the doorway, and included lots of glass in and around the front door. The result is both welcoming and inviting.

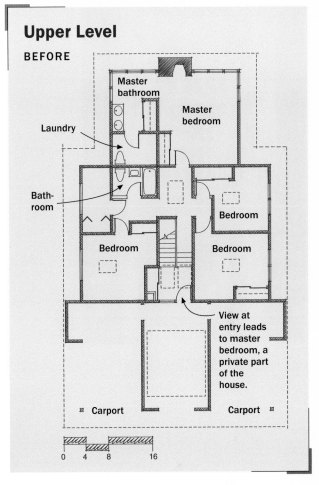

Upper Level

BEFORE

Master bathroom

Master bedroom

Laundry

Bath-room

Bedroom

Bedroom

Bedroom

View at entry leads to master bedroom, a private part of the house.

Carport　　　Carport

0　4　8　16

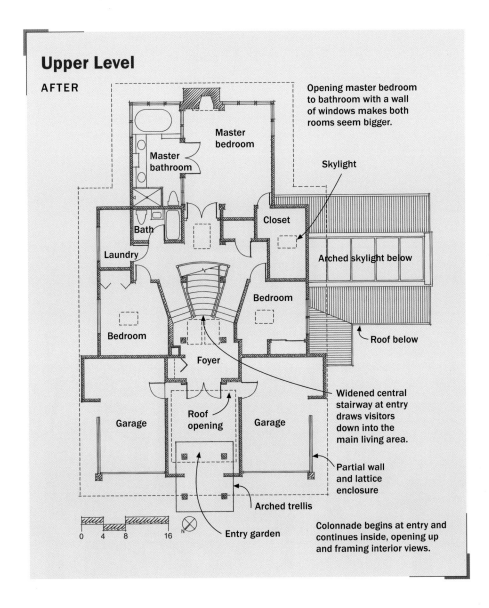

Upper Level

AFTER

Opening master bedroom to bathroom with a wall of windows makes both rooms seem bigger.

Master bedroom

Master bathroom

Skylight

Bath

Closet

Laundry

Arched skylight below

Bedroom

Roof below

Bedroom

Foyer

Widened central stairway at entry draws visitors down into the main living area.

Garage

Roof opening

Garage

Partial wall and lattice enclosure

Arched trellis

0　4　8　16

N

Entry garden

Colonnade begins at entry and continues inside, opening up and framing interior views.

Entering is an extraordinarily important part of experiencing a house. If you're not welcomed by the house as you enter, it's difficult to remedy the negative impression once you're inside.

Interior Views

Bernie established a colonnade that extends just beyond the face of the house, defining the entry and welcoming guests with its trellised arch. The colonnade continues inside and runs through the entire house, giving order and coherence to the existing structure. It becomes a device for opening up and framing interior views and serves to orient movement through the house: Where the eye is led, the feet will follow. By relocating the up-stairways to either side of the down-stairway, the inviting path lies directly ahead. As you stand at the doorway, your gaze is directed down through the gradually widening stairs to the living-room fireplace beyond. Although you can still see the master-bedroom fireplace, it's clear from the location of the railing that you're *not* invited to proceed this way.

The colonnade runs through the entire house, giving order and coherence to the existing structure.

ABOVE In the old house, the front entry gave mixed messages about which way to go. Now, the widened and centered down-stairway clearly indicates that this is the way to proceed. Although the distance up to the master bedroom suite is shorter, the railing sends a clear but subtle signal that this view is just for looking.

RIGHT The colonnade continues down to the lower level, where the final two columns flank the fireplace. Having such a focal point to walk toward helps draw people into the heart of the house.

Designing for the Way You Live

Once you are down the first flight of stairs, you're met with a surprise—another level of living space quite invisible from the entry foyer. Here, significant changes have been made to reconfigure this space to work with the way Sally and Gary really live. Instead of an enclosed kitchen that's dark, uninspiring, and isolated from the main living spaces, the kitchen opens to an informal sitting area, where Gary (who is not the cook in this household) can sit and talk to Sally while she prepares dinner.

Sally and Gary both love to entertain, and the only added space in this remodeling project is a formal dining room—a spectacular room that is delightful to look at, even when it's not in use (see the photo on p. 244). For people who seldom entertain or who like to entertain only informally, a dining room is a largely superfluous space today. But for people like Sally and Gary, who really enjoy putting on a spread in a room with a special ambiance, the dining room is one of the most important rooms in the house. The Not So Big philosophy doesn't dictate that you get rid of all formal spaces. If you actually use a formal dining room for formal dining (and not just as a place to drop off the mail), by all means include one. The point is to design for the way *you* live.

Sally prepares dinner for friends and family several times a month, and this new dining space provides the perfect stage for her culinary productions. A 20-ft.-long skylight stretches across the new space and extends into the kitchen, making a once-dark

TOP **The remodeled kitchen has been opened up and made into the nerve center of the house. A sitting space adjacent to the kitchen allows Gary to chat with Sally as she prepares dinner.**

ABOVE **A television is cleverly concealed in the back side of the kitchen cabinetry. When the doors are closed, there's no sign it's there at all.**

Lower Level
BEFORE

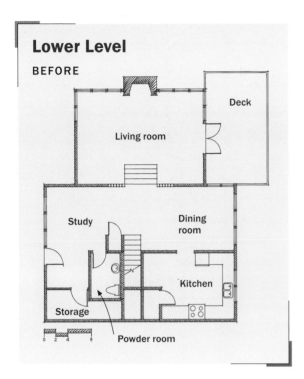

Deck

Living room

Study

Dining room

Storage

Kitchen

Powder room

0 2 4 8

Lower Level
AFTER

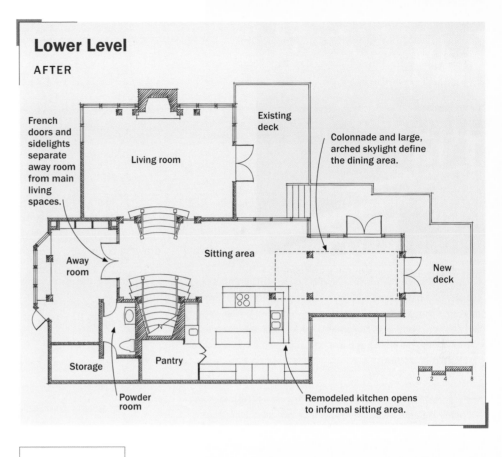

French doors and sidelights separate away room from main living spaces.

Existing deck

Colonnade and large, arched skylight define the dining area.

Living room

Away room

Sitting area

New deck

Storage

Pantry

Powder room

Remodeled kitchen opens to informal sitting area.

0 2 4 8

---

and inhospitable area into a room filled with light and warmth. In a sunnier climate, such a large skylight might cause serious overheating, but in the Pacific Northwest, such concerns are minimal. With so many cloudy days, finding ways to introduce natural light becomes the governing issue.

The kitchen itself is like the helm of a ship—a place from which all others can be seen—and very much in keeping with the style of the rest of the house. A wide, beamlike soffit lowers the ceiling height around the kitchen, defining the room without the use of walls. Here, Sally keeps her collection of pottery and china in glass cabinets surrounding the double ovens. With internal lighting, they become a beautiful backdrop to the main work area. When it's just the two of them, Sally and Gary will often eat at the small table in the middle of the kitchen, which also doubles as a kitchen island. Substituting a table for a built-in island can lend a farmhouse informality to a room, making it seem homey and approachable.

Architect:
Bernie Baker
Architect, P.S.
Size: 2,600 sq. ft.
Location:
Mercer Island, Wash.

RIGHT **A raised countertop shields kitchen work areas from view without the need for enclosing walls. The lowered soffit further defines the room and provides a place from which to hang pendant lights.**

OPPOSITE **For many families, a dining room is superfluous. Not so for this couple, who entertain in this garden-room setting two or three times a month. The room is so enchanting that guests will linger long after the meal is over.**

Storefront Windows

Another space that hadn't worked well in the original house was the study, which was too open to the rest of the house for concentrated work. By separating this area from the main living spaces with French doors and flanking sidelights—what Bernie refers to as "storefront windows"—the room has become an ideal away room. Sally uses this space for her business (writing children's books) and when the television is on in the sitting area beside the kitchen, the study can become a quiet retreat without losing its visual connection to the social hub of the house.

The master bedroom also uses a wall of windows to make both bedroom and bathroom feel bigger and to flood the bedroom with light. Bathrooms are often beautiful rooms, with built-in cabinetry and broad expanses of mirror. Opening this view to the master bedroom gives a gracious and airy feel without adding any square footage. This same trick is used throughout the house, where almost every sight line, whether to another interior space or out to the trees beyond, is captured or framed by a wall of glass. The effect is much more dramatic than settling for one or two windows set into a wall surface, as is the norm in most new construction.

Clearly, this was not an inexpensive remodel. It would have cost only slightly more to build new. But for a couple whose goal was to take what they already had and transform it, this remodeling responds masterfully—not by adding

The Away Room

One of the biggest problems in today's homes is the pervasive presence of noisy entertainment like television and computer games. When the TV is on in a room, it tends to capture everyone's attention—even those who would rather be doing something else. As we build more open floor plans, the problem gets worse. What we need is a space in the home that allows the activities that require peace and quiet to be separated from those that generate noise.

One solution, and a common feature of a Not So Big House, is an away room. This is a compact, multipurpose space, usually about the size of a small bedroom, that opens onto the main living area with French doors. Its primary role is to provide an acoustically private activity space that's still visually connected to the living area and kitchen. It can also serve as a study during the day and can even convert to a guest bedroom for visitors. In this home, Sally's study is an excellent example of an away room. The wide French doors and surrounding windows offer ample connecting views to the living area and kitchen, so she doesn't feel isolated. But with the doors closed, the TV can be on and Sally can still get her work done.

The away room is also wonderfully effective when there are children in the house. With the television and electronic toys confined in this room, children can enjoy themselves to their exuberant hearts' content, and the sounds of Nintendo won't prevent adult conversation. The glass doors allow parents and children to see one another, which is great for supervising, and also provides kids with a comfortable sense of family togetherness.

more square footage but by revising what was already there to meet the needs of today. Even the plainest of houses often has good bones that, with the vision of an architect, can have new life breathed into it. Why throw away what you don't want anymore just because your lifestyle has changed? Instead, why not tailor it to fit who you are today?

A House in Harmony

THERE'S GROWING CONCERN IN OLDER suburbs today about a building phenomenon known as "tear-downs." This happens when a house in an established and desirable neighborhood is purchased, torn down, and replaced with a new house. The sad reality is that the new house is frequently a massive and ostentatious structure, similar to the starter castles so prevalent in newer housing developments across the country. Such a house is of a completely different scale and character than its older neighbors, and it often offends the residents of the existing community.

This is rarely done intentionally. The buyers of the older house select it because they like the neighborhood. But when it comes to remodeling versus starting from scratch, there's no contest. A new house will invariably end up costing less than renovating the old one and will provide more of the amenities we expect in a home. So the new owners select a house from a plan book, with no consideration of how the house will relate to the neighborhood.

This house makes more with less at every turn, using restraint to create a composition with depth and beauty.

OPPOSITE The fireplace in the family room is a marvelous composition of fireslate and wood that plays off the proportions of both the house and the Golden Mean. Although nothing is quite symmetrical, everything is beautifully balanced to appeal to the eye. If you look closely, you'll see that even the slate on the floor has been cut to line up with the edges of the materials on the wall.

> *A Not So Big House is a good neighbor, custom-made to fit the needs of its owners and also to fit into its surroundings.*

ABOVE **Though this house is more highly designed than its neighbors, the goal was to fit in rather than stand out.** (PHOTO COURTESY PAUL LUKEZ.)

ABOVE Colors and textures were carefully selected to give the house a subtle distinctiveness. Because the lines of the windows are so fine, their bright red coloring is not over-bearing but, like well-applied makeup, draws the eye back for a second look. In texture, the plywood panels of the upper story contrast with the narrow lap siding of the area below. But because they are both stained the same color, the effect is one of restraint.

Good Neighbors

It was just such a situation that Amy and Frank faced when they purchased a house for themselves and their two small children in an upscale Lexington neighborhood of 1960s split levels. Although they had originally planned to add on, they quickly discovered that it would be far less expensive to start from scratch with a new home. But they were also concerned about their neighbors and wanted to help maintain the character of the community they'd just joined.

Fortunately, they found an alternative to the teardown syndrome. Their architect, Paul Lukez, designed a house for them that is a wonderful example of what is so special about building Not So Big. A Not So Big House is a good neighbor, custom-made to fit the needs of its owners and also to fit into its surroundings, adding both beauty and vitality to the community. Paul assured Amy and Frank that the house they wanted, though slightly larger than most of its neighbors, could be made to fit in gracefully. He accomplished this by including the neighborhood's character as one of the site considerations that are a normal part of the architectural process.

Making the new house an exact replica of neighboring homes was not the goal. But by duplicating certain stylistic traits, such as roof slope, window alignments, and the scale of the house facade, the new home would seem a natural and integrated part of the existing fabric of the community. And this indeed is what resulted. The exterior has an understated confidence that lets it blend in with its neighbors while still maintaining its own distinctive character.

Music to Live By

The longer you look at this house, the more there is to see, both inside and out. This is largely because the house has been carefully and beautifully composed. Because the budget was relatively tight, the plan was kept very simple, the rooms straightforward in form, the ceilings flat in most places, and the palette of materials limited. Money was spent instead on making the most of the combinations of materials and the interplay among them.

Gracefully integrating a stairway's handrails is always a challenge. Here, the architect has used a wood that contrasts with the cherry railing and has separated the two rails at the landing. They're almost like arms reaching around the wall and drawing the composition together—a lot more elegant than the standard solution.

LEFT Throughout this home there's an intriguing interplay of dimension and proportion. The side light next to the front door is adjacent to a copper-covered panel with the same dimensions. The two combined exactly match the width of the door.

Main Floor

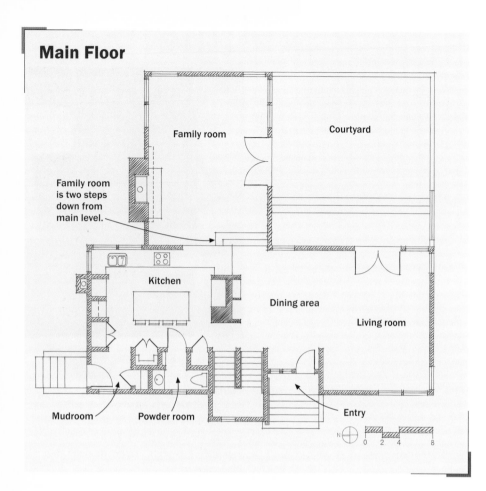

Family room

Courtyard

Family room
is two steps
down from
main level.

Kitchen

Dining area

Living room

Mudroom

Powder room

Entry

N
0 2 4   8

Architect:
Paul Lukez
Architecture

Builder:
Merrill Nearis,
MBN Construction

Size: 3,000 sq. ft.

Location:
Lexington, Mass.

RIGHT Although nothing on the outside of the house seems to align precisely with the elements above or below, there's an underlying order here that makes it look "right." Trace a line down from the edge of each window on the second floor, and you'll see that it lines up with a center divider of either a door or a copper panel below.

It was Goethe who said that architecture is frozen music, and just like a fine piece of music, this house has rhythms and patterns that ripple through the work. Look at the way the materials are used on the exterior. Instead of every surface receiving the same treatment, there are variations in texture, ranging from exterior-grade plywood to lap siding to copper panels, all subtly interlaced with trim bands of a slightly lighter color. In addition to this creative use of materials, there is a proportional relationship among the parts of the house that helps give it its lyrical quality.

Paul likes to set up an architectural language of elements for each house he designs, based on a repetition of connections, materials, and geometric proportions—much like the tempo and key signature of a musical composition. The motif for this house includes an 8-ft. module that can be subdivided into 4-ft., 16-in., and 4-in. dimensions as appropriate. The windows and their surrounding trim, for example, are 4 ft. wide and, when doubled for two windows, 8 ft. wide. Each window contains a pattern of mullions that are based on a 4-in. module. Though they vary slightly from window to window, there's an obvious similarity among them. To borrow a musical term, you can think of this subtle repetition of elements as a theme and variations.

Proportion and Geometry

These relationships don't stop at the windows; the same dimensions are repeated in all the major design features of the house. Both the backsplash behind the cooktop and the fireplace in the family room are dramatic and playful variations on the modular theme. As Paul puts it, "The rules I set for myself provide the constraints for the composition, but the poetry comes from breaking a rule or two. It's a bit like jazz that way." And the backsplash and fireplace are definitely the soloists.

Both of these features comply with most, though not all, of Paul's own constraints, but in addition they engage a propor-

ABOVE Materials are elegantly combined wherever you look. Cherry, aluminum, and copper panels below the Fireslate countertop are interwoven with a narrow lacing of darker wood strips. At the far end of the kitchen, sections of cabinetry have been separated by vertical walls. This avoids the generic look that standard kitchens often have and gives the room a distinctive rhythm.

RIGHT The family room is two steps down from the rest of the main level, giving it a higher ceiling and a sense of definition much like that of a quiet pool at the end of a stream. The fireplace and its surrounding woodwork give the room a sense of movement, accentuated by the pencil-line U-channels set between sheets of drywall.

BELOW Natural light was an important design element in this house, with windows situated for maximum effect throughout the day. There are occasional surprises, too, like this window that seems to break through the ceiling to allow in light from above, washing the wall with afternoon sunshine.

tioning system known as the Golden Mean, which appeals to the eye like a harmonious chord does to the ear. In fact, if you study the history of architecture, you'll discover that many of the best-loved buildings have been developed around the proportions of the Golden Mean. Paul doesn't always try to lay out those proportions when he's designing, but intuitively they seem to arise.

This house makes more with less at every turn, using restraint to create a composition with depth and beauty. Its modular theme allows materials to be conserved, at the same time providing the impetus for the creativity that is woven throughout the house. With the kind of discipline that Paul uses to evolve his designs, every material plays its part in making architectural harmony. And it does so while staying in tune with its community. It's a neighbor that all of us could live with.

Phi and the Golden Mean

A proportion is a relationship between lengths that always stays constant, no matter the size. So, for example, a rectangle with the proportion 1:2 ("one to two") retains that proportion whether it is 10 ft. by 20 ft. or 2 in. by 4 in. The proportion called the Golden Mean is 1:1.618. It is also known as phi, the 21st letter of the Greek alphabet.

Like its better-known relative pi, phi has some truly astonishing characteristics. For example, the length of each bone in each finger of our hands has the ratio of phi with respect to the adjoining bone. Its proportions are present throughout all living things, from the distribution of leaves around a stem to the pattern of seeds in a sunflower to the spiral of divisions in a nautilus shell. Phi also underlies the structure and geometry of much in our world that strikes us as beautiful. It's like a hidden harmonic scale—one we have no words for but which many of us can see and feel, even if we have no training in the visual arts. It's the spatial equivalent of having an ear for music.

The house shown here is finely tuned to the Golden Mean. In the drawing below, you'll see the phi proportion occurring over and over, as it spirals down from the plane of the wall to the smallest details on the fireplace. Though we don't yet have the language to describe the harmonics of the Golden Mean, many Not So Big Houses are pleasing not only because of their crafting but also because they are tuned to this hidden scale.

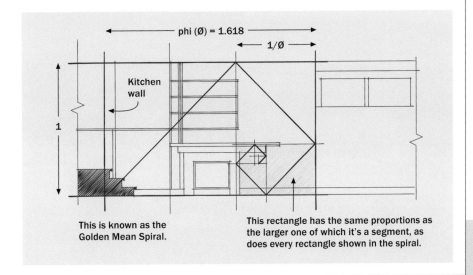

phi (Ø) = 1.618

1/Ø

Kitchen wall

1

This is known as the Golden Mean Spiral.

This rectangle has the same proportions as the larger one of which it's a segment, as does every rectangle shown in the spiral.

The backsplash behind the cooktop and the fireplace in the family room are dramatic and playful variations on the modular theme.

Affordable Comfort

ABOVE Although the form of this house is simple, the dark green trim, corner boards, and columns highlight its shape and bring out its personality. The diamond motif above the dormer window adds a playful touch that distinguishes it from a standard builder home at very little expense.

THIS HOUSE, DESIGNED BY ARCHITECT Ross Chapin for a family of four in Amherst, Massachusetts, presents another view of the archetypal qualities that speak to us of home. Like the house in Pennsylvania designed by Jeremiah Eck (see p. 190), it has a steep roof with living space below, a magnificent brick chimney, a front dormer with a focal window, and a central front door under its own sheltering roof. This home, however, was constructed on a much tighter budget, proving that you can build a truly beautiful home even if there isn't a lot of money available. You simply have to evaluate what's important to you and distribute the money accordingly.

When a house is small, it's important to have at least one area that gives a sense of spaciousness.

For Rene and Susan and their two teenage children, the location of the house was a high priority, and like many people, they

OPPOSITE The brick chimney is a dramatic feature that the owners decided to spend extra money on. The layout of the bricks in the chimney recalls the diamond motif from the front of the house. A belt line divides the gable end, separating the cedar shingles above from the lap siding below. The total composition looks both cozy and inviting. (PHOTO BY CHARLES MILLER; COURTESY *FINE HOMEBUILDING* MAGAZINE.)

ended up spending more of their overall budget on land than they had intended. So when it came time for the design process, they knew they'd have to make some compromises. Ross helped them identify what spaces they really needed and explained how to design them to get the most value for their money.

Common Ground

Rene and Susan's previous home had a formal living room, a dining room, and a tiny kitchen on the main level. As in many households, even though there was no family room, the living room still didn't get used much. Instead, the living happened mostly in the kitchen and adjacent dining room. So in their new home, Ross suggested making one large common room, with a

ABOVE **A wood stove at the center of the common room shares the chimney with the exterior fireplace. The detailing on the surrounding brickwork gives it the look of a real fireplace, but the wood stove offers a more controllable and efficient heat source. The door to the right of the hearth leads to the deck, which is an extension of the primary living space.** (PHOTO BY CHARLES MILLER; COURTESY *FINE HOMEBUILDING* MAGAZINE.)

Architect:
Ross Chapin
Architects

Builder:
Bill O'Bremski

Size: 1,750 sq. ft.

Location:
Amherst, Mass.

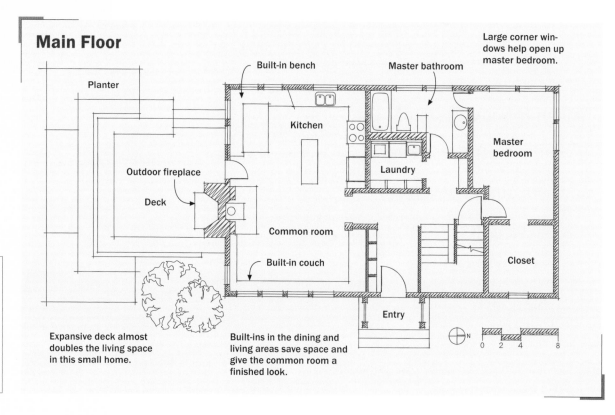

Main Floor

Planter

Built-in bench

Master bathroom

Large corner windows help open up master bedroom.

Kitchen

Outdoor fireplace

Deck

Laundry

Master bedroom

Common room

Built-in couch

Closet

Entry

N
0 2 4 8

Expansive deck almost doubles the living space in this small home.

Built-ins in the dining and living areas save space and give the common room a finished look.

> *Built-in furniture can save a significant amount of square footage and give the room a cozy feel at the same time.*

high ceiling and lots of light, where the family could congregate to cook, eat, do homework, and socialize. It would be beautiful and filled with warm materials that encouraged both family and friends to linger.

When a house is small, it's important to have at least one area that gives a sense of spaciousness, and in this house the common room serves that function. At 16 ft. by 24 ft. with a 10-ft. ceiling, it's still not a large space for what is essentially three living areas: kitchen, dining room, and living room. But combining them into a single large space creates the illusion of being in a bigger house while using far less square footage than building a separate room for each function.

ABOVE Windows surround the built-in couches in the living room, flooding the space with light and views during the day. By night, the lighting is very simple but effective, with inexpensive wall sconces pointed both up, to bounce light off the ceiling, and down, to create warm pools of light for reading.

Built-In Benefits

Another interesting spatial trick helps the common room stretch even farther. An everyday dining table typically requires at least 3 ft. to 4 ft. between the table edge and the wall, so that there's

ABOVE The kitchen occupies one corner of the rectangle of the main room. To the right, the lowered soffit helps to give the space a sense of shelter and its own identity. To the left, a built-in bench on two sides of the table allows the eating area to occupy less space than usual because there's no need to allow for chair clearances on these sides.

room for chairs and some additional circulation space. Here, the chairs are replaced with a built-in bench, so there's no need to allow for that extra space. Built-in furniture can save a significant amount of square footage and give the room a cozy feel at the same time.

The same space-saving design is used in the living area, where the couch is built in along the window wall (see the photo on p. 259). Pushing standard furniture tight against a wall tends to suggest that a room is too small, as if the furniture had to be shoe-horned in. Built-in furniture lets you use a reduced amount of space but gives the opposite effect, making a room look more finished. The continuous lines of the built-in couch, together with the wide windowsill that serves as a shelf, give this room a tailored look and provide ample seating in a modest amount of space.

When you build in couches and benches like this, it's critical that they fit the people who sit in them. Not all chair shapes are comfortable for all people, so Ross arranged for a mockup to be made prior to final construction to make sure that the proportions were just right. Although this is a little extra work and expense, it's money and effort well spent. Remember, you're tailoring a house that is designed to fit *you*.

The Warmth of Wood

The common room also has some finishing details that you wouldn't normally find in an inexpensive home. The cherry cabinetry, made by a local cabinetmaker, is of exceptional quality and beauty. Spending a little extra on the cabinetry can lend the whole house an aura of quality and craftsmanship.

LEFT Kitchen cabinets can be designed to suit your individual needs and to create a custom look. This cabinetry includes an island that's more like a freestanding table. Narrow drawers below the upper cabinets and open shelving in the hard-to-reach areas above the refrigerator and range hood give this inventive kitchen a well-proportioned and hospitable feel.

Up Close

Granite is a beautiful and durable material for countertops and backsplashes, but its cost can be prohibitive. An alternative is to use 12-in. by 12-in. granite tiles, which have the feel and durability of solid granite at a fraction of the cost.

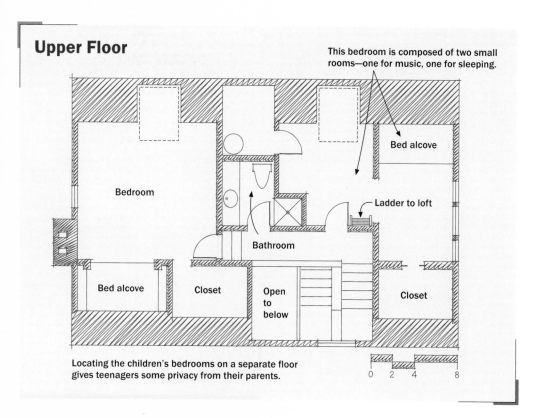

Upper Floor

This bedroom is composed of two small rooms—one for music, one for sleeping.

Bedroom

Bed alcove

Bathroom

Bed alcove

Closet

Open to below

Ladder to loft

Closet

0 2 4 8

Locating the children's bedrooms on a separate floor gives teenagers some privacy from their parents.

By spending more of your budget on highly visible features like the cabinetry and doing some creative compromising elsewhere, the quality of the whole house increases.

The ceiling is another place where a little extra detailing has been added to great effect. Ross had been studying traditional Japanese architecture and was inspired in the creation of this design by the ceiling support system of beams and purlins in the famous temple at Ise. Its open structure allows light to play over the tops of the beams, giving the whole ceiling a floating, latticed quality.

The beams and purlins (the crosspieces) provide the support for the upper level and are made of construction-grade wood, complete with knots and other blemishes. This provided an opportunity to use a lower grade of trim around the windows and doors, to echo that look and save money at the same time. It's very different from the refinement of the cabinetry, yet it works well in this eclectic space.

The trimwork in a house can be a significant expense, so if you can make a less expensive product work for you, it can add up to substantial savings. It's a common fear that choosing a lower grade for one material will ruin the whole effect of the house, but this is seldom the case. By spending more of your budget on highly visible features like the cabinetry and doing some creative compromising elsewhere, the quality of the whole house increases.

Comfort Zones

Beyond the common room, the house is basically unadorned and the spaces are small. But Ross used some interesting design concepts to help make a little go a long way. He separated the private areas of the house into different zones—a children's zone and an adults' zone. This strategy gives family members some privacy from one another, a desirable feature for everyone during the teen years. The second floor of the house is given over to the children, and the adults have their private territory in the main-floor master bedroom. This room isn't intended for socializing, so it was kept intentionally small, with no separate sitting area or extra floor space.

The children's rooms are somewhat larger, to give each child his or her own private realm, well away from mom and dad. Placing the beds in alcoves in the eaves leaves more usable space for everyday activities. Suzanne has a bedroom with lots of floor space, while Stephen's room is actually two small rooms with a wide doorway in between. An aspiring musician, he practices his guitar in one room and uses the other for sleeping. Since both kids' bedrooms are built into the roof form, they have sloped ceilings, which adds some personality without additional expense.

LEFT In a Not So Big House, it's important to make the most of the space that's available. This house employs a number of clever storage ideas, like these staircase bookshelves. Adding 10 in. to the width of the stairway created over 16 lineal feet of book storage, where typically there's just a wall.

BELOW The sloped ceiling of the second floor, which is tucked snuggly into the roof form, makes a wonderful, tentlike place for a child's bedroom. A skylight introduces the same amount of light as an expensive dormer, at a fraction of the cost. (PHOTO BY CHARLES MILLER; COURTESY *FINE HOMEBUILDING* MAGAZINE.)

Section

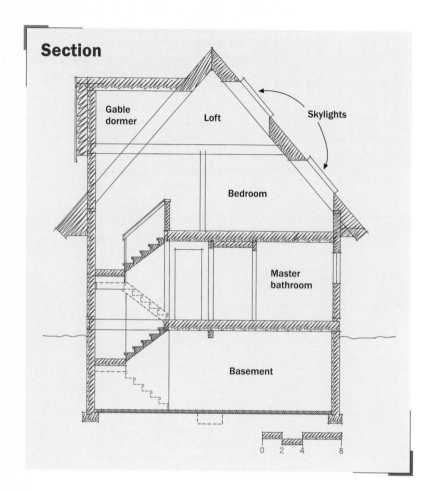

Gable dormer

Loft

Skylights

Bedroom

Master bathroom

Basement

0 2 4 8

RIGHT **A small loft accessed by a ship's ladder is a place for individual family members to be alone. Providing a retreat place can make a small house seem larger, because there is room to get away.**

OPPOSITE **A beautifully designed exterior fireplace extends the season for outdoor socializing and is a great attraction for friends and family alike. With its encircling wooden bench, it becomes an outdoor room—a wonderful place to congregate toward evening around the welcoming warmth of the fire.**

Room at the Top

Making full use of all the available space, there's one more room at the top of the house—a loft that's accessed by a ship's ladder. The space is tiny and only 7 ft. high at the ridge, but its diminutive size doesn't mean it's not frequently used. Since the home was built a decade ago, the loft has served as both in-home office and retreat space—a place to go to meditate or simply to sit quietly and be alone. Although this function is not commonly accommodated in most American homes, its inclusion can make an enormous difference in the feeling of spaciousness. You don't need large rooms to make space for privacy. Just the knowledge that there's a getaway at the top of the stairs is all it takes.

It's thoughtful touches like these that give this simple house such a feeling of home. Standing outside, you know instinctively that you'll feel comfortable the moment you step inside. It's not a pretentious house. It's not designed to impress the neighbors. Instead, it's built to nurture and delight the people who really count—the people who live in it. It has the genuineness that comes from designing for real people and real lives, lived within the confines of a real budget. Most of us know those constraints but don't know how to transcend them. This house admirably shows how it can be done.

Comfort, Pueblo-Style

When designing with an unconventional palette, let the materials work for you to create a house with personality.

ARCHITECT DANIEL HOFFMANN fell in love with the look and feel of Southwestern architecture when his parents moved to Santa Fe 30 years ago. When it came time for retirement, Daniel and his wife, Georgia, decided to make nearby Taos their new home. They found a site in town, just a half block from the historic district, and decided to design a home in the Pueblo style, using adobe bricks for walls and peeled logs for roof support. The native Pueblo Indians added rooms to their houses as they needed them, resulting in structures that appeared to have grown organically over time. Following the same approach, the Hoffmanns' house was planned as an assemblage of cubes rather than as a unified whole.

OPPOSITE The house has few interior doors, allowing long sight lines throughout to connect the main living spaces. Lowered beams are used to differentiate one room from another without obstructing the views. The sculpted wall between kitchen and dining areas, which mirrors the wall flanking the fireplace, hides the kitchen work area.

BELOW Located just half a block from the historic section of Taos, this home for a retired couple is built in the Pueblo style to look as if it had grown up over time.

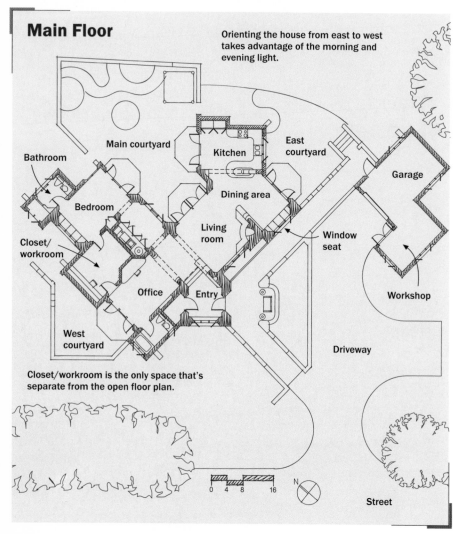

Main Floor

Orienting the house from east to west takes advantage of the morning and evening light.

Bathroom

Main courtyard

Kitchen

East courtyard

Garage

Bedroom

Dining area

Closet/
workroom

Living room

Window seat

Office

Entry

Workshop

West courtyard

Driveway

Closet/workroom is the only space that's separate from the open floor plan.

0 4 8   16

N

Street

Architect:
DWH Architects,
Inc.

Builder:
Las Colonias
Construction

Size: 1,985 sq. ft.

Location:
Taos, N. Mex.

Site and Light

Daniel wanted to make the most of the rare quality of the light in Taos, located atop a high mesa that allows light to enter almost horizontally at the start and end of the day. Since the street runs southeast to northwest, orienting the windows to the east and west also placed the house at a 45-degree angle to neighboring homes, which has the advantage of opening up longer views that don't look directly at the adjacent structures.

Because the building site has a drop of 7 ft. from one side to the other, the decision was made to sink the garage 4 ft. into the ground and to raise the master-bedroom wing 3 ft. above grade. In this way, all living spaces are kept at the same level. The adobe walls surrounding the courtyards provide privacy and help to disguise the height of the bedroom wing, while the sunken garage all but disappears from the street.

Open-Plan Living

Since it was just the two if them, Daniel and Georgia had few concerns about noise, so they chose to minimize the number of interior doors. They preferred a house that felt open, that allowed views from place to place, and that was all on one level for accessibility. Although they are both healthy and mobile

TOP To avoid the predictable monotony of banks of cabinet doors, upper kitchen cabinets were kept to a practical minimum, leaving room for open shelves and a broad expanse of windows.

ABOVE Oversized drawer pulls and hand-carved doors give the whole kitchen an air of crafted playfulness.

LEFT Two graceful archways frame a view from the entry to the window beyond. Without the window, the view would be far less welcoming. The antique desk is out of the way of the main living space, but its beauty can still be appreciated every day as the owners enter and leave the house.

The kitchen fits with the look and feel of the rest of the house—an important characteristic when building Not So Big.

today, they wanted to design a home they could stay in even if they became physically impaired.

Entering through the front door, you're greeted by a long view through two archways to a perfectly aligned window. The window is actually part of the master bedroom, but this is not apparent to a visitor. It simply looks like part of a graciously proportioned hallway. Without the window, the view would be much less appealing. The optical effect is to make the house look significantly larger than it really is—an important Not So Big concept.

The Hoffmanns wanted to make sure the kitchen blended in with the other living spaces, so they decided to minimize the number of upper cabinets, replacing what they could with windows and open shelving. A built-in wall pantry next to the refrigerator more than compensates for the lost storage space. The cabinet doors are custom carved, and the drawers have oversized pulls—painted wooden fish—created by a local artist. The refrigerator panel is also unique. Here, painted canvas has been stretched over the original black glass panel on one side. The result is a kitchen that looks more like living space than work space. And most important, it fits with the look and feel of the rest of the house—something to keep in mind when building Not So Big, where one space flows directly into the next.

ABOVE **A painted canvas stretched over the black glass panel of the refrigerator door makes it look less like a kitchen appliance and more like a work of art. The adjacent pantry provides plenty of storage space to make up for the limited number of cabinets.**

The only space that isn't part of this open flow is a room originally intended as the master-bedroom closet. While the house was under construction, it occurred to Daniel and Georgia that, given its size, this space could really do double duty as a storage room for other things as well. They've dubbed this the Fibber McGee room, after the beloved 1930s radio character and his famous overstuffed closet. Here, the Hoffmanns store the supplies for their art and architecture projects. A large layout table in the center makes it an excellent "messy projects" room. Meanwhile, it works just fine as an everyday dressing room as well.

ABOVE AND LEFT Originally intended as a master-bedroom closet, the Fibber McGee room (named after the radio character who had a closet to end all closets) still stores clothes but also does double duty as a project room.

RIGHT The embracing wall of the beehive fireplace was sculpted to provide some separation between the sitting and dining areas. When you're seated in either space, your view is focused on the activity before you; but when you stand, the separation disappears as the wall steps back to reveal the adjacent room.

BELOW The window seat in the dining area has a lowered ceiling, making a wonderful sitting nook for one or two. It's connected to the kitchen visually but quite separate from the living room, thanks to the thick wing wall of the fireplace.

OPPOSITE The owner's home office opens off the skylit front foyer. The beamed opening between rooms has thickened walls at the base, making use of the sculptural quality of adobe. The desk is tucked neatly into an alcove with a lowered ceiling and similar beamed opening—a very comfortable place to work.

Adobe offers some wonderful opportunities for alcoves, wall niches, and creative storage.

Live-In Sculpture

The Hoffmanns' decision to build with native materials opened up some interesting design possibilities. Adobe, because of its thickness, offers some wonderful opportunities for alcoves, wall niches, and creative storage. Adobe walls were originally made of mud bricks reinforced with straw and were about 24 in. deep. Today the process is much the same, with bricks made to a standard 10-in. by 4-in. by 4-in. size. In this home, walls vary from 10 in. thick at walls without windows to 36 in. at the window seats. Once in place, the raw bricks can be sculpted with a pneumatic chipping tool. This is how the armrests on the window seats were made, as well as the stepped wing walls on either side of the beehive fireplace, the beveled openings surrounding the windows, and the bases of the beamed openings between rooms.

Lighting with a Personal Touch

*L*ighting can be an expensive part of a new home, but the Hoffmanns put Georgia's artistic flair to good use, saving a bundle in the process. All the wall sconces are simple porcelain fixtures, with wonderfully creative metal and wood shades made by the resident artist. This gives the house a highly personal touch, with walls adorned with everything from angels in the bedroom to fish in the kitchen. Lit from behind, these whimsical sculptures shine forth and make it eminently clear that this is the home of people who enjoy making their house a personal expression.

ABOVE **The thickness of an adobe wall makes it possible to bury a deep cupboard into the wall. Known as an** *alacena,* **this is a typical feature of Pueblo architecture. The doors of the** *alacena* **match the kitchen cabinets, but with dancing gecko door pulls instead of fish. The owners haven't missed an opportunity to make everyday utility into a work of art.**

Another traditional element in an adobe house is the *alacena*, a storage cupboard built into the wall much as we would set a medicine cabinet in place. But since adobe walls are so much thicker than the standard 2x4 walls we're used to, these cupboards can be almost 2 ft. deep. The Hoffmanns took advantage of this concept for their wood storage box adjacent to the fireplace. The doors, when closed, recall the motif of the kitchen cabinetry, integrating the two spaces.

When designing with an unconventional palette, as in this adobe example, you can explore the special characteristics of the materials and let them work for you to create a house with personality. Using the depth and sculptural qualities of adobe, as

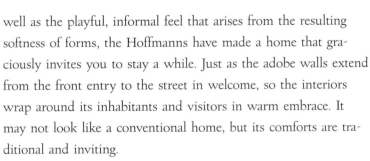

LEFT Throughout the house, lighting is cleverly disguised as wall sculpture. Here, a wooden angel above the bed lights up at night to provide a soft glow for the master bedroom.

BELOW The view from the master bedroom extends across the courtyard to the mountains beyond.

well as the playful, informal feel that arises from the resulting softness of forms, the Hoffmanns have made a home that graciously invites you to stay a while. Just as the adobe walls extend from the front entry to the street in welcome, so the interiors wrap around its inhabitants and visitors in warm embrace. It may not look like a conventional home, but its comforts are traditional and inviting.

Thinking outside the Box

ABOVE Designed as a separate addition to a small existing house, the new house was built over a number of years by the owners themselves. Many of the construction materials were salvaged, including the big round-top window at the gable end, which became a focal point for the design.

OPPOSITE The clerestory windows, which capture the low south light in the winter months, are set in slightly from the end wall, allowing the form of the gable to be expressed. The round-top window is centered below the ridge of the gable, giving it a frame that completes the gable form. (PHOTO COURTESY JACOBSON SILVERSTEIN WINSLOW.)

TODAY'S HOUSEHOLDS COME IN MANY different shapes and sizes, from blended families to separated ones, from couples with kids to individuals who choose to stay single. Rather than attempt to force all of them into the standard "three bedrooms up" house plan, it makes sense to rethink the house to fit the myriad needs of families, couples, and singles. This northern California home does just that. Designed for a specific situation, it is flexible enough to work in different ways according to changing circumstances.

Two small, separate houses allow for a variety of living arrangements.

When Fred and Barbara moved into the tiny concrete-block house on their new property in 1978, they were going through a difficult time in their marriage, and they knew that they would need some space to be apart. At the same time, they both wanted to be close to their three young children. They came up with an unusual solution: build a second house on the property, adjacent to the existing one (see the site plan on p. 280). Each adult

ABOVE **This east-facing window, salvaged from an old schoolhouse, allows light to stream into the bedroom each morning, a welcome to the day. It's trimmed differently than every other window in the house, the unadorned sash and mullions emphasizing its simplicity and beauty.**

RIGHT **This alcove just off the master bedroom, designed originally as a meditation space, now serves as a secluded desk nook, with a view onto the courtyard below. It's an ideal "place of one's own"—a tiny spot in the house just for one, to make of what you will.**

would live in one of the houses, and the children could move between them as they chose. Although this may seem like an uncommon solution to marital problems, Fred and Barbara were "thinking outside the box" of convention, creating an environment in which their children could flourish.

Working Together

Barbara, who is an architect, designed a house that would be simple to build. She also made extensive use of salvaged materials to keep costs down. Since Fred and Barbara did most of the construction themselves, they were able to collect materials gradually. Over time, they accumulated an assortment of found items: fir flooring that had once been siding on a military base, posts and beams from an old bridge, stair railings and treads, a schoolhouse window—literally everything but the kitchen sink. Though it took them many years to complete the construction, they were able to live on the site throughout the process, refining and embellishing as they went. And their salvaging, though labor intensive, paid big dividends, both in character added and money saved.

Once complete, the two small, separate houses allowed for a variety of living arrangements. When the couple needed time apart, there was a space for each of them, without it causing a major disruption to either their children's lives or their own. When the whole family wanted to get together, there were communal gathering spaces both inside the new house and out.

LEFT The area under a stairway is often unused or at best made into a closet. But the sloped ceiling below the stair can make a cozy corner for one or two chairs. Combined with a wood stove, as here, it becomes a warm spot to settle in on rainy days and in the evenings.

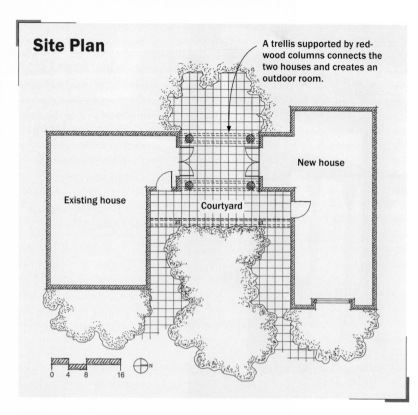

Site Plan

A trellis supported by redwood columns connects the two houses and creates an outdoor room.

New house

Existing house

Courtyard

0 4 8   16   N

An Outdoor Room

To make a connection between the old house and the new, Barbara decided to create an outdoor room that would be defined much like any interior space, with a ceiling and four (implied) walls. The ceiling takes the form of a trellis, covered with wisteria and other flowering creepers that fill the connecting garden court-yard with year-round color. The walls are suggested by the four columns that support the beams above. Nothing more is required to make this a thoroughly delightful place and one of the most used "rooms" in the two houses.

In a Not So Big House, outdoor space can be just as important as indoor space, and it can be defined in the same ways: with alcoves, varying ceiling heights, connecting views, and comfortable proportions. It benefits from thoughtfully designed and crafted details, such as the doubled rafters in this connecting trellis. And, when considered in conjunction with the interior of the house, the outdoor room can extend the living space into the surrounding landscape. This is easier to do in California than in a colder climate, but even in a less hospitable environment, a view of well-designed outdoor rooms can help make your perception of the house extend beyond the walls.

ABOVE In near-perfect climates (with no bugs to speak of), French doors can be thrown open to allow interior and exterior spaces to flow together. A vine-entwined trellis blurs the distinction between inside and out, extending the sense of home into the surrounding landscape. (PHOTO COURTESY JACOBSON SILVERSTEIN WINSLOW.)

An outdoor room extends the living space into the surrounding landscape.

Doing Double Duty

The dining area in the new house was designed as the primary gathering spot for the family, but it also needed to work for entertaining. One of the keys to making a small house work is to make each space do double duty. If a space can be expanded or modified easily for an occasional use, you need to build only half as much space as if you were to build a separate room for each "once in a while" function.

Here, the dining area is close to the kitchen and to the French doors that open onto the arbored connection between the two houses, making it an inviting central location for the family to congregate. When guests come for dinner, the table can be extended all the way to the wood stove at the bottom of the stairs, allowing up to 20 people to be seated comfortably. For even larger gatherings, a long table can extend the full length of the house, from kitchen to living room. With such an open plan, there's a lot of flexibility for special occasions, yet each space still has its own definition.

The inglenook also does double duty. By day it's a cozy spot by the fire, the columns and half walls separating it psychologically—though not acoustically—from the main space. But when guests are visiting, this small alcove turns into a guest room with two beds. Wide drawers below the benches hold the neces-

LEFT The kitchen has few upper cabinets so there's room for a large window above the sink, which brings light and views into the work area. A spacious pantry serves the same function as cupboards, and a 4-ft.-long counter stores all the appliances: mixer, breadmaker, coffeemaker, and food processor. It's like a walk-in appliance garage.

BELOW The dining area, which works well for both everyday needs and larger gatherings, opens out onto the terrace beyond. A sheltering trellis bridges the two houses, creating an outdoor room with a wisteria ceiling. (PHOTO COURTESY JACOBSON SILVERSTEIN WINSLOW.)

An inglenook makes a wonderful conversation area for two or three people or a place to curl up in the evening and read while others socialize in the adjacent living room. The benches on either side of the fireplace are sized to double as guest beds.

When space is well designed, its special nooks and crannies can change function over time as the needs of family members change.

sary bedding. Though not completely private, it provides a comfortable sleeping place, with a bathroom conveniently nearby.

Another double-duty space is located on the upper level. The spacious master suite could readily be made into two bedrooms should the need arise. In its current configuration, it serves both as bedroom and adult retreat. When Barbara originally designed it, the south-facing alcove was intended as a meditation corner. Today it contains a desk and chair. Small spaces like this can change function as needed—from dressing area to in-home office to exercise room. When space is well designed, its special nooks and crannies can change function over time as the needs of family members change.

Weathering Change

Fred and Barbara's willingness to think outside the box to meet their family's housing needs has paid off. Their unusual design for living proved flexible enough to weather not only changes in their own family structure but also the inevitable changes that occur in all families with the passing of time. The two-house concept worked well while the children were growing up, and the arrangement continued even after Barbara and Fred's marriage ended. The original concrete-block house was ultimately turned over to the teenagers, and Barbara eventually moved away. The new house is now Fred's home, and when the kids—now fully grown—come to visit, the original house serves them as a guest house.

Although it's sometimes hard to admit that family life is not picture-perfect, when it's not, we need to find ways of designing that allow us to accommodate change gracefully over time. This is a wonderful example of a Not So Big House designed for the way this family really lived, with an unusual configuration that adapted readily as needs changed. It is impossible to predict how our lives will evolve, but if a house is well designed and built with materials that will last, it will mold easily to a new set of circumstances. An unconventional approach is often eminently sensible and will likely become more common as we tailor our homes to fit reality.

Architect: Jacobson Silverstein Winslow Architects

Builder: Fred Winslow

Size: 1,200 sq. ft. (new house)

Location: Lafayette, Calif.

Up Close

The head of the bed is set in a shallow window alcove with a low sloped ceiling. The windowsill is aligned with the top of the mattress. Although it's unusual to place a bed adjacent to a window, the views are wonderful, and provide a great connection with the outdoors. Just because an arrangement isn't typical doesn't mean you shouldn't do it.

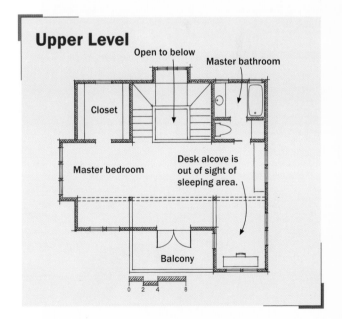

Main Floor

Pantry

Sitting area under stairs

Inglenook doubles as guest bedroom.

Kitchen

Living room

Dining area

Entry

French doors open onto trellised patio.

0 2 4 8 N

Upper Level

Open to below

Master bathroom

Closet

Master bedroom

Desk alcove is out of sight of sleeping area.

Balcony

0 2 4 8

Playfully Sustainable

THE HOUSE THAT TED MONTGOMERY designed for his family near Burlington, Vermont, is an example of what's possible when you build with sustainability in mind. When you think of sustainable design—doing the right thing for the planet—you probably assume you have to settle for a house that's less than what you want: less waste, fewer luxuries (it's a bit like eating your vegetables). But Ted Montgomery wasn't willing to settle for less, and he designed a model of what's possible when you integrate a concern for energy efficiency with an irrepressible flair for invention.

The house is one of 13 in Ten Stones Intentional Community, a development in which people brought together their shared visions of home and neighborhood on 88 acres, 80 of which remain common open space. On their own half acre, Ted and wife Sarah tried a number of different locations and orientations for their home

Combine invention, economy, beauty, and whimsy, and you have the ingredients for a really delightful place to live.

on paper before deciding on the current relationship between site, house, garage, and studio.

Because an energy-efficient house typically has few if any windows on the north face, Ted located the garage there, to buffer the main house from the north wind without compromising desirable window area. Originally the community had planned to have cars parked a distance away from the houses, but the cold, harsh reality of the Vermont winters changed some minds. So Ted instead disguised the garage by berming two sides with earth and adding a roof deck, which also offers a lookout over the community. In the spring, the sloped roof is planted with grass, further downplaying the garage.

ABOVE The siting of an energy-efficient house is critical. This house is oriented toward the sun, and the north and west sides are bermed (mounded with earth) to reduce the amount of wall surface exposed to the elements.

OPPOSITE In locating the house on the site, Ted wanted to minimize the number of trees cut down. The white ash that sprouts through the roof inspired the room that became the focus of the entire house.

A Room with a Viewpoint

One of Ted's goals was to minimize the number of trees that had to be cut down to make room for the house. He also wanted to ensure that it was oriented toward the sun. What evolved was a house designed around a passive solar sunspace—the garden room—with a 75-ft.-tall white ash growing through the middle of it. The trees that did have to be removed to make way for the house were milled into lumber that was used to finish the interior.

Windows opening onto the garden room can be thrown open on sunny days to let in warmth and the fragrance of earth and plants, even in the middle of winter.

The garden room became the primary organizational focus for the house. The room is flooded with southern light, so it heats up over the course of a sunny winter day and acts as a passive solar collector. Ted placed all the main living spaces and bedrooms so they open onto this indoor-outdoor area. In this way, the garden room provides a major source of heat for the house.

The garden room itself opens onto an outdoor courtyard, created by the placement of the studio—Ted's workplace—at a 90-degree angle to the house. Just as interior spaces can be defined with two perpendicular walls to create a shelter around a specific activity, so too can exterior spaces. A beautiful trellislike gateway links the studio to the main house, adding further definition to the courtyard.

Up Close

An arched gateway between the house (left) and the studio marks the entry into the south-facing courtyard. This intriguing opening between buildings welcomes visitors and offers a glimpse of the surprises this house has in store. (PHOTO COURTESY TED MONTGOMERY.)

The window seat in the kitchen has a lowered ceiling, which provides a bridge between pantry and refrigerator. It creates a wonderful sense of enclosure—a personal cocoon, a place to chat with the cook, and a great spot for a cup of coffee and the morning paper.

Connecting Views

As soon as you step inside the house, you know it'll be a fun place to spend time. No matter where you are in the house, there are long views through the space, which gives an airy, spacious feel to the 1,200-sq.-ft. main level. When you look at the floor plan, you can see that the entryway, living area, dining area, and kitchen are all open to one another, yet they are clearly identified as separate places by the walls that define them.

This is a key to making Not So Big feel bigger without losing a sense of intimacy and comfort. Connect activity areas with views from one place to the next, but don't make the space so undifferentiated that it all looks and feels the same. In the Montgomerys' home, the variety of shapes the space takes, the connecting views, and the feast of color and pattern make this a home that really works. Here, invention has been substituted for scale, to make a house that draws you in and invites you to take a second look.

LEFT **LEFT** Long diagonal views connect all the main living spaces, making the house appear larger than it really is. The view here is from the kitchen to the living room.

Architect:
Indiana Architecture & Design

Builder:
Ted Montgomery

Size: 2,300 sq. ft.

Location:
Burlington, Vt.

Connect activity areas with views from one place to the next, but don't make the space so undifferentiated that it all looks and feels the same.

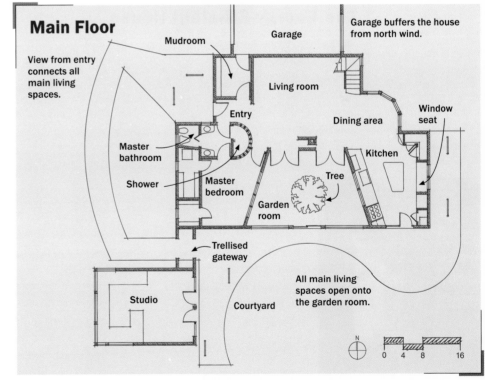

Main Floor

Garage buffers the house from north wind.

Mudroom

Garage

View from entry connects all main living spaces.

Living room

Entry

Dining area

Window seat

Master bathroom

Kitchen

Shower

Tree

Master bedroom

Garden room

Trellised gateway

All main living spaces open onto the garden room.

Studio

Courtyard

N

0 4 8 16

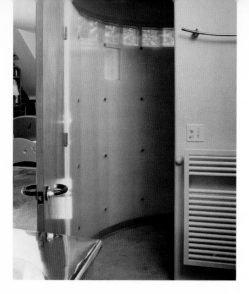

The shower in the master bathroom, lined on the walls with recycled plastic instead of tile to facilitate cleaning, is wheelchair accessible. The house's copper motif continues in the towel bar at right.

Making Magic with Materials

The interior of the house is filled with unique details, created with a sense of whimsy that fills the house with a lightness of spirit. Ted made most of the cabinetry and modular furniture himself out of plywood and Medite, a formaldehyde-free particleboard, that he painted with nontoxic paint. The couches pull apart into individual chairs, with storage for magazines and papers built into the backs. The furniture's bright colors and whimsical cutouts add a playfulness that's in keeping with the informality of the house. The same is true of the door panels on the front of the two pantry cupboards, which sport a motif evocative of Swiss cheese and soap bubbles (see the photo on p. 288). Who says you can't have fun with design?

The Energy-Efficient House

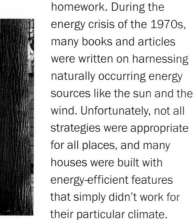

*N*o matter where you live, it's important to design with energy efficiency in mind. What that means, however, varies depending on your location. Understanding which strategies are appropriate for your region and climate requires some careful homework. During the energy crisis of the 1970s, many books and articles were written on harnessing naturally occurring energy sources like the sun and the wind. Unfortunately, not all strategies were appropriate for all places, and many houses were built with energy-efficient features that simply didn't work for their particular climate.

In a northern climate like Vermont's, the winters are long and cold, and the sun is intermittent.

Given such conditions, a south-facing passive-solar sunspace is one of the best ways to capture the available heat. When the space warms from the sun's rays, windows between the house and the sunspace can be opened to heat the home's interior; on cloudy days, the sunspace simply acts as a buffer, providing welcome relief from the snowy vistas beyond.

In areas with plenty of winter sunshine and less extreme temperatures, a more direct approach makes sense. By facing most of the windows to the south, the sun enters the living spaces and warms the interior without the need for a sunspace buffer.

Whether or not you employ passive-solar features, the most important strategy in building energy efficiently is to do an excellent job of insulating and controlling air infiltration. This is true even in hot climates. Instead of

using insulation to keep the heat in, you're using it to keep the heat out. And to keep cooling loads to a minimum, windows need to be located to minimize solar gain during the months when air temperatures are above the comfort range.

When a house is built tightly to minimize air infiltration, there's one additional energy-efficient feature that's crucial. An air-to-air heat exchanger is a device that automatically introduces fresh air into the house while retrieving the heating or cooling energy of the outgoing air. This can save about 85 percent of the heating or air-conditioning energy and helps avoid problems with stagnant air and poor indoor air quality. All new houses that need heating or cooling systems should have air-to-air heat exchangers. It's a matter of health and not something to be left out. Insist on it.

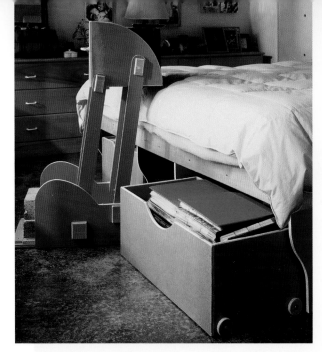

ABOVE Creative storage ideas are evident throughout the house. In the typically little-used area below the bed, the owner has made storage chests on rollers for books and treasures.

LEFT The bathroom countertop is made of copper, a long-lasting, relatively inexpensive surface that will weather and age beautifully over time. The sheet copper is wrapped around a 1½-in. layer of plywood.

The kitchen-island countertop is made from one of the ash trees felled on the site, and the rest of the countertops are made of plywood covered with copper sheeting, which ages beautifully over time and costs about the same as plastic laminate. Copper is also used in the stair railing but in tubular form. Reminiscent of the Art Nouveau style, it's a work of art in its own right. The towel bars in the bathroom continue the copper motif. The floors on the main level are concrete that has been colored with an acid-based stain to make it look like mottled leather.

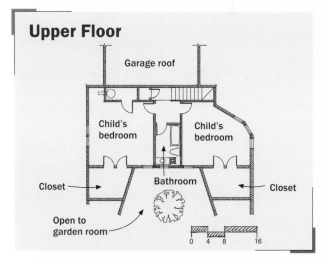

Upper Floor

Garage roof

Child's bedroom

Child's bedroom

Closet

Bathroom

Closet

Open to garden room

0 4 8 16

You can create the effect of an expensive built-in using inexpensive materials.

Another material that's used creatively throughout the house is paint. Instead of making all the walls the same color and using moldings or wood trim to decorate each space, Ted used color to provide visual interest. By layering an element of one color over a surface of another color, you can create the effect of an expensive built-in using inexpensive materials. In the living-room bookshelves, for example, the back wall is painted purple while the shelves themselves, made of plywood, are green. This makes the room appear larger and the overall composition more interesting.

Although there's a lot to take in here, the number of basic materials used is surprisingly small. This limitation of the palette is key. By being innovative with each element, you can make a house that has a lot going on without becoming overwhelming. There's a fine line between whimsy and cacophony.

What is most impressive about this house, though, is the apparent ease with which it brings together considerations of sustainability, energy efficiency, playfulness, and comfort. The effortlessness is deceptive. To design and build a home that integrates so many concepts in a way that looks natural requires significant skill. This is the art of good design. Combine invention, economy, beauty, and whimsy, and you have the ingredients for a really delightful place to live.

OPPOSITE **Materials and color are used creatively throughout the house. Built-ins are made of plywood painted with nontoxic paints. The couch is designed to be pulled apart into individual chairs to seat a crowd, with storage built into the backs.**

Up Close

Copper tubing is used in the stair-railing design to turn an everyday necessity into a work of art.

One Phase at a Time

FOR SEVERAL YEARS AFTER THEY found the perfect property on the shores of Maine's Penobscot Bay, Stephanie and Sandy couldn't bring themselves to build on the land because it had such a raw magnificence. But camping with two small children eventually lost its charm, and they realized that without a house to come home to, their opportunities to enjoy the site were limited. So they asked architect Robert Knight to design them a low-impact house that would initially serve as a vacation home and, over time, become their year-round residence. With two children, they knew that once they moved into the house full-time, they would need more bedrooms, but that was still in the future. They weren't sure exactly what they would need when the time came, so they decided to build the house in two phases.

Building in phases is a basic principle when designing Not So Big.

Building in phases is a basic principle when designing Not So Big. So often, in an attempt to see into the future, houses are

ABOVE **With such a magnificent piece of property, the owners wanted a house that was unobtrusive and had a low impact on the land.**

OPPOSITE **The second-floor landing is both circulation space and closet, utilizing the normally unused area under the eaves. Above the door, transom windows extend to the ceiling, giving a continuous flow to the space. Make these areas solid and the house would feel smaller and more closed in.**

Main Floor

FIRST PHASE

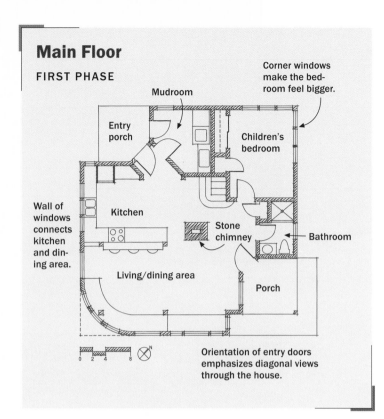

Mudroom

Entry porch

Corner windows make the bedroom feel bigger.

Children's bedroom

Wall of windows connects kitchen and dining area.

Kitchen

Stone chimney

Bathroom

Living/dining area

Porch

0 2 4 8 ⊗N

Orientation of entry doors emphasizes diagonal views through the house.

Upper Floor

FIRST PHASE

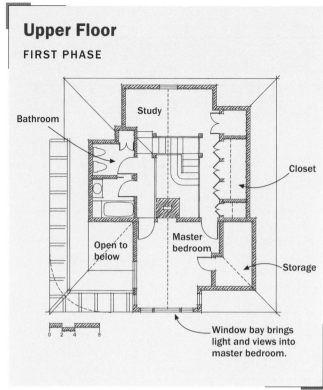

Bathroom

Study

Closet

Open to below

Master bedroom

Storage

0 2 4 8

Window bay brings light and views into master bedroom.

ABOVE The first phase of the design was an almost square, 1,400-sq.-ft. house with a hip roof and lots of windows and skylights to bring in the light and views. (PHOTO COURTESY ROBERT PERRON.)

overdesigned and overbuilt for circumstances that never come to pass or that are radically different than imagined at the start of a project. Phasing allows you to build what you need now and add on only when you fully understand your new needs.

Bob Knight designed a house that was quite compact, with just 900 sq. ft. of finished space on the main level and 520 sq. ft. on the upper level—an ideal vacation retreat, with an informal floor plan and lots of windows to take in the breathtaking views. The house site was selected to minimize the number of trees that would have to be cut down, while still allowing views of the water and the tidal flats to the southeast. Stephanie and Sandy knew they would add a gabled wing onto the north side of the house in the future, and Bob simply designed the original house with that in mind, postponing any formal plans for the addition until the need arose.

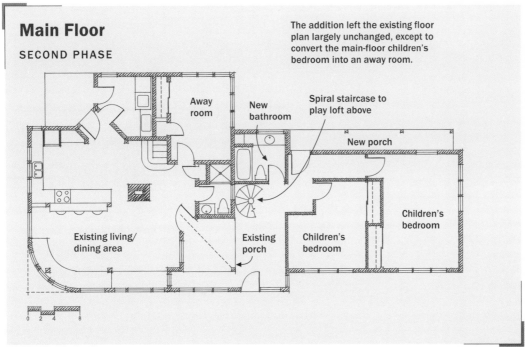

Main Floor

SECOND PHASE

The addition left the existing floor plan largely unchanged, except to convert the main-floor children's bedroom into an away room.

Away room

New bathroom

Spiral staircase to play loft above

New porch

Existing living/dining area

Existing porch

Children's bedroom

Children's bedroom

0 2 4 8

ABOVE The addition, built 12 years after the original house, added bedrooms and a bathroom for the children but left the heart of the original floor plan untouched. The house works just as well as a year-round residence as it did as a vacation home.

Architect:
Knight Associates

Builder:
Stewart Construction

Size: 1,420 sq. ft. (original house); 930 sq. ft. (addition)

Location:
Penobscot Bay, Maine

RIGHT Surrounded by windows and skylights and with a wraparound window seat that allows you to climb right into the view, the corner eating area is one of the highlights of the house. This inviting space upstages the adjacent living area and has become the main gathering place in the house.

We live in our homes much more informally than most standard floor plans would suggest.

OPPOSITE Long views throughout the house extend to the beautiful property beyond, making the house seem significantly larger than it actually is. When you can see along the diagonal from one corner of the house to the other, you are effectively extending the length of the view beyond the rectilinear dimensions of the house.

When they did, in fact, add on some 12 years later, the new wing included bedroom and bathroom space for the kids but little else. The main part of the house, the informal living space, turned out to be as perfect for year-round living as it was for vacationing. This highlights the fact that our homes today can learn a lot from how we live when we're "officially relaxing"—we live in our homes much more informally than most standard floor plans would suggest. Despite the fact that they were transforming a casual vacation place into a year-round home, Stephanie and Sandy saw no reason to add a formal dining or living area. They knew how they lived in the house and how they entertained there. It was the informality that made them feel comfortable, and their friends enjoyed this aspect of the design just as much as they did.

Taking the Long View

The plan itself is very simple—basically a square covered by a hipped roof, with two corners removed, one for the front entry and one for the deck, with the roof extending down to shelter these two spaces. The front entry and porch doors are oriented at a 45-degree angle to the rest of the floor plan, emphasizing a diagonal view through the house. The views within the house are also mainly on the diagonal, which makes the house feel larger than it actually is. It's an important trick in making Not So Big feel bigger. You can sit in the dining area, for example, and look back past the wood stove to the stairway; or you can be

working in the kitchen and look out through the living-area window to the ocean beyond.

The corner windows in the dining area and the main-floor bedroom are further elaborations on this motif. When you take away the visual solidity of the outside corner of a room by replacing a wall with windows, the room feels significantly bigger, provided there's an open view beyond. It's as though the great outdoors becomes part of the room itself.

ABOVE The wall of windows with skylights above, connecting the kitchen and dining area, seems to float past the work space. Defined by the lower wood ceiling and corner column, the kitchen is wide open yet still distinct—almost like a house within a greenhouse.

OPPOSITE By raising the counter between the kitchen and eating area, dirty dishes are hidden from the table. With no walls to separate the kitchen from the living areas, the whole main level benefits from the easy informality of the light-filled kitchen hub.

Rooms to Live In

In this home, the eating area—with its window seats, corner windows, and skylights—is such a wonderful place to be that the living room takes a subordinate role. This is where people gather, and with the table extended, it can accommodate a large party if necessary. The kitchen counter is raised 6 in. on the dining side, which allows family and friends to socialize with the cook during meal preparation and has the added benefit of hiding the kitchen mess while people are eating. Many people hesitate to give up a formal dining room because of concerns about looking at dirty dishes. This organization of space eliminates that problem. Why build two eating areas when you can have one extra-

ordinary one that brings you pleasure every day and delights your guests as well?

When the addition was built, the first-floor bedroom, which had previously served as the kids' bunk room, was turned into an away room. This space, near the main social areas of the house, lets adults get some work done or make a quiet phone call without separating themselves completely from family activities. Some people prefer to install a French door, so a room like this one can also serve as a place for noisier activities like television or video games—to be isolated acoustically but not visually. Children often want to be close to the adults but don't want to do the same things. This simple solution can avoid a lot of irritation caused by competing activities and the high-decibel levels that generally go along with kids.

A Simple Stack of Stones

A powerful aspect of the design is the spectacular stone chimney that extends directly up through the center of the house, creating impressive views from every angle. This is an excellent example of how craftsmanship can enhance a home. Initially, the house had been designed to have a brick chimney, which hadn't been thought of as a "statement piece." However, Stephanie and Sandy found a local stone mason, Jeff Gamelin, who could work magic with the stones found on local beaches. Although it is essentially just a straight, square assemblage of stones, his work transcends the medium, and the chimney becomes

ABOVE **The master bedroom is relatively small, but the visual connection with the landing through the upper transoms gives it a feeling of spaciousness. The stonework of the chimney provides a wonderful contrast in texture to the rest of the room.**

RIGHT **A window bay brings the view of woods, water, and sky right into the master bedroom. Though the alcove is small in terms of square footage, its impact is great.**

"When you start with a smaller area and then really finish it beautifully, you end up with a far better place to live."

the focal point of the house, both upstairs and down.

This is the kind of craftsmanship that makes a Not So Big House special. Thanks in large part to the conscious decision made at the beginning of this project to minimize its impact on the land, the house itself was kept small, and the money that would have otherwise gone into square footage went instead into quality of craft and materials. With all the wood and stone in the house, it's not inexpensive per square foot. But if you have only 1,400 sq. ft., it's still within a reasonable price range. As Bob Knight says, "When you start with a smaller area and then really finish it beautifully, you end up with a far better place to live."

Up Close

A stone chimney can be so much more than just a pile of rocks. In this chimney, made from local beach stones, craft becomes art, bringing beauty to almost every room in the house. The tiny built-in niche halfway up the chimney provides an opportunity to display a treasured object.

LEFT Skylights are sometimes referred to as roof windows, yet they're seldom located in such a way that they really act as windows—places that allow access to both light and view. When you have a steeply sloped roof, as in this house, locating the skylight's sill below ceiling level gives you all the benefits of a normal window in an area that would normally require a dormer to access the view.

Updating a Not So Big House

BARRY KATZ CAUGHT ON TO THE IDEA of building Not So Big early. As the owner of a high-end, custom homebuilding company, he'd seen what can happen when homeowners spend all their money on square footage and volume. He was all too familiar with the bigger-is-better philosophy of the '80s—and with houses where one or more rooms remain unused, often even unfurnished, for years after construction is complete. This just didn't make sense to him, so for his own family he chose a very different approach. Barry and his wife, Susan, found a site they liked within walking distance of downtown Westport, Connecticut, Susan's hometown. They asked New Haven architect Barry Svigals to help them design a house that they could build with their limited budget and later remodel to include more bells and whistles as finances allowed.

To save on expensive square footage, the house they built in 1982 had no separate formal spaces. When friends came to visit, they were welcomed into the family's living area, where the

The remodeling didn't require the addition of a lot more space, but what already existed clearly needed to be redefined.

OPPOSITE The remodeled living room works better than it did before, even though it is technically smaller. A 10-ft.-high ceiling replaces the original cathedral ceiling, making the room more intimate. If a space feels comfortable, it's much more likely to be lived in, even if it doesn't look as dramatic.

Main Floor

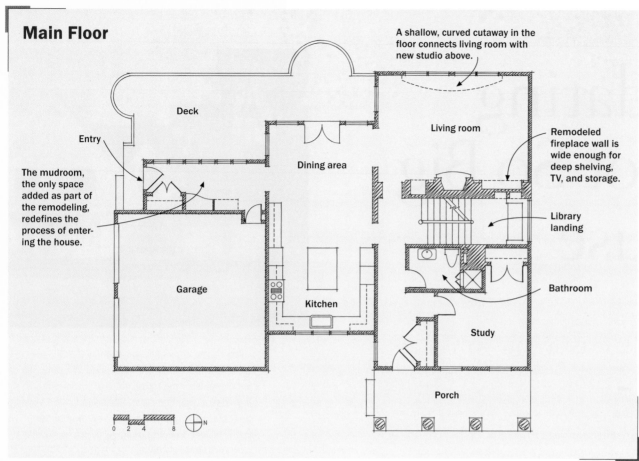

A shallow, curved cutaway in the floor connects living room with new studio above.

Deck

Entry

The mudroom, the only space added as part of the remodeling, redefines the process of entering the house.

Dining area

Living room

Remodeled fireplace wall is wide enough for deep shelving, TV, and storage.

Library landing

Garage

Kitchen

Bathroom

Study

Porch

0 2 4 8 N

Architect:
Svigals Associates
Builder:
Barry Katz Homebuilding
Size: 2,700 sq. ft.
Location:
Westport, Conn.

Upper Floor

Bedroom

Studio

Closet

Hall

Bathroom

Closet

Bedroom

Bedroom

Bathroom

0 4 8 16

The upper part of the living room, open to below in the original house, has been converted into a studio.

New steps from the landing at the top of the stairs provide access to the studio.

kitchen, dining room, and living room were open to one another. The finishing details, which Barry and Susan knew they would eventually want to upgrade, began as inexpensive builder standards. With his building background, Barry Katz knew that changing the interior structure and adding windows would be prohibitively expensive if done later. So the couple spent the money they saved on square footage and expensive millwork to fill the house with light and to make rooms that would be big enough to be comfortable even when their two young children were strapping teens. In many ways, you could say that they built a Not So Big starter house.

Fast forward 15 years. The money for more details and refinements is available, and it's time to remodel. Barry and Susan again called Barry Svigals, and together they evolved a plan for the remodeling. The basic house still served the functions of family living just fine. But now Susan needed an in-home office; an ever-expanding collection of books was spilling from their makeshift shelves; and there was an overflow of coats, hats, shoes, and pet supplies, all without a home. The remodeling didn't require the addition of a lot more space, but what already existed clearly needed to be redefined.

ABOVE **The upper section of the cathedral-ceilinged living room was converted into a studio, with a curved cutout and railing that opens up the studio to the living room below. The windows in the gable end wall remained unchanged, and both levels now benefit from the light and view they provide.**

LEFT **Extra windows, like this round top in the master bedroom, were included in the original design to fill the house with light. Even though the budget was limited, the owners knew how much more expensive it would be to add these elements later.**

One Room Becomes Two

One feature of the original house that Barry and Susan found less attractive than they'd expected was the cathedral ceiling in the living room. Although it looked impressive, it made the room uncomfortable to sit in. They always felt as if they were on display

when they were in the room, because the shape of the space made it seem very formal. Even when guests were over, it didn't function very well, because the high ceiling turned the room into an echo chamber.

Svigals's solution was to turn the upper part of the room into a studio for Susan, accessible by four new steps from the landing at the top of the stairs. To avoid the need for a major redesign of the west facade, the window configuration was left intact, with a shallow opening and railing connecting the study with the living room below, allowing both to benefit from the light and view.

Now that the remodeling's done, Barry and Susan find that the living room is a far more comfortable room to be in—both for the family and when guests are over. The remodeled room has a 10-ft.-high ceiling, so it's by no means a low space, but it is no longer an echoing cavern. Best of all, the cutaway to the studio is a beautiful form, intriguing to visitors, and a graceful way to let in light.

ABOVE The only addition to the remodeled house is a mudroom, connected to the dining area with a pocket door. Rather than use a door that's solid and impenetrable, this one is made of translucent glass, which lets in the light but not the view.

RIGHT A small desk surface just around the corner from the mudroom door provides a place for mail sorting, menu planning, and family scheduling. The pigeonhole slots above allow mail to be sorted on the spot, before the piles form.

OPPOSITE When a mudroom is the family's everyday entry, it deserves to be more than just a space to store coats and shoes. With a wall of windows, this new mudroom is a wonderful light-filled transition space between outside and in. The bench is a great place to sit and take off muddy shoes, and its curve is echoed in the soffit above, adding a playful touch. There's even a lookout post for the canine welcoming committee.

An Everyday Entry

The only space added as part of the remodeling was the mudroom, which runs the length of the garage and brings you into the dining area through a translucent pocket door. Because this would be their primary entrance into the house, Barry and Susan wanted it to be a cheery place. A Not So Big House should not only welcome guests but also family members—if they enter through a back door, that's where the design effort needs to be. By making the west wall of the mudroom entirely

out of windows, this space is constantly bathed with light. There are places for all the outside gear, the pet supplies (and the pet), and a general message board. And when the Katzes step through the door into the dining area, they already feel at home.

Compare this to the earlier entry process. They used to move directly from the garage into the kitchen, with no transition space—an unsettling experience. There was no place to take off coats, and perhaps more important, no place to be received by the house before entering the family realm. Whether it's a mudroom or a small vestibule that helps make the transition, when such a space exists, it's as though the house greets you. This space serves far more than just a practical function. It's the spatial equivalent of the family's welcome mat.

Bookshelves and Built-Ins

The Katzes had managed to acquire a small library of books since they'd built the original house in 1982, and they wanted to add plenty of built-in shelving to accommodate the ever-growing collection. When you're a book lover, every available surface must be considered for shelving. It's important to be creative when you are looking at wall surfaces to find places where your shelves will be well integrated and add character to the space. It helps, in fact, if you think of books as extra-thick wallpaper.

ABOVE Space was borrowed from the reconfigured wall between the stairway and the living room to create additional shelves for the owners' growing collection of books. The built-in couch at the landing, with ample cushions and reading light, is a wonderful place to sit and read.

OPPOSITE The owners worked with an interior designer to create this wall of shelves. By building the shelves 4 in. out from the wall surface, the painting above the fireplace has a framed, inset appearance and space is made for the full depth of the television.

Many landing nooks look appealing but don't get used. This one is big enough and inviting enough that it really does work.

Svigals suggested that they take the wall opening that formerly overlooked the living room and make it into a library wall. Barry and Susan were initially hesitant about making the change, but they now agree that the new library landing is a wonderful addition. When combined with the built-in couch (with its own swing-arm reading light), it provides a great spot to curl up with a good book. Many landing nooks look appealing but don't get used. This one is big enough and inviting enough that it really does work.

Bookshelves were added in other places, too. In Susan's new studio, a double row of shelves runs the length of the north wall, under a new row of small windows (see the photo on p. 307). The windows have a head height of 4 ft. 6 in., just right for someone sitting at the desk. Both the windows and the bookshelves are lower than normal to encourage you to sit down and see them at comfortable eye level. When there's a low kneewall, as here, employing such strategies can make the space both more usable and more comfortable.

In the living room, the whole fireplace wall has been made into shelving and storage, with places for books, CDs, tapes, and audio/video equipment. The wall itself has been thickened substantially (to 24 in.) to make room for the television and the lower cabinets. Although this makes the room slightly smaller in terms of usable square footage, you barely

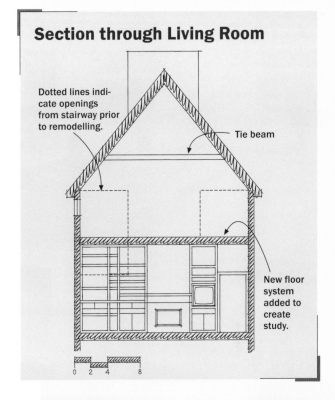

Section through Living Room

Dotted lines indicate openings from stairway prior to remodelling.

Tie beam

New floor system added to create study.

0 2 4   8

Instead of a combination refrigerator/freezer unit, the owners opted for a larger refrigerator and located freezer drawers in the island. When the drawers are closed, you'd never suspect they were anything other than regular cabinetry.

notice the difference in a room this size. People are often loath to give up floor space for storage, yet the result is a more functional and more beautiful room. In a Not So Big House, the built-ins are designed to do more with less. They become works of art in themselves, and the room is far more useful with them in it.

An Old-World Look

Barry and Susan had been collecting ideas and clipping pictures from design magazines for years, and when it came time to remodel, they put them to good use. They both loved the traditional detailing that gives a house a sense of permanence and the feeling that it was built in an earlier era. Trimwork is one of the key details that has changed significantly over the years, becoming narrower and less detailed. But just because a house is new doesn't mean it has to use today's standard moldings. Throughout the newly remodeled house, the moldings are suggestive of a house that's much older, and the kitchen and bathrooms have the kind of detailing typical of the end of the 1800s. It's details like these that give a house its personality, telling you a lot about what's important to the people who live there.

When you design a starter house with future remodeling in mind, you can initially keep detailing and its associated costs to a minimum, while children are young and elegant surfaces are in danger of being damaged. A decade later, when the kids have outgrown the desire to color on the wallpaper and you're ready to remodel, there's usually more money available to personalize the house. In the meantime, collecting design and decorating ideas is an excellent way to keep the vision of your dream house alive and well. And the result, like the Katzes' home, will be a truly delightful, eminently comfortable, and better-than-ever Not So Big House.

Just because a house is new doesn't mean it has to use today's standard moldings.

ABOVE Just because a house is new doesn't mean it has to look it. Here, everything from the floor tile and high wainscoting to the faucets and built-in medicine cabinets has been lovingly detailed to look like a bathroom from an earlier era. In its earlier incarnation, the finishes in this room were standard 1980s fare.

Tight Quarters

THE IDEA OF BUILDING SMALLER
and better houses strikes a chord with people in many parts of
the country because they recognize that just having a lot of space
doesn't necessarily make a place feel like home. But in a large city
like New York, the issues are a little different. Here, almost everyone lives in a space that's tiny and cramped, and you don't consciously decide to build small—the decision is made for you. The
idea of building Not So Big is a perfect fit for city spaces. As architect Josh Heitler, owner of a 560-sq.-ft. co-op apartment in
East Soho, puts it, "You're always up against the challenge of a
limited amount of space, so you're always looking for tricks to
make something look and feel bigger."

*When you focus on ideas per square foot rather
than on dollars per square foot, you find you can
live more comfortably in less space.*

ABOVE This apartment is located in an old
tenement building built in the 1860s. The two
windows farthest to the right on the third floor
open into the living room.

OPPOSITE One of the apartment's main features is the long, unobstructed view from one
end to the other, drawing daylight from the two
ends toward the middle. When you can see
daylight at the end of a hallway, the space
becomes far more appealing and vital.

RIGHT An old medical-office cabinet stripped of its original paint provides additional storage space in the kitchen. Using a stand-alone piece rather than built-in cabinetry keeps the old brick wall uncluttered, thus adding a feeling of spaciousness.

BELOW In older apartments there are often challenges to work around, such as the plumbing stacks for the building, which run up through the thick wall between the dresser and the bed. A gas meter adjacent to the window is cleverly disguised behind a hanging mirror that can be moved aside when the meter reader calls.

When Josh purchased the apartment in the summer of 1997, it was in a sad state of repair. The space was dark, with a tiny bathroom and kitchen monopolizing the two windows at one end of the 50-ft.-long space. The floor was covered with layer upon layer of carpet and linoleum, the edges peeling up to expose the old flooring below. When Josh invited his mother to come and see his new home, she burst into tears. Clearly this was not the future she'd had in mind for her son.

When a space looks this inhospitable, it takes some imagination to see its potential. But Josh had just completed his architectural training and had done his thesis on adaptive reuse, which is all about making older buildings serve new functions in innovative ways. His new residence gave him the opportunity to test some of his theories.

Down to the Bare Bones

The first step was to gut the place. Everything was stripped down to the studs and the original floor boards. The floor had a noticeable slope from side to side, so Josh decided to level it out with a new 2x4 floor-joist system set on top of the existing surface. He liked the character of the old structure, though, so he decided to leave at least one area with both the floor boards and ceiling joists exposed. He also liked the texture of the brick wall that ran the length of the apartment and opted to leave this as it was, making it a key feature of the new design.

If you move from a small area into a larger area, you subconsciously compare the two and feel the relative spaciousness of the larger one.

To make the most of the four existing windows for the primary living spaces, Josh wanted to relocate the kitchen and bathroom to the middle of the apartment. However, when you're redesigning within the confines of an apartment block, you have to tie into the existing vertical plumbing runs and vent stacks, which limit your options for relocation. Josh figured he could run the new pipes underneath the slightly raised floor he'd planned, but the toilet was a major limiting factor. It had to have sufficient slope to the main vertical sewer pipe and to the vent stack. So the first floor-plan decision, and one that dictated the layout of much of the rest of the apartment, was the location of the toilet. Once this was determined, everything else fell into place.

Extending the View

If Josh hadn't made the effort to place the rooms needing less natural light in the narrow middle section of the apartment, the overall design would have been far less inviting. Locating the two main rooms at either end of the space and allowing the full extent of the long brick wall to be visible throughout the apartment creates the impression that the space is much larger than it actually is. When you can see a full 50 ft. of unobstructed view, your mind tells you this is a big space, even when it's only 10 ft. wide.

Architect:
Lacina Group, Architects
Builder:
Josh Heitler and JK Remodeling
Size: 560 sq. ft.
Location:
New York, N.Y.

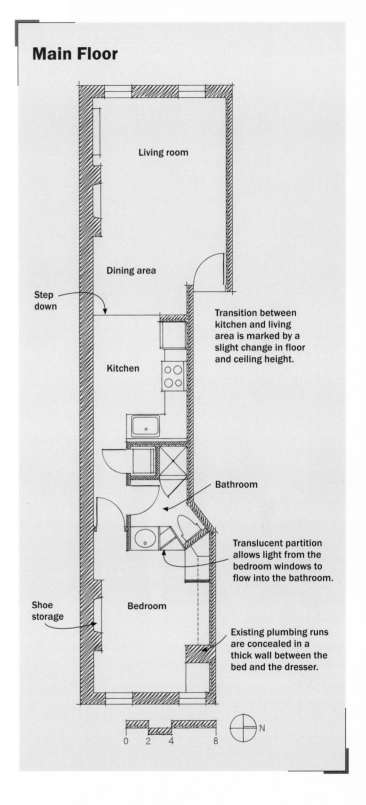

Main Floor

Living room

Dining area

Step down

Kitchen

Transition between kitchen and living area is marked by a slight change in floor and ceiling height.

Bathroom

Translucent partition allows light from the bedroom windows to flow into the bathroom.

Shoe storage

Bedroom

Existing plumbing runs are concealed in a thick wall between the bed and the dresser.

0   2   4   8

N

RIGHT The mirror above the sink stands in for the window you'd typically find in this location; its reflection provides a view of the living-room windows. Mirrors can be used creatively like this to bring daylight into areas that would otherwise be dark or far from outdoor views.

Up Close

Because the fireplace in the bedroom no longer works, it has been put to new use as a place to store shoes. When you are designing Not So Big, any nook or cranny—whatever its original purpose—is fair game for creative reuse.

The layout also breaks the apartment into three distinct zones. The narrower center zone is more compressed, while the larger rooms at either end create a sense of release. This is a technique that architects use frequently to increase the sense of size. If you move from a small area into a larger area, you subconsciously compare the two and feel the relative spaciousness of the larger one. When this is combined with a change in floor or ceiling height, the experience is further enhanced. Even though the difference in height between the kitchen and the living room is only a matter of a few inches, perceptually the effect is dramatic, and the 12-ft. by 14-ft. living room seems significantly larger as a result.

Weaving Old and New

When space and natural light are restricted, it's critical to give the interiors some vitality. You can do this with expensive materials and special details, but when money is limited, you have to be more creative. Josh's research into adaptive reuse had brought

home the fact that if you can lay bare some of the original building materials, they add a character and quality that new construction simply doesn't possess—and they're essentially free, because they're already in place. Still, some new construction was obviously going to be needed to accommodate the practical necessities, such as cooking, bathing, and storage. So Josh combined the old with the new, keeping the design spare to create a contemporary look and keep costs to a minimum.

Rather than attempt to make the old materials look new or the new materials match the character of the old, the two stand in distinct contrast to one another, giving the apartment a more animated spirit than if it were composed of either one alone. The kitchen, for example, has a smooth white ceiling and tile floor—all new materials—while the living room shows off the original joists and floor boards, which gives that space a very different quality and visual weight. It's more rustic, more textured, and it allows you to experience the full breadth of the space—from one side to the other and right up to the rafters. This is another trick used by architects and designers to make a small space feel bigger. As Josh describes it, "If there's a place where you can see the measure of the whole space, it can make an enormous difference and greatly increase the sense of scale."

LEFT **Even the area over the bed has been used to provide extra storage. This shelf has standard under-cabinet lights—the kind you'd normally find in a kitchen—attached to the bottom, which serve as reading lights.**

BELOW **Suspending the bookshelves from the wall leaves the floor area of the living room fully visible, making it appear larger. Limiting the amount of furniture and placing the television on a rollaway cart helps this small room feel ample rather than cramped.**

Dining in the Big Apple

In New York, space is at enough of a premium that many apartments have no eating area at all. The living room often serves as the dining room as well, with plates set on the coffee table or perched on laps. Another common solution in a tiny living space is to have an equally tiny table set in the kitchen, with just enough room to get to the refrigerator and stove. Josh didn't like either of these alternatives, so he did something that might initially seem to be a waste of space. Instead of extending the kitchen cabinetry all the way to the end of the wall, he held it back a couple of feet. Then he placed the dining table along the long brick wall, just beyond the break between the kitchen and living room, and thus a few inches lower than the kitchen.

There was in fact just enough room for the table in the kitchen, but moving it into the living room like this gives it quite a different personality. Its separation from other activity areas is accentuated by the step down from the kitchen and the drywall enclosure around the living-room fireplace. The composition of this tiny dining area shows how little is required to create a sense of shelter around activity. Take away its boundaries, and it's just a table in a hallway.

ABOVE **The dining area is defined on the left by the change in floor and ceiling height from the adjacent kitchen area and on the right by the enclosure for the fireplace. The pool of light created by the hanging lamp further accentuates the sense that this is a separate place, with its own distinct personality.**

Through the Looking Glass

Although there are no windows in the middle zone of the house, there's still plenty of natural light. Josh used mirrors and interior windows to borrow light for areas that would otherwise be dark and unwelcoming. In the kitchen, instead of the typical window above the sink, he placed a mirror that reflects the windows at the end of the living room. He can still see outside, even though his back is turned to the exterior wall.

Instead of building a standard, solid wall between the bedroom and the bathroom, Josh installed a translucent membrane that allows light from the bedroom windows to flood the bathroom as well. The mirror above the bathroom sink has a matching mirror on the bedroom side, which reflects additional light into the bedroom.

That such a long, thin space should seem so light filled and airy is a testament to the inventiveness of its architect. To have accomplished this on a shoestring budget is even more impressive. When you look at this truly tiny living space and see all the amenities it provides, it's easy to see that what our homes are really lacking isn't space, it's inventiveness. When you focus on ideas per square foot rather than on dollars per square foot, you find you can live more comfortably in less space.

BELOW Because access to daylight is so limited in this long, narrow space, the bathroom wall is made of Plexiglas rather than studs and wallboard, which allows natural light to flood in. The etched look was accomplished by hand-sanding the surface—a labor-intensive process but much less expensive than buying etched glass.

LEFT The bedroom side of the translucent wall is cleverly composed to offer a tiny built-in bedside table. Every inch of extra space has been used for storage. Surrounding the bed alcove are cubbies for clothes, shoes, and a few hanging items.

Southern Comfort

A QUESTION I HEARD OFTEN AFTER
The Not So Big House came out was, "Can I build a traditional-style
house with a Not So Big floor plan?" The answer is an unequivo-
cal yes. Not So Big concepts can be interpreted in any style. And
to prove it, here are examples from Habersham and Newpoint,
two planned communities near Beaufort, South Carolina, with
details based on the best of the past but
with updated floor plans for the way we
live today.

Eric Moser, who has designed many of
the houses for these two New Urbanist
developments, loved the look of the traditional houses of the past even as a boy,
but he always wondered how people
could live in them. They didn't seem to fit
their residents' lifestyles, with all the
socializing taking place in the kitchen while the formal front
rooms sat vacant. In true Not So Big style, two of Moser's design
hallmarks are making the kitchen the heart of the home and
eliminating the unused formal spaces in order to make money
available for special details.

*The main floor layout is
hardly what you'd expect
to find in a house with
such a traditional exterior.*

ABOVE **Many people are captivated by
the look of older homes, with their
simple gabled roofs and gracious front
porches, but their interiors are often ill-
suited to present-day lifestyles. A growing number of planned communities
around the country, like Habersham in
Beaufort, South Carolina, are filling the
void, with exteriors that hark back to
an earlier time and interiors designed
for today.**

OPPOSITE **The wraparound porch is a
wonderful extension of living space
that's relatively inexpensive to build. It
has the added advantage of making the
house appear significantly larger than it
really is.**

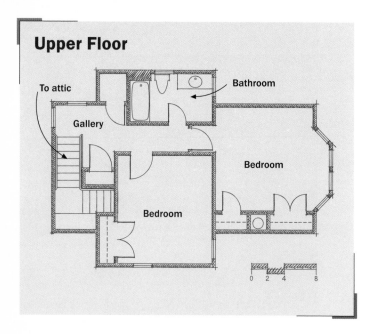

Upper Floor

To attic

Gallery

Bathroom

Bedroom

Bedroom

0 2 4 8

If you look at the plan for this home, which was built first in Newpoint and then in Habersham (the house interior shown here), you'll see that the kitchen is centrally located and open to both dining and living areas. An away room opens off the front entry and looks into the living room through double doors. It's hardly the kind of main-floor layout you'd expect to find in a house with such a traditional exterior. But as Eric points out, "Just because you're manipulating the interior spaces doesn't mean you have to give up all the character of these traditional homes."

Modifying an Old Plan

Eric broke with the pattern of the standard floor plan, where each activity has a defined room, usually rectangular or square, and where doors or archways connect one room to the next. By removing the walls between spaces—especially those between the kitchen, living room, and dining area—and by adding wide openings to create long, diagonal views, he made the design work for today's more informal lifestyles. In general, when a space can be seen, it is used. When it can't be seen, it sits dormant.

Main Floor

Laundry

Master bathroom

Dining area

Walk-in closet

Kitchen

Living room

Master bedroom

Entry

Front porch

Away room

N

0 2 4 8

Hallway separates master-bedroom suite from living area.

Centrally located kitchen opens to dining and living areas.

Designer:
Moser Design Group, Inc.

Builder:
Southern Traditional Custom Homes

Size: 2,100 sq. ft.

Location:
Beaufort, S.C.

A hundred years ago, the owners of a house would no more socialize in the kitchen than we would today in our laundry rooms. It was a workspace, the realm of the wife and (if she was lucky) the servants. The kitchen didn't need to have views to other spaces—in fact, it was specifically designed *not* to be seen. But today our lives revolve around the kitchen, and this is where we congregate. If we can't see any other living spaces from here, we tend to crowd into this utilitarian room, while the rest of the house—where we've spent most of our decorating budget—sits unused.

Details Make the Difference

So what gives this updated southern belle her traditional character? It's all in the scale and style of the details. Look at the two columns that mark the entrance from the entry to the living room, for example (see the top photo on p. 326). They're 14 in. square, much larger than required structurally. But their width makes room for some classic panel detailing that is evocative of a much older home. The crown moldings, door and window casings, and baseboards are also much larger than is typical in a new house today. Certainly these special features add dollars per square foot, but when compared to the savings generated by the elimination of entire rooms, the cost is minor. This was not an expensive home to build, and every-

ABOVE The kitchen is centrally located and opens to both the dining and living areas. The raised countertop serves to hide a messy work surface, but there's no visual separation between cook and company either during meal preparation or cleanup.

LEFT This home's interior detailing is characteristic of its 100-year-old relatives, but the plan is based on Not So Big principles. The away room, visible through the double doors, is close to the front door and can be used as a quiet retreat space, an in-home office, a guest bedroom, or a combination of all three.

where money has been used wisely, making an otherwise standard set of parts into an expression of old-world charm.

Imagine this same interior without these special details. The two columns could have been 4 in. square and sheathed with drywall. The ceilings could have been spray-textured, with no crown moldings to mark the division between walls and ceiling. The openings into the kitchen could have been walled over. And the result? A standard, unadorned developer house.

It really doesn't take a lot to give a house some character, but someone *does* have to design for it, draw it into the blueprints, and make sure it gets built properly. If detailing like this is done sloppily, it can look worse than if it weren't there at all. Although it's important to spend a budget sensibly, this doesn't always mean that you should necessarily select the low bidder. Craftsmanship counts when it comes to building Not So Big, and though it will cost more, it's an investment you'll rejoice in every day.

ABOVE Columns like these are a rarity in new homes today and are generally considered a possibility only in a very expensive home. But when the square footage is kept to a reasonable minimum, there's money available for the kinds of special features that add a timeless quality to an otherwise simple structure.

RIGHT The master-bedroom suite is on the main level but separated by a hallway from the everyday living spaces, giving it plenty of acoustical privacy. The stairway's painted risers and natural treads, with three spindles per tread, give it a classic look.

Furnishing for Comfort

A real challenge when building a period-style home with the kind of floor plan and detailing illustrated here is to resist the urge to decorate with chairs and sofas from that same era. There's only one thing that can sabotage the livability of a Not So Big House, and that's not so comfortable furniture. Fill a room with furnishings designed for looks but not human bodies, and you'll still find yourself leaning on the counter in the kitchen.

This can be a real dilemma for people who've inherited heirloom pieces or spent a

New Urbanism and Traditional Neighborhood Design

*F*or the last few decades, housing developments have focused on expedient construction and automotive convenience rather than on the resulting quality of the neighborhood and community. Trees are stripped from the site, houses are isolated from one another as lots get bigger, and you need a car just to go to the corner store. Front porches have disappeared because there's no pedestrian activity on the streets to watch or share with neighbors, and even the picket fence has been regulated out of existence by well-meaning but misguided development covenants.

Given this state of affairs, it's hardly surprising that there's a nostalgia for a simpler time, when neighbors looked out for one another, lots had mature trees, and streets were just wide enough for two cars to pass.

A movement is taking place across the country to rehumanize the process of residential development. It's known both as New Urbanism and Traditional Neighborhood Design (TND). This concept may be familiar to readers who saw the movie *The Truman Show*, which was filmed at Seaside, Florida, one of the first and best-known new urban communities.

Just as with the Not So Big House, TND emphasizes quality over quantity. Streets have sidewalks, lots are smaller, and the focus on community is brought back by preserving existing landscape features (especially large trees), building front porches, and using carefully proportioned and well-crafted details. Newpoint has been in existence for only six years, but it looks as though it's been around for centuries. And Habersham, which was

started just two years ago, promises to have this same timeless quality. In our search for home, there's a lot we can learn from the TND movement.

lot of money in the past on furniture for a large, formal house. One strategy is to locate prize pieces in an out-of-the-way corner where they can be admired without monopolizing a primary living space, as has been done here with the very pretty but not particularly inviting wooden love seat next to the French door (see the photo on p. 328). Meanwhile the furniture in the living room has an overstuffed comfort that, though not something you'd find in an antiques magazine, invites you to stretch out and settle in. It's an unfortunate reality that much of what we consider stylish today inhibits the very living we long to do in our homes.

There's only one thing that can sabotage the livability of a Not So Big House, and that's not so comfortable furniture.

ABOVE Ceilings throughout the main level are 9 ft. tall, and moldings are ornate and substantial, in keeping with the proportions of an older home. But instead of traditional rooms, here spaces flow from one to the next without doors and dividing walls to define them—a more contemporary approach to interior design.

A Change of Face

Another lesson that can be learned from this house is just how different an exterior can look with variations in its detailing. This same basic house has been built several times in the communities of Habersham and Newpoint. Though the plans are essentially identical, the finishing details are quite different.

Looking at the front elevations of two of the homes, you can see that both have a wraparound porch on the main level that looks both gracious and welcoming. But the version built in Newpoint (top right) has significantly more gingerbread decorating its surfaces. It also has a steeper pitch to the main roof and an additional balcony on the second floor. The closely spaced porch columns with their connecting brackets make this house seem more introverted than its less-decorated sister. It feels more private, as though in stepping onto this porch you move behind a veil. By contrast, the Habersham house (bottom right) has a more open demeanor.

It's not uncommon for people to reject a plan because they don't like the house "face," when in fact this is very easily altered. Just like the interior, it's the details—the slope of the roof, the special moldings, the width of the trimwork, and the proportions of each element in relation to one another—that give a house much of its character. When arranged with an eye for composition, learning from the past but designing for today, the options for variety and personal expression are almost infinite.

Although I don't advocate a retreat into the past, there's much we have forgotten about how to make a house look and feel like home. We can learn by looking and listening to our senses and, in so doing, rediscover those things we miss while eliminating those that no longer work today. Communities like Newpoint and Habersham, and houses like this one, are a major step in that direction.

ABOVE These two houses have the same house plan as the house featured in this chapter but with different clothing. What makes them appear so different is the detailing. If you count the columns on the porches of both houses, for example, you'll see that the one in Newpoint (top) has a different visual rhythm from its sister in Habersham (bottom). The location of the steps up to the wraparound porch in Habersham invites you into this house, while their central positioning in Newpoint, surprisingly, makes the entrance a more private affair. This is because when you arrive at the former you are aligned with the front door, while the latter delivers you to a living-room window.

An Accessible House for One

OPPOSITE The bathroom has been designed with plenty of room for a wheelchair to turn around, but the room doesn't have an institutional feel. The goal throughout the house was to integrate accessible design features in an unobtrusive way.

LEFT Designed as a quiet retreat with a Not So Big budget, this cabin quickly became a year-round home. The construction materials are off the shelf and inexpensive—4x8 sheets of Hardipanel, concrete blocks, and standard asphalt shingles—but artful design makes the whole more than the sum of its parts.

W HEN YOU'RE DESIGNING A NOT SO Big House, it's important to think not only about your present lifestyle but also about your future needs. For example, a far-sighted couple designing a house for their young family might want to allow for a future bedroom on the main level for when they are older. The reality is that we all age, and if we build for a lifetime, we have to keep future needs in mind.

In recent years, there's been much written about universal design, inclusive design, and life-span design. These are all names for the same intent: to design products and environments for the widest possible variety of people. Although in public buildings it's important to make such accommodations from the outset, in residences, design solutions can be more specific to the individual's personal needs and can be modified over time as those needs become clear. The difficulty comes in determining

By designing an open plan and building in only the most crucial elements from the beginning, you can create a house that will be easy to remodel as needs change.

ABOVE **Each French door has a canopy and opens out onto a narrow deck with a cable railing that doesn't obstruct the view.**
(PHOTO COURTESY PRENTISS ARCHITECTS.)

just how much to build in from the start and how much to leave for remodeling when the day comes.

Sometimes life throws us an unexpected curve ball, and there's no way of anticipating what needs we'll have even a year or two down the road. This was the case for the owner of the home shown here. She had been diagnosed with multiple sclerosis, and her doctor suggested that she could benefit from having a stress-free environment in a natural setting to get away to now and then.

The owner approached architect Geoff Prentiss, who found her a secluded piece of property on Orcas Island surrounded by marsh and trees, which perfectly met her needs. The house he designed for her there, which started out as a place of retreat to be used primarily for day trips from her home in Seattle, is very simple: a long gabled structure with just one main room, a bathroom, and a closet.

What was originally intended for daytime use quickly became a year-round home, as the owner discovered the restorative quality of the site. Although the amenities are minimal and the plan is rendered down to its simplest components, it serves her needs and feeds her spirit. It is an excellent demonstration of the fact that for many of us, it's the quality of a place, far more than the specifics of a floor plan, that makes a house a home.

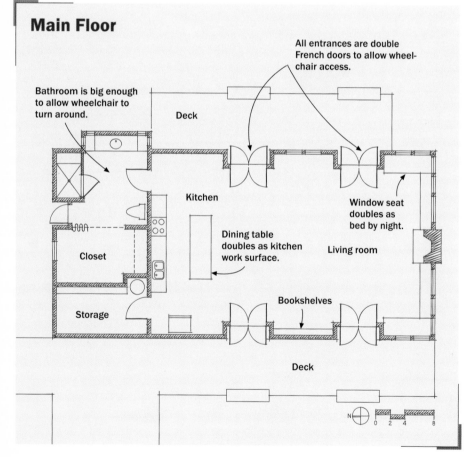

Main Floor

All entrances are double French doors to allow wheelchair access.

Bathroom is big enough to allow wheelchair to turn around.

Deck

Kitchen

Window seat doubles as bed by night.

Dining table doubles as kitchen work surface.

Living room

Closet

Storage

Bookshelves

Deck

N 0 2 4 8

Architect:
Prentiss Architects, Inc.
Builder:
Ravenhill Construction
Size: 1,215 sq. ft.
Location:
Orcas Island, Wash.

Getting Around

Although the owner was fully mobile during the design process, she needed to plan for an uncertain future, which included the strong possibility of her eventually needing a wheelchair to get around. She didn't want the house to look like it was built for a wheelchair, however, and Geoff made that a primary design objective. As a result, you'd never guess that this house was designed for someone with impaired mobility.

One of the most difficult issues to address when it comes to accessibility is how much to anticipate in the design process. For some, the most functional solution once the wheelchair is a full-time necessity may not be aesthetically or practically acceptable until then. By designing an open plan and building in only the most crucial elements from the beginning, you can create a house that will be easy to remodel as needs change.

This is an important consideration for those who want to design their homes to allow for the possibility of future mobility issues. It's possible to spend a lot of money on universal-design features that may not ultimately be useful, while other unanticipated features become a must. My suggestion to clients contemplating this issue is to make the walls and doors work for wheelchair accessibility, and accept that if mobility becomes an issue, some remodeling

ABOVE **For accessibility, the house is primarily one large room with an attached bathroom and closet. Four sets of French doors open wide to connect inside with out. Kitchen, dining, and living areas are all housed under the long gable roof.**

It's the quality of a place, far more than the specifics of a floor plan, that makes a house a home.

ABOVE The dining-room table doubles as a kitchen work surface and, as in an old farmhouse kitchen, is flexible enough to accommodate all sorts of tasks, from eating to creating art projects to paying bills. The kitchen counter itself is set 4 in. lower than normal to allow easy access for the owner, who may someday be dependent upon a wheelchair to get around.

RIGHT Doorways are wide, and the shower stall has no lip to trip over or roll over in a wheelchair. Although this makes the shower a little less convenient for someone without impaired mobility, if a wheelchair is a likely eventuality, there'll be no major remodeling required when it happens.

OPPOSITE The birch plywood ceiling gives a golden glow to the light as it bounces around this room. When that effect is combined with the many windows, contrasting walls, and radiant concrete floor, the room has a warmth to it, despite the hardness of the surfaces. In the Pacific Northwest, making the most of the diffuse daylight is crucial, since sunny days are rare in the winter and spring.

will be needed. You can then tailor that remodeling to suit the particular disability rather than a generic standard.

This is the strategy that Geoff employed. All the entrances into the house are double French doors, specially designed to be opened with one hand. The extra width allows for a wheelchair to move through with ease, without the oversized look that comes with extrawide single doors.

The kitchen counters are not open below, as they typically would be in universal design, but they are only 32 in. high, 4 in. lower than a standard countertop. This height allows comfortable access from either a standing or a sitting position. The dining table, which is of course open below, also doubles as a kitchen work surface. And the bathroom is designed with plenty of room for a wheelchair to circulate, complete with lipless shower and strategically located grab bars.

Alcoves Make the Room

In many ways, this small house is like one spacious great room. But there are some apparently insignificant details that make it far more livable than most such rooms. If you look at the floor plan, you'll see that the main rectangle of the room has a number of small alcoves added, which house window seats, bookshelves, and places for freestanding furniture.

Now, if you look at the photos of the space, you can see that the ceiling is brought down over these areas, defining each as its own space and creating shelter around each activity, a fundamental strategy in making Not So Big work. It's such a simple gesture, yet without it the room would feel very different.

Beneath the window seats that flank the fireplace, open shelves store everything from blankets to books to briefcases. The vertical dividers between shelves are finished with madrona branches from the neighboring woods. Introducing a natural element from the site lends a spirit and uniqueness often missing in contemporary homes.

BELOW The main room has some subtleties of design that make it work better for everyday living than the typical great room. Along both side walls, small alcoves create places for a variety of activities and functions, like this small library nook.

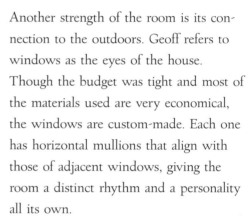

Try this with the photo on p. 335: Imagine the French doors to the outside being pushed out to align with the windows on either side. And then bring the sloping roof down to the outside wall. Suddenly, there's no differentiation of spaces and no more alcoves. The room is bigger by a few square feet, but the number of comfortable places has actually decreased and the character of the room has diminished.

Window Patterns

Another strength of the room is its connection to the outdoors. Geoff refers to windows as the eyes of the house. Though the budget was tight and most of the materials used are very economical, the windows are custom-made. Each one has horizontal mullions that align with those of adjacent windows, giving the room a distinct rhythm and a personality all its own.

The tall windows flanking the fireplace serve an important role. First, they bring the room into proportion. Had these windows been the same size as their neighbors, the end wall of the house would have seemed top heavy and the room less humanly scaled and less comfortable. Place your thumb over the upper window in the photo on p. 335 to see what I mean.

But also these windows almost look like eyes. Remember how, as a child, you'd see faces in the forms of clouds,

rocks, and tree branches? As adults we still have this reflex, but most of us are not as consciously aware of it. Still, it has an influence on how we feel about a place. A house or room with a friendly "face" tends to make us feel more warmly toward it. One without such a harmonious composition can make us feel uncomfortable, without our knowing why. This effect, which we recognize easily in a two-dimensional surface like a painting, is just as important—if not as apparent—when you are working in a three-dimensional space.

A great lesson of this house is that when we design a place that we think of as a cabin retreat rather than a year-round house, we allow ourselves to accommodate our needs in innovative ways. The results typically require less space and often fit our real lifestyle better than a conventional house. This spirit of innovation gets to the heart of building Not So Big. For those trying to plan for a less mobile future, the attitudes embodied in this house are based on practicality, but they are life affirming rather than life diminishing. If we surround ourselves with images of the depletion that's ahead of us, we're likely to reflect that attitude in how we live. But if we surround ourselves with the warmth of forms and colors we love, we are likely to live much more fully. By building Not So Big, there's money available to add some special features to accommodate mobility needs and still make a home that's beautiful and filled with places of inspiration.

Double-Duty Window Seats

Where do you sleep in a house without bedrooms? If you're living alone, wherever you like. The owner of this house had originally planned to buy a sleigh bed, but she liked the window seats so much that she decided to use one as her bed at night. Just a pane of glass away from the outdoors, it's more like a sleeping porch than an interior room.

As in a Japanese house, where futons are rolled out for sleeping and put away during the day, the room changes use from day to night, rather than requiring the owner to move to a different part of the house. This can work well for one person, although it may be less acceptable for couples or families. Still, it illustrates how a single space can be made to do double duty in unconventional ways that are particularly suited to the occupant's preferences. Just because something is unusual doesn't mean you shouldn't do it.

Elegant Simplicity

ABOVE Designed to fit into a neighborhood of 19th-century Quaker summer cottages, the simple form of this home belies its beauty and strength. A house doesn't have to be complex to have impact.

OPPOSITE When the entry door and the French doors across the living room are open, there's excellent cross-ventilation, making air-conditioning unnecessary. The view through beckons you out to the water side of the house.

THE SUMMER HOME DESIGNED BY architect Jim Estes for a retired couple in Jamestown, Rhode Island, is a study in simplicity. Created with an unerring eye for proportion and a careful execution of classic details, this house captivates anyone who enters it. It gracefully illustrates how beauty can be the result of economy of means and how a plan does not have to be complex to have impact.

When Marion and Bill originally approached their architect, they were envisioning a much larger house—a place with plenty of room for visiting children and grandchildren. But after the first round of design work with Jim, they realized that what they really wanted was a place with a more intimate scale—a place that the two of them could enjoy together. A large, rambling house can be great for family reunions, but it's often overwhelming for day-to-day living. Here, visitors would be welcomed, but they would not be made the focus of the design.

There's nothing flamboyant about this house, yet it is masterful in its understated presence.

339

It is often the simplicity of a plan that gives the resulting home its charm. The key is in the third dimension.

Whether to size a house for yourself or for your extended family is a common dilemma. In an effort to accommodate everyone, houses can get very large, when in fact the people who live there every day need very little space to feel at home. Jim solved the problem by designing an open floor plan with a main living area that can serve comfortably for a couple or a crowd. This allows the house to be considerably smaller yet actually work better for both purposes.

Main Floor

The fireplace is centered under the ridge beam, reinforcing the symmetry of the floor plan.

Master bedroom

Porch

The dining area is tucked in an alcove off the living room.

Living room

Bedroom

Garage

Entry

Pocket doors allow the kitchen to be closed off from the dining area.

0 4 8 16

N

Architect:
Estes/Twombly Architects, Inc.
Builder: Allan Randall, Construction
Size: 1,800 sq. ft.
Location: Jamestown, R.I.

A Simple Plan

Marion and Bill wanted the house to fit unobtrusively into its neighborhood, a 19th-century Quaker summer colony near Jamestown. Many of the homes have strong, simple forms, with symmetrical exteriors and wide porches facing the water. Jim suggested a straightforward plan based on what he calls "bilateral symmetry." This means that the house is organized around a central axis, which in this case bisects the fireplace. The floor plan is essentially symmetrical on either side of this axis, with segments of space carved out under the broad sheltering roof.

RIGHT **Although this room has a high cathedral ceiling, it is not overwhelming when only one or two people are using it, as so many great rooms are today. The exposed rafters and the pattern of woodwork above the fireplace break up the scale of the room and add a texture reminiscent of houses of the past.**

The kitchen is small, with pocket doors that allow it to be completely separated from the dining area on formal occasions and open when only family or friends are present. As might be expected, the doors are almost always open.

A mistake often made in houses today is that every ceiling is the same height, leaving no way to differentiate between spaces.

Many homeowners want a plan with more complexity, which automatically adds to the cost, since every angle and curve has construction ramifications. Marion and Bill were unusual in accepting a plan that, on paper at least, looked undistinguished. But as Jim admirably demonstrates, it is often the simplicity of a plan that gives the resulting home its charm. The key is in the third dimension.

The living room is at the heart of this plan and acts as a focus for activity, with dining area and stairway alcoves opening onto it. With its high ceiling, the room could easily have become sterile and overwhelming. But here—with the ridge centered above the fireplace, the beams and rafters exposed, and the height variations introduced in the alcoves—the result is an ample gathering space for friends and family that's just as comfortable for two.

Say It with Contrast

A mistake often made in houses today is that every ceiling is the same height, leaving no way to differentiate between spaces. This house works because of the contrasts, both in ceiling height and in the exposed structure. Take away the beams and rafters, and make the dining area the same height as the rest of the living room, and you have your typical, palatially proportioned drywalled barn— hardly the place you'd want to curl up with a good book. It doesn't take a lot to bring a space down to human scale. In this house, the shape and size of the dining area help do the trick. The roof here runs perpendicular to the main roof, which helps give the vaulting heights of the living room a more manageable and intelligible dimension. It's almost as if this sloped ceiling slows down the space, and brings it to a gentle halt. This is mirrored on a smaller scale in the kitchen ceiling, which opens off the dining area.

LEFT There is a clear hierarchy of activity areas in this house, and their importance is defined by the ceiling height. The dining area is attached to the living room like a lean-to, with its ceiling descending to only 7 ft. at the far windows. The room becomes an inviting alcove off the living room, subordinate in both floor area and ceiling height.

Up Close

Shutters on most modern houses are merely decorative, but on this house they really work and

are closed in the winter months, when the house is largely unused. Because they are sized to fit the windows, the proportions look right.

The textural quality created by the beams and rafters is also important in creating a comfortable scale. In conventional stud-frame construction, we cover the rafters and fill the space with insulation. Here, Jim put the insulation above the rafters and roof sheathing, to get the look and feel of an old summer cottage. When our eye receives visual information that allows us to interpret scale, we often feel more secure. Subconsciously, we know how much distance there is between one rafter and the next. We see the pattern of shadow and light made by the sequence of rafters. And together these visual cues add up to a place that feels like home.

Grandmother's House

Many Not So Big Houses draw their inspiration from houses of the past. An archetypal image of home that we carry in our minds is what I like to call "grandmother's house," an assemblage of images composed of memories from childhood—perhaps a special window seat in the kitchen, a cozy fireplace, or a wonderful porch swing. Parts of this composite home may also be drawn from images we remember from cherished childhood fairy tales and paintings, like Carl Larsson's images of idyllic Scandinavian home life.

It's often the easy comfort of a grandmother's house that encourages children and grandchildren to visit; the closer a house is to the archetype, the more at home they feel and the more they want to return. The simple home shown here embodies many of the necessary characteristics, including generous porches, window shutters, exposed rafters, and a classic cottage form. It's very helpful to keep this archetype in mind when you're planning a Not So Big House, which is by its nature a smaller, cozier home.

This gracious porch, sheltered by a wide overhanging roof, is a perfect width for enjoying the natural surroundings—even when it's raining. Any wider and the proportions wouldn't feel right for the house.

Getting It Right

Because the house was designed primarily for summer living, the porch was a key area. The main living spaces open onto it, and the long views through the house to the porch beckon you to sit quietly and gaze at the water. At 8 ft. wide, the porch is the perfect size for sitting. Make it much wider, and you start to feel too far away from the surrounding landscape. Make it much narrower, and it's difficult for people to get by.

During the winter months, when the house is largely unused, the heat is turned down to around 40°F and the window shutters are closed for the season. Shutters today are typically used as a decorative motif, but we forget that they used to serve a real function—and, as in this house, sometimes still do. One of the most satisfying aspects of the exterior of this house is the size of the shutters. They really do cover the windows when they're closed. So when they're open, they look right. We instinctively respond to good proportions, even if we don't always know why.

All told, there's nothing flamboyant about this house, yet it is masterful in its understated presence. Beauty arises not from cleverness so much as from care, from taking time to scale each element appropriately in relation to the next, and from paring down to the essentials: simplicity and elegance. It sounds deceptively easy, but the art is in knowing how we respond to space and light. Proportion is key, as this house illustrates so well.

ABOVE The master bedroom is just off the porch, and its alignment takes full advantage of the landscape. Its doorway acts as a wonderful picture frame, setting off the view down the length of the porch and inviting you to come out and enjoy the sunrise. It speaks of peacefulness and relaxation.

LEFT Daylight pours down the staircase and into the living room below. The stair is designed as an alcove of sorts—almost a room in its own right. The upper landing that leads to the guest bedroom creates a hallway with a low ceiling on the floor below. It's largely the contrasts in ceiling height that make this house so appealing.

A Not So Big Remodel

ABOVE From the back of the house, you can see the flat-roofed section that connects the old house with the new addition. Just visible to the left is the backdrop of Long Island Sound, one of the main reasons the owners chose to remodel rather than move.

DREAMING OF A NEW NOT SO BIG House is all well and good, but for many people the money for such a major undertaking simply isn't available. Adding on or remodeling, however, is often an option, and when accomplished with restraint, it can transform the living environment at an affordable price.

The owners of this house bought their early 1980s rambler because it had wonderful views of Long Island Sound. The house itself was less than wonderful, however, with many of the problems typical of the small, undistinguished ramblers that fill postwar suburbs around the country. It was built from a standard floor plan and designed for a flat lot, but their lot was anything but flat, with a steep slope down toward the Sound. To accommodate the site, the house had been built with a basement and tuck-under garage. But the original builder hadn't stopped to figure out how to get guests and family members up to the main level—where the entry would have been if the house were on a flat lot. It was, for all intents and purposes, a house without a front or back door.

> *If you can minimize the added square footage and change only the necessities, it's usually less expensive to remodel.*

OPPOSITE The new front door is located beneath the main-level deck, adjacent to the garage at left. Most entries bring you into the house at the main level, where the living spaces are, so if you have a lower-level entry, it's important to send guests a clear message that this is indeed the one they should use. The new addition helps give this entry a main-level feel.

ABOVE **This 1980s rambler with a tuck-under garage presented some interesting remodeling challenges. The main entry was the three-panel sliding door, just visible on the left of this photo, presenting a wide-open view into the main living space of the house—not a pleasant greeting for either visitor or homeowner.** (PHOTO COURTESY CENTERBROOK ARCHITECTS.)

RIGHT **A new addition accommodates a master bedroom suite, with office space and an entry below. The deck has been widened slightly to make it work better for sitting and socializing, but the rest of the exterior remains the same—except for a fresh coat of paint and a warmer color scheme.** (PHOTO COPYRIGHT JOHN WOODRUFF, WOODRUFF AND BROWN PHOTOGRAPHY.)

The makeshift entry for the family was via a spiral staircase from the garage, winding up into a drafty sunroom off the living room. The space was very tight, making it difficult to bring in groceries, let alone anything larger. Guests had an even stranger entry experience. From the driveway, there was a beautifully landscaped path leading up the hill to what all indications suggested must be the front door. But at the top of the path, visitors found themselves at a wide sliding door, looking directly into the living room. People would turn quickly and descend the path in confusion, assuming they must have missed the proper entry, but this was the only one.

There were a few other problems with the house as well. The kitchen and dining areas were tiny and drab, there was only one bedroom on the main level, and despite its magnificent location,

the house didn't provide places to take advantage of the views. The deck off the dining area commanded the best view of the Sound, but it was too narrow to be of much use. And the exterior color scheme was dark and unwelcoming.

Rethinking the Plan

After living with these problems for a decade, the homeowners decided it was time to remodel. They asked their architect, Jim Childress of Centerbrook Architects, to help them solve their entry problems and to reapportion the space to increase the size of the kitchen, dining area, and bedroom. They also wanted to add a guest bedroom and bathroom somewhere on the main level.

When you are doing major surgery to the structure of an existing house, it can get very expensive. To keep costs down, Jim adopted the time-tested design strategy that says "If it ain't broke, don't fix it." Spend money only where there are problems and leave the rest of the

Architect:
Centerbrook
Architects & Planners

Builder:
Deich Construction
Co., Inc.

Size: 1,950 sq. ft.

Location:
Mystic, Conn.

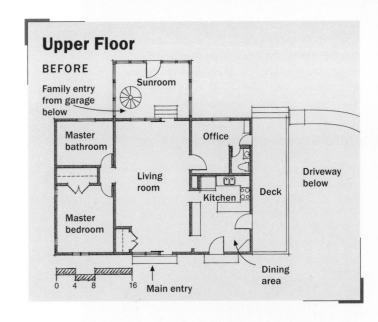

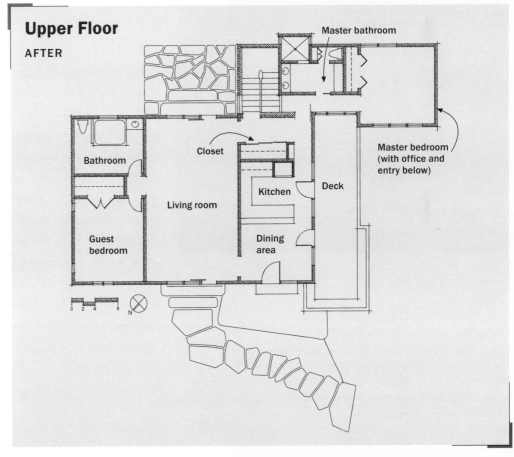

BELOW The brightly painted walls of the stairway and the natural-wood treads give a contemporary flair to the entry sequence. When there's limited daylight, as here, the lighting becomes very important. It's the combination of light and artwork that draws you on to explore the next level.

By adding the new area as a separate structure, the existing roof could remain untouched, which was a major money saver.

house alone. In this case, although the living room and bedroom wing could have been improved, they worked well enough and were left as is.

Jim concentrated instead on the heart of the design problem: improving the entry process for both family and guests. Often it's both easier and cheaper to add on what's needed, especially when there's a need to connect levels, as was the case here. And if one entry could provide both formal and informal access, there'd be less work to be done and fewer associated costs. So Jim proposed building a two-story addition off the northeast corner of the house that would incorporate a new bedroom suite on the upper level, an office space and entryway below, and a stairway to tie everything together.

By adding the new area as a separate structure, connected to the old house by a flat-roofed section, the existing roof could remain untouched, which was a major money saver. And by turning the existing master bedroom suite into the guest suite and placing the new master suite in the addition, Jim gave the couple's private realm a greater sense of remove from the main living areas, as well as better access to the views of the Sound.

RIGHT The brightly colored sliding door to the right has been made to look like a section of wall rather than a door. It remains open most of the time, but when privacy for the master bedroom suite is desired, the door can be closed.

Moving the office to the lower level of the addition allowed the kitchen and dining areas to be expanded to a more comfortable size. And by keeping the kitchen in the same general area, there was less need for rewiring and plumbing, both major expenses in kitchen remodeling. The remainder of the old office space became an entry closet and landing for the new stairway from the lower-level entry.

An Elegant Solution

The final design has elegantly solved all the old entry confusion with a minimum of means. The new entrance on the lower level, which serves both visitors and family, is next to the office space, with its three big windows creating the look of a main floor. This is enough to give guests the visual cues they need to know that this is indeed the front door. Once inside, even though there are few windows on this level, color and lighting have been used effectively to enliven the space and to draw people up and into the main level—not an easy thing to do gracefully in a constricted space.

ABOVE **At the top of the stairs, you can look along the hallway to the new master bedroom suite. The long view helps increase the sense of scale.**

Jim's solution may look obvious now, but when you are first contemplating a remodeling, the problems can seem overwhelming and the various needs contradictory. This is why you often see huge additions that don't fit the original house. Rather than taking the time to analyze, develop, and refine a design that does the most with the least, the more typical approach is to solve the problems with square footage. The solution may be expedient, but it's rarely elegant—and often fails to solve the problem.

Making a Little Go a Long Way

An attitude of simplicity and restraint runs throughout this remodeling. The deck, for example, was in perfectly good condition, so rather than tear it off and start over, a new bench was cantilevered out from the existing structure, widening the west corner to create a more comfortable sitting area at a much lower cost than building an entirely new deck.

The kitchen uses sleek but inexpensive custom cabinets with flush doors and very few extras in the cabinet interiors—a strategy that can save a lot of money. Most people don't realize that a custom cabinet is not necessarily more expensive than a stock one. If the door style is simple, requiring only a minimum

ABOVE **The original deck was too narrow for anything but a linear arrangement of chairs—not a comfortable way to socialize. By cantilevering a bench from the existing deck, the dimensions have been increased to allow for a sitting circle without rebuilding the deck.** (PHOTO COPYRIGHT JOHN WOODRUFF, WOODRUFF AND BROWN PHOTOGRAPHY.)

OPPOSITE/TOP **Although the kitchen/dining area is still small even after the remodeling, it seems larger thanks to the long view down the light-filled hallway to the bedroom. Adding French doors along the southwest wall gives the impression that the room extends all the way to the deck railing.**

of crafting, and the cabinet interiors don't have a lot of pullouts or other special features, costs can be kept down. And since such cabinets are designed to work with the space available, they can lend the whole kitchen a quality that goes far beyond their cost.

Other features that give this room its personality are the use of color, trim alignment, and unique drawer pulls—all low-cost items. A new refrigerator was not in the initial budget, so an enclosure was made to fit the future refrigerator, which didn't get installed until a year later. If you can allow some small things to be completed as money becomes available, you build in a flexibility that makes it possible to transform your house, over time, into the home of your dreams.

LEFT **A trim line extends from the bottom of the upper cabinets over to the raised countertop at the peninsula, defining the upper edge of the back-splash and unifying the design of the room without the expense of another wall of cabinetry.**

Move or Remodel?

Whether to move or remodel is a question that most home-owners face at some time in their lives. Like the owners of this house, many people love their location but find their house constricting and inconvenient. Building a new house is an option, but new construction typically costs more than remodeling, even though the actual cost per square foot for remodeled space can be higher than brand new. When you are remodeling, though, there are usually many things that don't need to be redone. If you can minimize the added square footage and change only the necessities, you'll find that it's usually less expensive to remodel.

But if you don't really like where you live and are simply contemplating a remodel because you think it will be easier than moving, think again. Anyone who's remodeled will tell you that living through the construction process is one of the hardest things they've ever done. By all means remodel if you feel connected to a place, but if not, look around for a location that you feel better about.

If you're not sure what to do, consult a local architect and an appraiser or realtor to help you assess your needs and come up with some possible solutions, their probable cost, and the potential increase in property value. Weigh the costs, consider what you will get in return, and you'll be able to determine what makes sense for you.

A Cottage Community

*F*INDING GOOD EXAMPLES OF SMALL houses with the kind of detailing and tailoring that building Not So Big entails was harder than I'd imagined. Finding an entire community of Not So Big houses was an unexpected bonus. Third Street Cottages on Whidbey Island in Washington State is a community of eight tiny houses, located on just two-thirds of an acre. The houses themselves have a main-floor square footage of 600 sq. ft. to 650 sq. ft., with a loft above. They are clustered around a central commons, which in-cludes a lawn and "pea patch" garden. Parking is located in small pockets of three to five cars along the west edge of the property. To enter the neighborhood, you park, come into the commons through an implied gateway, and arrive at each house via its front gate and porch.

The two cottages illustrated here—Hilltop, and Pears and Cherries—give a sense of the overall community and a glimpse of the charm of each individual home. Filled with simple but beau-tifully designed details reminiscent of the bungalows of the Arts

By spending less on the overall square footage, there's more money available to make a place that's comfortable, well crafted, and personal.

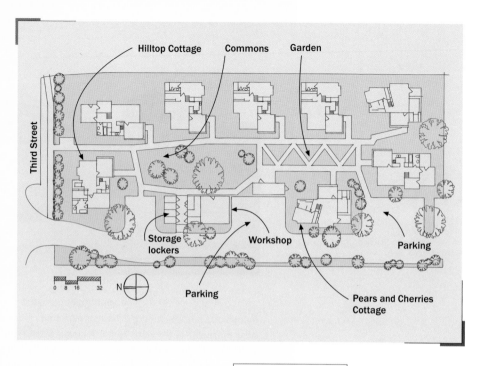

Hilltop Cottage   Commons   Garden

Third Street

Storage lockers

Workshop

Parking

0 8 16   32   N

Parking

Pears and Cherries Cottage

Architect:
Ross Chapin Architects

Developer/builder:
The Cottage Company

Size: 710–930 sq. ft.

Location:
Whidbey Island, Wash.

Filled with simple but beautifully designed details, these homes exemplify what building Not So Big is all about.

and Crafts movement, these homes exemplify what building Not So Big is all about. By spending less on the overall square footage, there's more money available to make a place that's comfortable, well crafted, and personal. Architect Ross Chapin and developer Jim Soules built with this philosophy in mind. As Ross says, "We placed a high value on craftsmanship and design because we wanted to build in character. Yet we didn't want to get too fussy or precious with the details." So they used simple, off-the-shelf items that allowed them to keep costs down while keeping quality and craft up.

Nooks and Crannies

The diminutive size of these cottages means that every square foot must be put to use. Rather than making one large, undifferentiated room for the main living area, Ross created alcoves, window bays, and other pockets of space to make a small area seem much larger and to accommodate more activities. For example, Pears and Cherries has a 2-ft. by 10-ft. alcove that increases the usable living-room space by far more than its square footage would suggest. It creates a cozy corner with a lowered ceiling, set off from the vaulted main space.

Other alcoves are smaller still. In Hilltop, there are two tiny bays, each only 16 in. deep. The shallow window bay in the living room brings in more light than if it were flush with the adjacent wall, because the surrounding surfaces reflect the light and bounce it into the room. The window's height from the floor also increases the sense of privacy. The bay in the bedroom

LEFT In the Pears and Cherries Cottage, access to the loft above is via a steep stairway. The bedroom and bathroom are nestled under the loft. The living-room alcove to the left has a lowered ceiling, to distinguish it from the main living area, and the top of the adjacent built-in bookshelves creates a shelf for displaying treasures, which continues around the room.

BELOW Using exposed joists with pine decking instead of drywall gives the ceiling between the bedroom and the loft a lot more character. The window seat shown here is actually more like a skylight seat: The windows are located above ceiling height, bringing in an abundance of light while maintaining privacy from neighboring cottages.

encloses a high window that brings light into the space from above, giving it a warm glow. There's something inspiring about light from above, especially when the source of the light is not visible, as here. It's no accident that this technique was used in churches and cathedrals of the past. But it doesn't take a huge space to create the same uplifting spirit.

A Sense of Entry

This subtle sense of the way spatial experience affects us is evident throughout the cottages. The framed openings for the kitchens in both cottages act as wide doorways, indicating that you are entering a new activity area without obstructing views from one place to another. When space is limited, using this

technique to identify a transition can make a space feel much larger.

An obvious example of this principle is Hilltop's kitchen, seen at right. In the plan, you can see that the room is simply an extension of the living room. Its ceiling height and finish are the same as that of the adjacent space. What distinguishes it as a separate room is the surrounding trimwork and lowered header as you enter. Picture the room without these elements and you can see that the result would look more like a makeshift trailer than a house. It's the detailing, the wing wall adjacent to the refrigerator, and the change in ceiling height that make it work. It doesn't require a dividing wall, just a psychological gateway.

Loft Living

Each cottage has at least one full-height loft, accessed by a steep or alternating-step stair. The lofts provide some bonus space that can be used in a variety of ways—anything from storage space to meditation retreat to home

ABOVE The walls of the Hilltop Cottage kitchen are paneled with reclaimed Sitka spruce. Although the room is small, everything is beautifully detailed. Notice the cabinetry support bracket below the countertop's bar overhang. It's details like this that give a home a personal quality.

OPPOSITE The kitchen in the Pears and Cherries Cottage is designed to be welcoming. Aligning the framed entryway with the window beyond invites you in, and the eating alcove tucked away to the left intrigues you with a glimpse of what's there, making you want to see more.

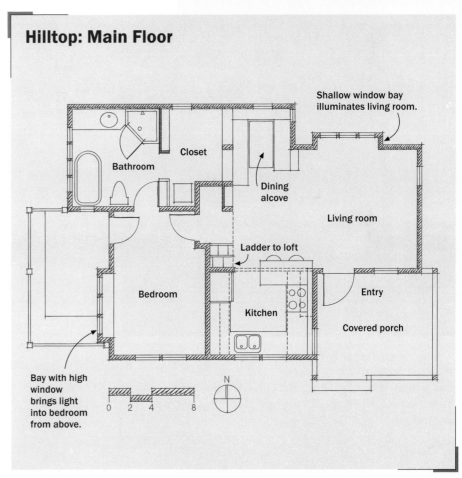

Hilltop: Main Floor

Shallow window bay illuminates living room.

Bathroom

Closet

Dining alcove

Living room

Ladder to loft

Bedroom

Kitchen

Entry

Covered porch

Bay with high window brings light into bedroom from above.

N

0 2 4 8

Although Hilltop Cottage has only 650 sq. ft. on the main level, there's an additional 200 sq. ft. of loft space, room enough for a cozy in-home office. The ship's ladder (a design purportedly invented by Thomas Jefferson) takes up much less space than a standard staircase.

office. The lofts also serve to increase the apparent scale of the main living areas in each cottage by extending the sight lines. When you can see that there's additional living area above and just out of view, it makes the whole main floor seem larger—especially when it's bathed in sunlight.

Building Smaller, Building Smarter

Ross and Jim pared the cottages down to a reasonable minimum in terms of square footage. To give each home its own unique charm, they spent time on design and used materials that had inherent beauty. The houses were also sustainably made, by using fewer resources in their construction than most similar houses built today and materials that are themselves sustainable. The interior walls, which add such warmth to the rooms, are paneled with Sitka spruce that was rejected by a local piano factory and was on its way to a paper mill. The flooring is Medite, a formaldehyde-free particleboard, which has been cut into 24-in. by 32-in. tiles, stained to look like aged leather, and then finished with linseed oil. The exteriors are sided with Hardiplank fiber-cement boards.

These eight houses were designed on spec for singles and couples, a market that is currently largely ignored by mass-market developers. Although more than half of all households in the country consist of only one or two people, almost all new single-family construction is based on a model that's best suited to a much larger family. Despite the fears of lenders, the cottages sold almost immediately, and they have generated enormous interest, both locally and nationally.

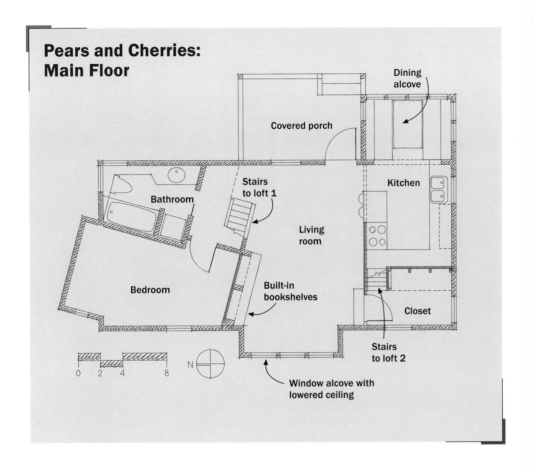

Pears and Cherries: Main Floor

Dining alcove

Covered porch

Kitchen

Stairs to loft 1

Bathroom

Living room

Built-in bookshelves

Bedroom

Closet

Stairs to loft 2

0 2 4 8

N

Window alcove with lowered ceiling

The diminutive size of these cottages means that every square foot must be put to use.

The Cottage-Community Concept

When we imagine the towns and villages of the pre-automobile era, a prominent feature is the strong sense of community that was created by the proximity of homes—and people—to one another. Neighbors went about their daily business on foot, greeting one another or stopping for a brief conversation. People looked out for each other, and a sense of safety prevailed. The Third Street Cottages project taps into this time-honored method of creating community, for those interested in living simply but beautifully.

The project was developed to form a neighborhood with a true sense of home for all of its residents. In order to do this, priority was given to "place making"—creating spots to gather, to work together in the garden, or to greet a neighbor in passing—rather than designing around automobiles, as is invariably the case today.

The emblem of our longing for this sort of community is the front porch—such a predominant feature of homes of the past. A porch provides the opportunity to chat with the neighbors or just watch the world go by. Add to this a low split-cedar fence, perennial hedge, and common area, and there's just the right balance between public and private space to allow a community to flourish through the chance interactions of daily life.

RIGHT The cabinetry throughout each house has a personal touch, with simple details added to the door panels and well-chosen hardware, which distinguishes it from run-of-the-mill cabinetry. The painted-wood walls and exposed ceiling joists add far more interest and texture than the standard drywall finishes we're used to.

BELOW When a house is small, you can have light on three sides of a room, an experience you don't get in a larger house, where there is more distance between exterior walls and usually more than one living area in a space. In fact the bigger the house, the darker the middle tends to be.

The days when a single person would never think of buying a home are long past, yet few houses are designed for this large and growing market. And too often, when small houses are built today, they are built cheaply, with little thought to character. But these cottages prove that there are many people out there who want to surround themselves with beauty, comfort, and practicality. And they want their dwellings to reflect their values. A drywalled shoe box just won't do.

ABOVE In the Pears and Cherries Cottage, an alcove surrounded by windows and wide sills provides the perfect ambiance for eating, reading the morning paper, or simply hanging out. It's the cozy size that makes this space work. If it were larger, it would lose the intimacy that makes you want to settle in and relax.

The Whole Nine Yards

WHEN YOU LOOK AT THE MAIN-LEVEL floor plan for the upgrade version of the 1999 *LIFE* Dream House (known by the architects at SALA as the Whole Nine Yards house), you can see the generic similarity to the basic house. There are the same four quadrants, the indented front porch, and the front door that lines up with the French doors opening to the backyard. The garage and mudroom are in the same position. You may notice that the upgrade plan is just slightly larger, that this house does have some bump-outs, and that the dining area and kitchen are reversed. Surely these aren't such significant differences. Yet the interior of the house looks quite different, and the cost of this house is substantially higher than the basic house—almost double, in fact. To find out why, let's evaluate the house piece by piece and analyze the differences between the two versions.

There's a quality of constant discovery in this house, an effect created by layering, which is one of the basic techniques that makes Not So Big work.

Main Floor

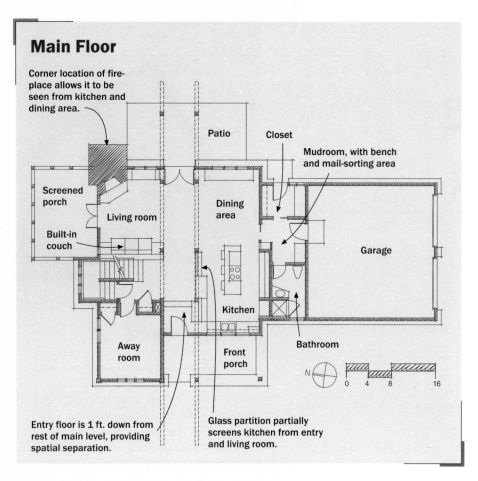

Corner location of fireplace allows it to be seen from kitchen and dining area.

Patio

Closet

Mudroom, with bench and mail-sorting area

Screened porch

Living room

Built-in couch

Dining area

Garage

Kitchen

Bathroom

Away room

Front porch

N

0 4 8 16

Entry floor is 1 ft. down from rest of main level, providing spatial separation.

Glass partition partially screens kitchen from entry and living room.

Architect:
SALA Architects

Builder:
Derrick Construction Co.

Size: 2,500 sq. ft.

Location:
Afton, Minn.

A House from Memory

The form of this house has a lot more detailing—what architects call "articulation"—than the basic house. This means that there's more depth, an effect created by the application of various materials to the surface. Look at the front face of the house, for example. There's the indented porch on the main level, just as on the other house. But there's also a smaller indented deck on the second level and an eyebrow created with shingles and trim above the second-floor windows, giving the house a wonderfully expressive face. The stucco base of the house stands proud of the walls by several inches and is flared out to make a solid-looking platform. As architect Michaela Mahady puts it, "It makes it feel as if the house is growing out of the ground." And then there are the dormers, which, when combined with the broad overhangs, call to mind a chalet in the Austrian Alps. All these elements add a unique quality and craft to the house, but of course each one also adds to the cost.

The alpine motif is no accident. The house sits high on a bluff overlooking the St. Croix valley, and Michaela used imagery from her own cultural memory (she has family roots in Austria) to make a house that, for her, is evocative of

home and comfort. Together with architects Wayne Branum and Katherine Hillbrand, she created a house that has an intimate feel and a sense of surprise around every corner. Like a good book, it makes you want to keep reading—to explore every nook and cranny and discover all its secrets.

The interior is welcoming and rich in both color and texture. As in the Back to Basics house, there's a lot of color used throughout, though here it is in a darker, more subdued palette. But there the similarity ends. Whereas expensive finishes were avoided in the Back to Basics house in favor of color, here materials such as wood and stone have been employed to give the

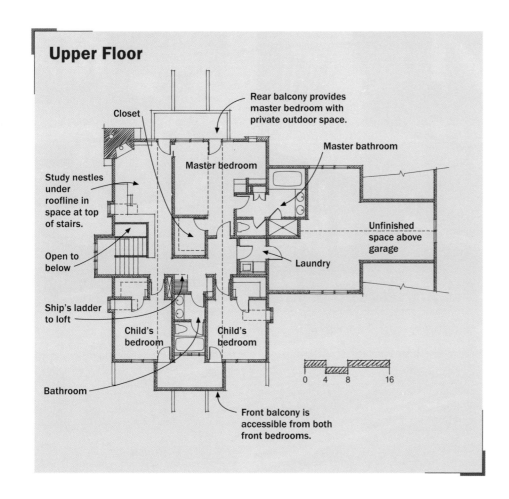

Upper Floor

Closet

Rear balcony provides master bedroom with private outdoor space.

Master bathroom

Master bedroom

Study nestles under roofline in space at top of stairs.

Unfinished space above garage

Open to below

Laundry

Ship's ladder to loft

Child's bedroom

Child's bedroom

0 4 8 16

Bathroom

Front balcony is accessible from both front bedrooms.

ABOVE The master bedroom has a cabinlike feel, with lots of wood paneling and a spectacular view of the valley. The bed sits in an alcove created by a lowered ceiling that's 7 ft. 6 in. from the floor. The alcove makes a cozy pocket of space in a room with an otherwise tall ceiling.

OPPOSITE The strong, simple form of the roof with its accompanying dormers evokes the image of an alpine chalet. Though it is reminiscent of vernacular architecture, it is anything but a reproduction. This is a design that learns from the past but transforms it into an innovative image for today.

home its warmth. When budget constraints are less of an issue, such natural materials can add a timeless quality and character to a house. But they're not critical to livability or personality; their effect is simply different.

Enduring Quality

The dropped ceiling that cuts through the center of the house is made of wood, where drywall was used in the basic version. And, although the usual wood casing is omitted around the windows, there's a lot of wood used in other places, with a plethora of built-ins and paneled walls and ceilings. Much of this wood was salvaged from the bottom of Lake Superior, where huge tree trunks have languished for centuries. Wood retrieved in this manner is of a caliber and hardness seldom found today and is an excellent sustainable material, but it comes with a hefty price tag. When built into a house like this one—a house designed to last for centuries—it will provide pleasure for many generations to come.

Rooms in the Roof

The ceilings throughout this house are higher than in the basic version, with an extra foot of height on the main level and the sloped form of the roof expressed in each room on the second level. This is a detail that costs more than standard 8-ft.-high ceilings but adds wonderful spatial complexity. Unlike the cavernous cathedral ceilings typical of suburban houses today, however, these sloped ceilings spring from a height that is more proportioned to human scale. In the study at the top of the stairs, for example, the ceiling comes down to 5 ft. behind the desk, rising

ABOVE **A comfortable study opens off the stairway landing on the second floor, a change from the basic house, where the upper level was significantly smaller. The darker colors of the painted walls and woodwork add to the intimacy of the space, and the ceiling seems to wrap down around the desk area, giving a sense of shelter to the activities below.**

OPPOSITE **The kitchen is designed for informal eating and is partially screened from the living room by a glass partition. The kitchen island is designed to be a functional work surface, an informal eating area, and a work of art. The raised section can also serve as a buffet during parties. The countertop material, a product called Fireslate, feels wonderful to the touch and looks like stone, though it's actually a combination of portland cement, silica sand, and fillers.**

ABOVE **The entryway is open to the main level but sits two steps down. The built-in bench provides a place for removing shoes, a feature that's particularly welcome in snowy Minnesota. As family and friends come and go, the photos displayed here tell something of the lives of the inhabitants—a simple personal touch.**

RIGHT **The screen between the stairway and the kitchen, made of obscuring glass, protects the entryway from direct views into the kitchen work area. The columns supporting the two beams that run the length of the house have an unusual and elegant design, giving the whole composition an Asian flavor and simplicity.**

to 12 ft. at the peak, and then descending back to 10 ft. on the other side of the room.

If you look at the section through the house on p. 373, you'll see that the slope could in fact have risen all the way to the wall opposite the desk, but in so doing the room would have lost all its coziness. Like a sculptor, an architect manipulates the space available to make every room into a place of comfort, beauty, and functionality. Just because the space is available doesn't mean that it will improve the room to include it. As with a well-tailored suit, often the fabric that is cut away is as important as the fabric that appears in the final article.

Layer upon Layer

There's a quality of constant discovery in this house, an effect created by layering, which is one of the basic techniques that makes Not So Big work. When talking about this effect, Michaela mentions an inspiration from her childhood. At Eastertime, she was sometimes given a large, scenic Easter egg. The egg was made with layer upon layer of spun sugar, suggesting a scene below and another below that. By breaking away the layers, she would discover more and more about the marvelous creativity of its making. A house can do the same thing.

As you walk through the front door, to your right is a wall that's not really a wall at all. Composed of built-ins and obscuring glass, it invites you to explore, just like the Easter egg. You want to know what's behind it, but you are also

By crafting every surface and sculpting every space, the whole house becomes a work of art, as well as an extraordinarily comfortable place to live.

drawn to the wall itself. You might stop and look at the pictures on the photo-display shelves. You might look through the peekaboo opening into the kitchen to catch a glimpse of the activities within. Or you might press your nose against the glass and enjoy the distorted view through to the kitchen island. How much more interesting than just a plain old wall made of studs and drywall.

Entering from the garage, you also have a clear sense of the layering that underlies the home's design. As you enter through the mudroom—a space complete with mail-sorting area, backpack storage, and walk-through closet—you see past the kitchen and the glass wall, past the column marking the edge of the stair, to the living room beyond. Although the distance is only 34 ft., it feels much greater, because of the layers you're looking through. They engage you, draw you into the house, and make you want to explore. The more layers you see, the more intriguing it becomes.

On the upper level, the layers are not quite as intricately detailed, but they still allow a sense of flow and an awareness of the whole as well as the parts. The transom windows above each door are a good example of this. The frameless glass tricks the eye into believing there's nothing there. The vault and roof ridge seem to extend endlessly, making the house seem significantly bigger than it really is, while the wall still does its job of providing acoustical and visual privacy where it's needed.

ABOVE **This is not just a house of beauty but also a house that's full of practicalities, like this mail-sorting area just off the entry from the garage. Why not create a place that's designed for handling the mail you walk in with every day right at the point of entry? It's a function we definitely need to design for today.**

What Makes a House Expensive?

The two versions of the *LIFE* Dream House—the Back to Basics (BTB) house and the Whole Nine Yards (WNY) house—beautifully illustrate the relationship between complexity and cost. By comparing the two, you can see just how much difference quality of materials and complexity of design can make. Both houses are similar in size—the WNY house is just 400 sq. ft. larger—and have similar floor plans, yet the WNY house is almost twice as expensive to build as the BTB house.

The following features contribute to the difference in cost between the two. As you look through this list, refer back to the plans and photos for each house to see the differences.

On the exterior, the WNY house has an intricately detailed pattern of cedar shingles at the gable end walls, with narrow lap siding below, as compared with Hardiplank fiber-cement board siding for the BTB house. The WNY house has a massive stucco chimney for a full masonry fireplace instead of a side-venting gas zero-clearance fireplace insert requiring no chimney at all. There are shed dormers on the WNY house, which greatly increase the complexity of the roof framing, versus easy-to-install skylights set between trusses in the BTB house.

On the interior, the WNY house has more woodwork, more built-ins, and a multitude of custom-crafted details. By contrast, the BTB house uses paint color for character instead of woodwork, and a limited number of built-ins in places where they'll have the greatest effect. The WNY house has Fireslate countertops and high-end appliances, whereas the BTB house has laminate countertops and mid-range appliances.

Spatially the houses are quite different, too. There are several bump-outs on the WNY house that make the foundation more expensive to build. It has higher ceilings throughout, with an opening between the main and upper floors adjacent to the staircase; exterior balconies from the bedrooms; and vaulted ceilings on the second level that add to the structural complexity. The BTB house keeps the ceilings at a standard 8-ft. height and omits the balconies and the opening between levels. It is also designed without a basement, allowing the space below the upper run of stairs to become part of the living room, which in turn reduces the length of the house by several feet.

Often we are unaware of the increased complexity caused by a bump-out in a foundation wall or an increase in ceiling height. If your goal is to keep costs down, make sure that the materials you use are consistent with your budget and that every effort is made to keep the structure simple to build.

Although this house is expensive, with a cost per square foot substantially higher than a typical home today, much of what makes it so livable comes from the quality of the design rather than the cost of the materials. Of primary importance is the fact that this home offers many more places for real living to occur than many much larger homes. By crafting every surface and sculpting every space, the whole house becomes a work of art, as well as an extraordinarily comfortable place to live. This is an intimate house, a house that embraces both its inhabitants and guests with its presence.

Back to Basics House

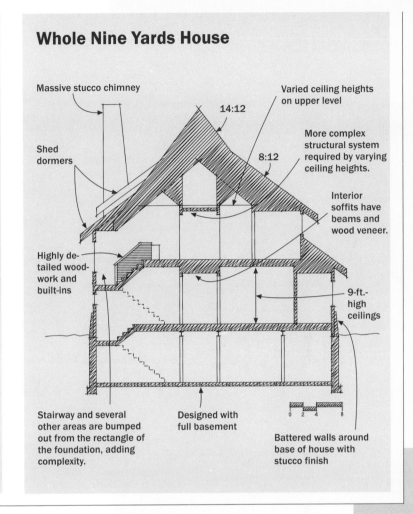

No chimney (gas fireplace)

Skylights (no dormers)

Simple woodwork and built-ins

14:12

Simple structural system throughout

Loft

Standard 8-ft.-high ceilings

6:12

Drywall interior soffits

Stairway within the rectangle of the foundation

Designed without basement

Wood boards and battens around foundation

0 2 4 8

Whole Nine Yards House

Massive stucco chimney

Varied ceiling heights on upper level

Shed dormers

14:12

8:12

More complex structural system required by varying ceiling heights.

Interior soffits have beams and wood veneer.

Highly detailed woodwork and built-ins

9-ft.-high ceilings

Stairway and several other areas are bumped out from the rectangle of the foundation, adding complexity.

Designed with full basement

Battered walls around base of house with stucco finish

0 2 4 8

LIFE Magazine asked SALA to put forth its vision for the house of tomorrow. In both versions, the answer is clear: a smaller, more tailored home that has a floor plan designed for today's informal lifestyle, with as much craft and personalization as the budget permits, built with sustainable techniques and materials that will allow the house to last for centuries. It's a far cry from the typical house of today. And it won't become the norm until we stop building big and start building Not So Big, tailoring our houses to become the homes our spirits crave.

OPPOSITE The transom windows above each bedroom door allow light and view to flow between spaces, while still providing an acoustical barrier. With no surrounding frame, the eye is fooled into believing there's no membrane at all. The roof seems to continue unobstructed, and the space seems larger as a result.

Credits

PAGE 2
Architect: **Sarah Susanka & James R. Larson**
Photographer: **Christian Korab**

PAGE 3
Architect: **Joseph G. Metzler with M. Christine Johnson, MSMP**
Photographer: **Susan Gilmore (© Meredith Corp.)**

PAGE 4
Architect: **Kelly Davis with Timothy Old, MSMP**
Photographer: **Karen Melvin**

PAGE 5
Architect: **Jean Larson & Mark Larson**
Photographer: **Saari & Forrai Photography**

PAGE 6
Architect: **Robert Gerloff**
Photographer: **John Danicic**

PAGE 7
Architect: **Michaela Mahady & Wayne Branum, MSMP**
Photographer: **George Heinrich**

PAGE 8 (TOP)
Architect: **Dale Mulfinger with Mark Malaby, MSMP**
Photographer: **Peter Kerze**

PAGE 8 (BOTTOM)
Architect: **Ross Chapin**
Photographer: **Charles Miller**

PAGE 9
Photographer: **Balthazar Korab**

PAGES 11, 12
Architect: **Joseph G. Metzler with Steven Buetow, MSMP**
Photographer: **Susan Gilmore**

PAGE 13 (LEFT)
Architect: **Sarah Susanka, MSMP**
Photographer: **Kevin Ireton**

PAGE 13 (RIGHT)
Architect: **Sarah Susanka & James R. Larson**
Photographer: **Christian Korab**

PAGE 14 (TOP)
Photographer: **Sarah Susanka**

PAGE 14 (BOTTOM)
Architect: **Greene and Greene**
Photographer: **Balthazar Korab**

PAGE 15
Architect: **Michaela Mahady with M. Christine Johnson, MSMP**
Photographer: **Phillip Mueller**

PAGE 16 (TOP)
Architect: **Michaela Mahady with M. Christine Johnson, MSMP**
Photographer: **Phillip Mueller**

PAGE 16 (BOTTOM)
Architect: **Frank Lloyd Wright**
Photographer: **Balthazar Korab**

PAGE 17
Architect: **Sarah Susanka with Steven Mooney, MSMP**
Photographer: **Christian Korab**

PAGE 19
Architect: **Sarah Susanka & James R. Larson**
Photographer: **Christian Korab**

PAGE 20
Architect: **Robert Gerloff**
Photographer: **John Danicic**

PAGE 21
Architect: **Sarah Susanka with M. Christine Johnson, MSMP**
Photographer: **Karen Melvin**

PAGE 22
Architect: **Sarah Susanka & Michaela Mahady, MSMP**
Photographer: **Karen Melvin**

PAGE 23
Architect: **Sarah Susanka with James R. Larson, MSMP**
Photographer: **Christian Korab**

PAGE 24 (TOP)
Architect: **Sarah Susanka with Richard Peterson, MSMP**
Photographer: **Karen Melvin**

PAGE 24 (BOTTOM)
Architect: **Sarah Susanka with James R. Larson, MSMP**
Photographer: **Christian Korab**

PAGE 25 (LEFT)
Architect: **Dale Mulfinger with M. Christine Johnson, MSMP**
Photographer: **Dale Mulfinger**

PAGE 25 (RIGHT), 26
Photographer: **Sarah Susanka**

PAGE 27
Architect: **Frank Lloyd Wright**
Photographer: **Balthazar Korab**

PAGE 28
Architect: **Michaela Mahady & Wayne Branum, MSMP**
Photographer: **George Heinrich**

PAGE 29
Architect: **Sarah Susanka**
Photographer: **Sarah Susanka**

PAGE 31
Architect: **Michaela Mahady & Wayne Branum, MSMP**
Photographer: **George Heinrich**

PAGE 32 (TOP)
Architect: **Leslie Barry Davidson**
Photographer: **Charles Wardell**

PAGE 32 (BOTTOM)
Architect: **Edwin Lundie**
Photographer: **Scott Gibson**

PAGE 35
Architect: **Sarah Susanka & James R. Larson**
Photographer: **Jeff Krueger**

PAGE 36
Architect: **Dale Mulfinger with Mark Malaby, MSMP**
Photographer: **Peter Kerze**

PAGE 37
Photographer: **Balthazar Korab**

PAGE 38
Architect: **Dale Mulfinger with Mark Malaby, MSMP**
Photographer: **Peter Kerze**

PAGE 40
Designer: **Laurel Ulland, MSMP**
Photographer: **Jenifer Jordan (courtesy *Renovation Style*, © Meredith Corp.)**

PAGE 41
Architect: **Sarah Susanka & James R. Larson**
Photographer: **Christian Korab**

PAGE 42
Architect: **Sarah Susanka & James R. Larson**
Photographer: **Crystal Kitchens**

PAGE 43
Architect: **Sarah Susanka with Steven Mooney, MSMP**
Photographer: **Jeff Krueger**

PAGE 44 (TOP)
Architect: **Sarah Susanka & James R. Larson**
Photographer: **Christian Korab**

PAGE 44 (BOTTOM)
Architect: **Kelly Davis with Timothy Old, MSMP**
Photographer: **Karen Melvin**

PAGE 45
Architect: **Sarah Susanka with Steven Mooney, MSMP**
Photographer: **Christian Korab**

PAGE 46
Architect: **Katherine Cartrette, MSMP**
Photographer: **Christian Korab**

PAGE 47
Architect: **Sarah Susanka, Katherine Cartrette, MSMP**
Photographer: **Christian Korab**

PAGE 48
Architect: **Sarah Susanka & James R. Larson**
Photographer: **Christian Korab**

PAGES 50, 51
Architect: **Sarah Susanka with M. Christine Johnson, MSMP**
Photographer: **Karen Melvin**

PAGE 52 (TOP)
Architect: **Sarah Susanka with James R. Larson, MSMP**
Photographer: **Susan Gilmore (© Meredith Corp.)**

PAGES 52 (BOTTOM), 53
Architect: **Sarah Susanka & James R. Larson**
Photographer: **Christian Korab**

PAGE 55
Architect: **Steven Gerber**
Photographer: **Roe A. Osborn**

PAGE 56 (TOP)
Architect: **Scott Neeley**
Photographer: **Steve Culpepper**

PAGE 56 (BOTTOM)
Architect: **Sarah Susanka with James R. Larson, MSMP**
Photographer: **Lisa Cicotte**

PAGE 57
Architect: **Timothy Fuller with Steven Mooney, MSMP**
Photographer: **George Heinrich**

PAGE 58 (LEFT)
Designer: **Paul Buum**
Photographer: **Christian Korab**

PAGE 58 (RIGHT)
Architect: **Michaela Mahady & Wayne Branum, MSMP**
Photographer: **George Heinrich**

PAGE 59
Architect: **Sarah Susanka, MSMP**
Photographer: **Jeff Krueger**

PAGE 60
Architect: **John Ferro Sims**
Photographer: **John Ferro Sims**

PAGE 61
Architect: **Sarah Susanka with Ollie Foran, MSMP**
Photographer: **Christian Korab**

PAGE 62 (TOP)
Photographer: **Benjamin Mendlowitz ©**

PAGE 62 (BOTTOM)
Architect: **Kelly Davis, MSMP**
Photographer: **Karen Melvin**

PAGE 63
Photographer: **Gilles de Chabaneix (from *Japanese Style*, © 1987 by Suzanne Slesin, Stafford Cliff, Daniel Rozensztroch, & Gilles de Chabaneix; published by Clarkson N. Potter, Inc., 1987)**

PAGE 64 (TOP)
Photographer: **J. Donald Larson**

PAGE 64 (BOTTOM)
Architect: **Sarah Susanka & James R. Larson**
Photographer: **Dana Wheelock**

PAGE 65
Architect: **Sarah Susanka & James R. Larson**
Photographer: **Jeff Krueger**

PAGES 66, 67
Architect: **Sarah Susanka & James R. Larson**
Photographer: **Christian ...**

PAGE 68
Photographer: **Christian ...**

PAGE 69
Architect: **Kelly Davis with Timothy Old, MSMP**
Photographer: **Karen Melv...**

PAGES 70, 71
Architect: **Sarah Susanka & James R. Larson**
Photographer: **Christian M...**

PAGE 72 (TOP)
Architect: **Michaela Maha... M. Christine Johnson, MS...**
Photographer: **Susan Giln... (© Meredith Corp.)**

PAGE 72 (BOTTOM)
Architect: **Sarah Susanka & James R. Larson**
Photographer: **Christian M...**

PAGE 73 (TOP LEFT)
Architect: **Sarah Susanka & James R. Larson**
Photographer: **Dana Whee...**

PAGE 73 (BOTTOM LEFT)
Architect: **Sarah Susanka & Steven Mooney, MSMP**
Photographer: **Christian M...**

PAGE 73 (RIGHT)
Architect: **Peter L. Pfeiffe...**
Photographer: **Bruce Gree...**

PAGE 74
Architect: **Sarah Susanka... M. Christine Johnson, MS...**
Photographer: **Christian M...**

PAGE 75 (TOP)
Architect: **Sarah Susanka... James R. Larson**
Photographer: **Sarah Susa...**

PAGE 75 (BOTTOM)
Architect: **Sarah Susanka...**
Photographer: **Sarah Susa...**

PAGE 76 (TOP)
Architect: **Kelly Davis wit... Timothy Old, MSMP**
Photographer: **Karen Me...**

PAGE 76 (BOTTOM)
Designer: **Laurel Ulland, MSMP**
Photographer: **Phillip Mueller**

PAGE 77
Architect: **Sarah Susanka &
Michaela Mahady, MSMP**
Photographer: **Karen Melvin**

PAGE 78 (TOP)
Architect: **Kelly Davis with Timothy
Old, MSMP**
Photographer: **Karen Melvin**

PAGE 78 (BOTTOM)
Architect: **Sarah Susanka &
James R. Larson**
Photographer: **Jeff Krueger**

PAGE 79 (TOP)
Architect: **Sarah Susanka &
James R. Larson**
Photographer: **Christian Korab**

PAGE 79 (BOTTOM)
Architect: **Sarah Susanka with Ollie
Foran, MSMP**
Photographer: **Christian Korab**

PAGE 80
Architect: **Sarah Susanka &
James R. Larson**
Photographer: **Christian Korab**

PAGE 81
Architect: **Sarah Susanka with
James R. Larson, MSMP**
Photographer: **Sarah Susanka**

PAGE 82
Architect: **John Calvin Womack**
Photographer: *Fine Homebuilding*

PAGE 83 (LEFT)
Architect: **Sarah Susanka &
James R. Larson**
Photographer: **Christian Korab**

PAGE 83 (RIGHT)
Architect: **Timothy Fuller, MSMP**
Photographer: **Christian Korab**

PAGES 84, 85
Architect: **Dale Mulfinger &
Timothy Fuller, MSMP**
Photographer: **Karen Melvin**

PAGE 86
Architect: **Sarah Susanka with
M. Christine Johnson, MSMP**
Photographer: **Chris Ostlind**

PAGE 87
Architect: **Dale Mulfinger with
Mark Malaby, MSMP**
Photographer: **Peter Kerze**

PAGES 88, 89
Architect: **Sarah Susanka with
Steven Mooney, MSMP**
Photographer: **Jeff Krueger**

PAGE 90
Architect: **Sarah Susanka with
James R. Larson, MSMP**
Photographer: **Christian Korab**

PAGE 91
Architect: **John Ferro Sims**
Photographer: **John Ferro Sims**

PAGE 92 (TOP)
Architect: **Sarah Susanka, MSMP**
Photographer: **Christian Korab**

PAGE 92 (BOTTOM)
Designer: **Philip S. Sollman**
Photographer: **Philip S. Sollman**

PAGE 93 (LEFT)
Architect: **Todd Remington**
Photographer: **Steve Culpepper**

PAGE 93 (RIGHT)
Architect: **Janet Moody**
Photographer: **Scott Gibson**

PAGE 94 (LEFT)
Architect: **Tony Simmonds**
Photographer: **Charles Miller**

PAGE 94-95
Photographer: **Charles Miller**

PAGE 95 (RIGHT)
Architect: **Dale Mulfinger &
Cheryl Fosdick, MSMP**
Photographer: **Karen Melvin**

PAGE 96
Designer: **John Hermannsson**
Photographer: **John Hermannsson**

PAGE 97 (LEFT)
Architect: **Sarah Susanka &
James R. Larson**
Photographer: **Christian Korab**

PAGE 97 (RIGHT)
Architect: **Sarah Susanka with
M. Christine Johnson, MSMP**
Photographer: **Sarah Susanka**

PAGE 98 (LEFT)
Architect: **Kelly Davis with
Timothy Old, MSMP**
Photographer: **Karen Melvin**

PAGE 98 (RIGHT)
Architect: **Michaela Mahady &
Paul Buum**
Photographer: **Christian Korab**

PAGE 99
Designer: **Fu Tung Cheng**
Photographer: **Charles Miller**

PAGE 100
Architect: **Sarah Susanka with
James Larson, MSMP**
Photographer: **Susan Gilmore
(© Meredith Corp.)**

PAGES 101-104
Architect: **Kelly Davis**
Photographer: **Karen Melvin**

PAGES 105-107
Architect: **Kelly Davis**
Photographer: *Fine Homebuilding*

PAGES 108-109, 111-112
Architect: **Sarah Susanka with
James R. Larson, MSMP**
Photographer: **Susan Gilmore
(© Meredith Corp.)**

PAGES 114-117
Architect: **Michaela Mahady
& Wayne Branum, MSMP**
Photographer: **George Heinrich**

PAGES 119-121
Architect: **Michaela Mahady
& Wayne Branum, MSMP**
Photographer: **Christian Korab**

PAGE 123
Architect: **Tony Simmonds**
Photographer: **Charles Miller**

PAGE 125
Architect: **Dale Mulfinger with
Mark Malaby, MSMP**
Photographer: **Peter Kerze**

PAGES 126, 128-131
Architect: **Kelly Davis with
Timothy Old, MSMP**
Photographer: **Lark Gilmer**

PAGE 132
Architect: **Victoria Holland**
Photographer: **Andrew Wormer**

PAGE 133
Architect: **Michaela Mahady**
Photographer: **Philip Mueller**

PAGE 134 (LEFT)
Architect: **Sarah Susanka with
Richard Peterson, MSMP**
Photographer: **Kevin Ireton**

PAGE 134 (RIGHT)
Architect: **Robert Gerloff**
Photographer: **John Danicic**

PAGE 137
Architect: **Joseph G. Metzler with
Steven Buetow, MSMP**
Photographer: **Susan Gilmore**

PAGE 138
Photographer: **Reese Hamilton**

PAGE 139
Architect: **Sarah Susanka, MSMP**
Photographer: **Christian Korab**

PAGE 140
Photographer: **Steve Culpepper**

PAGE 141
Photographer: **Roe A. Osborn**

PAGE 142-145
Architect: **Sarah Susanka, MSMP**
Photographer: **Christian Korab**

PAGE 146 (TOP)
Architect: **Sarah Susanka, MSMP**
Photographer: **Christian Korab**

PAGE 146 (BOTTOM)
Architect: **Dale Mulfinger &
Sarah Susanka, MSMP**
Photographer: **Sarah Susanka**

PAGE 148
Architect: **Sarah Susanka &
James R. Larson**
Photographer: **Sarah Susanka**

PAGE 149-152, 153 (TOP)
Architect: **Kelly Davis, MSMP**
Photographer: **Christian Korab**

PAGE 153 (BOTTOM)
Architect: **Kelly Davis, MSMP**
Photographer: **Sarah Susanka**

PAGE 154, 156, 157 (TOP)
Architect: **Kelly Davis, MSMP**
Photographer: **Christian Korab**

PAGE 157 (BOTTOM), 158 (TOP
& BOTTOM LEFT)
Architect: **Kelly Davis, MSMP**
Photographer: **Sarah Susanka**

PAGE 158 (RIGHT)
Architect: **Kelly Davis, MSMP**
Photographer: **Christian Korab**

PAGE 159
Architect: **Joseph G. Metzler with
Steven Buetow, MSMP**
Photographer: **Susan Gilmore**

PAGE 160
Architect: **Sarah Susanka with
Richard Peterson, MSMP**
Photographer: **Kevin Ireton**

PAGE 161, 162 (TOP)
Architect: **Sarah Susanka with
James R. Larson, MSMP**
Photographer: **Christian Korab**

PAGE 162 (BOTTOM)
Architect: **Joseph G. Metzler, MSMP**
Photographer: **Bruce Greenlaw**

PAGE 163
Architect: **Michaela Mahady &
Wayne Branum, MSMP**
Photographer: **George Heinrich**

PAGE 164
Architect: **Sarah Susanka with
Richard Peterson, MSMP**
Photographer: **Karen Melvin**

PAGE 165 (TOP)
Architect: **Michaela Mahady with
M. Christine Johnson, MSMP**
Photographer: **Christian Korab**

PAGE 165 (BOTTOM)
Architect: **Sarah Susanka, MSMP**
Photographer: **Sarah Susanka**

PAGE 166
Architect: **Sarah Susanka &
Michaela Mahady, MSMP**
Photographer: **Karen Melvin**

PAGES 167, 169-171
Architect: **Michaela Mahady with
M. Christine Johnson, MSMP**
Photographer: **Phillip Mueller**

PAGE 172 (LEFT)
Architect: **Sarah Susanka with
Richard Peterson, MSMP**
Photographer: **Karen Melvin**

PAGES 172 (RIGHT), 173
Architect: **Joseph G. Metzler with
Steven Buetow, MSMP**
Photographer: **Susan Gilmore**

PAGE 174
A Timeless Classic
Peter Twombly, AIA
Estes/Twombly Architects, Inc.
79 Thames St.
Newport, RI 02840
mail@estestwombly.com
interior designers: Peter Twombly
and Lisa Ballou

PAGE 184
A House for Today and Tomorrow
Murray Silverstein,
with Bill Mastin
Jacobson Silverstein Winslow Architects
3106 Shattuck Ave.
Berkeley, CA 94705
jsswarch@aol.com

PAGE 192
The Essence of Home
Jeremiah Eck, FAIA
Jeremiah Eck Architects, Inc.
560 Harrison Ave., Suite 403
Boston MA 02118
www.jearch.com

PAGE 202
Doing More with Less
Matthew Schoenherr, AIA
Z:Architecture
61 Jesup Rd.
Westport, CT 06880
zarchitecture@prodigy.net
interior designer: Beth Schoenherr, Sheridan Interiors

PAGE 212
**A Farmhouse
for Our Time**
Jean Larson, AIA, with
Steve Mooney
SALA Architects
43 Main St. SE, Suite 410
Minneapolis, MN 55414
www.salaarc.com

PAGE 200
A Jewel in the Suburbs
Jim Garramone
Garramone Design
9 Williamsburg Ct.
Evanston, IL 60203-1828
garrdesign@aol.com

PAGE 230
Three Easy Pieces
Frederick Phillips, FAIA
Frederick Phillips &
Associates
1456 N. Dayton St., Suite 200
Chicago, IL 60622
fpaarch@interaccess.com

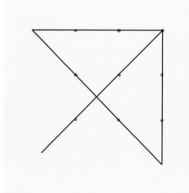